D1607388

SEBALD'S VISION

LITERATURE NOW

LITERATURE NOW

MATTHEW HART, DAVID JAMES,
AND REBECCA L. WALKOWITZ, SERIES EDITORS

Literature Now offers a distinct vision of late-twentieth- and early-twenty-first-century literary culture. Addressing contemporary literature and the ways we understand its meaning, the series includes books that are comparative and transnational in scope as well as those that focus on national and regional literary cultures.

CAROL JACOBS

SEBALD'S VISION

COLUMBIA UNIVERSITY PRESS
NEW YORK

Columbia University Press
Publishers Since 1893
New York   Chichester, West Sussex
cup.columbia.edu
Copyright © 2015 Columbia University Press
All rights reserved

Library of Congress Cataloging-in-Publication Data
Jacobs, Carol, author.
Sebald's vision / Carol Jacobs.
pages cm. — (Literature now)
Includes bibliographical references and index.
ISBN 978-0-231-17182-3 (cloth : alk. paper)—ISBN 978-0-231-54010-0 (e-book)
1. Sebald, W. G. (Winfried Georg), 1944–2001—Criticism
and interpretation. I. Title.
PT2681.E18Z644 2015
833'.914—dc23
2015004582

Columbia University Press books are printed on permanent
and durable acid-free paper.
This book is printed on paper with recycled content.
Printed in the United States of America

c 10 9 8 7 6 5 4 3 2 1

Jacket design: Jordan Wannemacher
Jacket image: © Getty

References to websites (URLs) were accurate at the time of writing.
Neither the author nor Columbia University Press is responsible for URLs
that may have expired or changed since the manuscript was prepared.

For Arnie and Ellen and their glorious clan:
Beryl, Willy, Isabella, Micaela;
A.J., Julie, Jasper, Lucas, and Zane;
and
for Henry,
who found the title for these musings
and has so lovingly stayed by my side all these years.

CONTENTS

PREFACE
"SEBALD'S VISION"

As a reader I therefore pay my tribute in what follows . . .
in the form of several extended marginalia which otherwise
make no particular claim.
(LOGIS IN EINEM LANDHAUS 7G)

A TITLE, NO doubt, should take the long view, describe, and cir-
cumscribe the textual matter to follow.[1] Sebald himself, however, often chose titles that no reader can mistake for simple deictic markers. Does *After Nature* (*Nach der Natur*, 1988) tell of a mode
of writing and art made according to, and perhaps in imitation of,
nature?[2] Or shall we understand the title to suggest a time after
nature, a pronouncement of an eco-apocalyptic foreboding suggesting that, from the outset, Nature might no longer be a viable
assumption? Or is it with certainty neither of these after all? *Schwindel. Gefühle.* (1990) in the German original punctuates *dizziness/
swindle/lie* (*Schwindel*), and then *feelings* (*Gefühle*) with the inter-
ruptive halt of periods—all lost in translation, of course, with the
title *Vertigo*. Is the German title then a dizzying suggestion that any
immediacy of feeling might needs be read in tandem with deception? *Austerlitz*, which seems unproblematically to name Jacques
Austerlitz, the central character of the narrative, is nevertheless

questioned by the boy of fifteen when he first learns his name: "what does it mean?" (*Austerlitz* 68E, 100G). It means as well, according to Austerlitz's teacher, a famous battle, the study of which makes evident that conventional, factual history simply will not do, that there is no way to make the telling of the past adequate to the object of its description. It names, moreover, one of the many train stations in *Austerlitz*, and specifically that from which the protagonist, Austerlitz, like his father before him, disappears. Something of this ambiguity, something of this deception, something of this evasion of factual narrative and of the inability of language to simply name, haunts *Sebald's Vision* as well.[3]

Three aspects of Sebald's writing must inevitably strike every reader.[4] To begin with, it is a question of a postwar German author addressing the Holocaust (and other historico-political and ecological disasters) in a manner the reading public had never before witnessed. In Sebald one encounters an ethics of melancholy outrage, but he also sets forth his moral position with an astonishing sense of self-certitude. Second: every reader is struck by the visual oddity of literary and essayistic works peppered with images: photographs, documents, diagrams, sketches, and reproductions of artworks. The temptation, of course, is to assume that, given the ethical stance, the visual materials are there as illustrations. In Sebald's writings one soon notices that this assumption is particularly vexed, since he openly plays with the purposeful uncertainty of what he places before our eyes. The visual materials, as Sebald admits in an interview, often serve the purpose of readerly disorientation. And then one encounters in each of his writings an astonishingly innovative writing style. Given his performances of meandering detours, his shattering of frames, crossing borders, writing tangentially, disintegrating the name, surreptitiously citing, and announcing blindness,[5] what is called for is a careful analysis of the highly unusual literary practices of his texts. How to reconcile such a radical stylistics with moral certitude? This is the question. How to understand, as Sebald will assert in interviews, that he can only speak indirectly? The task in reading Sebald, then, is to account for a whole range of concepts: what Sebald called our moral capacity alongside the vagaries of perception and, more generally, how representation in art and literature relates to the epistemological crises that he shows us arising out of the juxtaposition of all these.

That his writings are about vision as the ability to see can escape no reader. Alongside the unusual, interspersed visual materials that rightfully engage so many Sebald scholars a theme of sight is often woven into the text. In "Air War and Literature" Sebald reproves those writers who directly witnessed the Allied bombings. What was called for was a steady gaze at what was before them ("Air War" 51E, 57G) rendered in a concrete prose that might make the reader see.[6] Still in *The Rings of Saturn* the narrator will celebrate not only Rembrandt's verisimilitude (*Wirklichkeitsnähe; Rings of Saturn* 16E, 26G) but also his rebellion against mimesis. That refusal to copy nature emerges as Rembrandt's social commentary. Sebald also writes of the remarkable realism of the art of Jan Peter Tripp, while nevertheless insisting that it is less its identity with reality that is worth considering than the "far less apparent points of divergence and difference" ("As Day and Night" 84E, 178G).[7] In a late interview, Sebald will go on to insist that the Holocaust, which so concerned him, can only be spoken of indirectly: "So the only way in which one can approach these things, in my view, is obliquely, tangentially, by reference rather than by direct confrontation."[8] These are atrocities, he often takes the opportunity to remind us, that he himself, in any case, born in 1944, could not possibly have experienced head-on.[9]

The degree to which written texts are called upon to see and report a factual or historical world of the artist's experience fluctuates wildly in Sebald's works and, more crucially, also within each individual work. In the texts we are about to read, neat conclusions about vision-of-the-eye are impossible. And then we encounter the prolific acts of citation, both visual and verbal, that are bound to seem twenty-twenty from a certain point of view. As we all know, however—and no one better than Sebald—the play of montage alters the incorporated material and puts it into new relations that cause us to see and read otherwise.

Vision, of course, also implies not only acts of the eye but also those of the mind, or, as we like to imagine it, spirit, as when we say that someone has vision, a vision, or is a visionary.[10] Sebald's work is celebrated for its moral stand, for its turn not only to the Shoah

(*The Emigrants, Austerlitz, Rings of Saturn*) but also to other historical and natural scenes of violence: the 1525 massacre at Frankenhausen during the German Peasants' War (*After Nature*), the 1800 Battle
of Marengo (*Vertigo*), the bombing of German cities in the Second
World War (*Air War and Literature*), slave laborers worked to death
in the Belgian Congo, the nineteenth-century Taiping rebellion that
took tens of millions of lives in China, the devastation of the herring
population and then of trees in the hurricane of 1987 (*Rings of Saturn*).

Still, one takes away the rules of Sebald's engagement with difficulty and uncertainty. The puzzle in all this is due not only to Sebald's
inconsistencies and contradictions. What if such entanglements are
Sebald's game plan, which may be no plan at all? Sebald's writings
are a continuously changing meditation on these issues and a dizzying practice of thinking and representing them: Schwindel. Gefühle.,
one is tempted to say. What if to read Sebald (and perhaps this does
not distinguish him all that much from other writers) lies in the spec-
ificities of individual texts? Despite Sebald's frequent invocation of
the bird's-eye view (a vantage point shared by God and the dreamer),
any naïive attempt to assume that perspective as reader, to arrive at
an overarching thesis in relation to these particular issues in Sebald's
writings, is bound to fail. Even "Air War and Literature," which claims
for itself an extraliterary status while initially calling for documentary concreteness, eventually gives way to the suspicion that we may
not be able to learn anything at all, even when we step back or look
from above.

It is true: one ruins one's eyes with too much close reading. Still,
what I offer in the pages to come includes the practice of a stubborn
attention to detail. Sebald talks less openly of this than of "the eye /
of the crane" that allows one to overlook a wide terrain,[11] but even
a troubled nearsightedness nevertheless offers us flashes, now and
again, of a bigger picture. I take as my model an image from *The Emigrants* in which, as the artist Aurach/Ferber narrates,[12] he is represented as a young boy "deeply bent over his writing" (*The Emigrants*
171–72E, 255–56G). The photograph brings us right up to the face of
the child—also to his hands, his pencil, its point shining at the edge
of the frame. Only, just *what* he is writing is cut from our view. I take
as my model Austerlitz, who describes himself as a child—muttering

and spelling out the stories in his Welsh children's Bible yet certain something else lies there, completely different from the sense of the words produced as he runs his index fingers over the lines of writing (*Austerlitz* 55E, 80G), and Austerlitz repeatedly in that same Bible examining every inch of a bewildering, hatch-marked illustration of the camp of the children of Israel (*Austerlitz* 55–58E, 81–84G).

These are puzzling models, I know, for literary criticism, and they presage only modest accomplishments in the chapters to follow. Still, if there are any insights to come, it will have something to do with a self-imposed myopia as I trace Sebald's running, elusive, understated, meditations on the intersection of vision, our capacity to know, and of what Sebald called "our moral capacity": all these and his own narrative performances.[13]

Thus in *After Nature* (1988, chapter 1), the earliest published of Sebald's major literary works, it is at the title of the first of its three poems that one must pause: "Like the snow on the Alps." That title calls for particular attention, borrowed, as it is, from the poem's concluding line and not according to the usual convention of citing the first phrase. "Like the snow on the Alps" is devoted to the German painter Matthaeus Grünewald. In the opening lines of the poem the figures from the altar at Lindenhardt cross the border from the sixteenth-century artwork into our twentieth-century world. By the end of the poem it is we as readers who are openly called upon to cross the border into the linguistic demands of the text.

Along the way Sebald experiments with what it might be to take in what is outside the text. We think as we begin to read that we understand its obvious project. "Like the snow on the Alps" sets about describing the painter's work while sketching out a biography of the man: each of these tasks is embroiled in a sociopolitical critique. Such a project implies major presumptions about literary language and its practice of representation. Yet, as the poem progresses, ekphrasis gives way to a failure to capture the visual in language; and the biography describes the uncertainty of Grünewald's identity in the multiplicity of names attached to his works. Section 4 questions the identity of Grünewald because a jumble of different initials sign and claim authorship of his canvases. But, before and after this in Sebald's poem, that name appears in stranger form yet. Grünewald's wife-to-be falls in love neither with the man nor with the painter but with his "green-colored name" and is subsequently, we read, doomed to madness. Later, in the tale of the Aschaffenburg artist's death, broken fragments of the name *grün* and *Wald* are scattered through the lines.[14] They are the linguistic accompaniment to the coming blindness with which the poem closes, violent and ultimate blindness, it seems. We, the readers, who have been commanded to look sharply ahead, come upon those now famous phrases of Sebald, which announce: "So it becomes, when the optic nerve / tears . . . / white like the snow / on the Alps" (*After Nature* 37E, 33G). Following the details of these lines elsewhere in the book, one discovers that significance is generated in Sebald not by the gaze directed straight on but by a net of interconnections, or what Sebald elsewhere will call coincidences. A new mode of seeing and an odd mode of signification define his literary work. Thus culmination in loss of vision becomes the linguistic matrix of the possibility of signification throughout *After Nature*. One might wish to think it emblematic of Sebald's work as a whole, though Sebald himself warns us that no symbol, as he puts it, has a single, fixed meaning. Here, as elsewhere in Sebald's work, blindness and sight do not simply shut one another out. Signification in Sebald's poem often moves not by way of deictic pointing or simple nomination but rather by passages and phrases that gain their potential to signify through acts of repetition and echoing.

Four years after the appearance of *After Nature,* Sebald publishes *The Emigrants* (1992, chapter 2). The earlier work was announced in its German subtitle as a single poem (*Ein Elementargedicht*, "An Elemental Poem") divided into three long poems that tell of Grünewald, Steller, and Sebald. The new volume is divided into four, here too with each section devoted to a different figure. What binds *The Emigrants* together is not only what the title suggests, a loss of homeland in the form of four life stories, but also a literary landscape in which, in the spirit of its themes of dust and butterflies, a cross-pollination of recurring images proliferates across the texts. These are the coincidences of which Sebald spoke with light irony in his interviews. They are also, as in *After Nature*, what forces us to read, differently, even if that reading doesn't necessarily produce a certainty of delineated form. Once again, then, Sebald draws his characters together through the uncanny repetition of apparently arbitrary details, a new mode of drawing, one wants to say, that counters conventional figurative art. The art of Max Aurach in the last story is also of a piece with this. Wracked by losses of memory, what he treasures in his charcoal drawings is not the figure that remains for all to see, but the coal dust that falls away from the picture like lost traces of the past. As he paints a portrait, he does so by gouging out the paint he had previously laid on the canvas, not by producing but by undoing the representation.

The challenge to the conventions of the framed artwork and the cross-pollination of images are the experience if not the subject matter of a slide show early on in *The Emigrants*. The narrator, his wife, Henry Selwyn, and friend watch as images of Crete take flight in the narrator's thoughts, which carry us from place to place: Nabokov in the Swiss Alps (outfitted in butterfly-catching array) gives way to the Caucasus, to the Lasithi Plateau in Crete, until, like the specificity of place, the physical frame of the slide, it, too, cannot hold. It is a shattering of frame that shatters as well the capacity for circumscribed acts of narrative description. The story will take us from there to a film in which a caravan seems to pass out from the screen into the audience (passing the borders of art like Grünewald's figures), from this to a tale of madness in the story of Ambros Adelwarth's friend, another tale of another film that transgresses its borders—all in a manner, of course, that sweeps its reader audience along with it.

Still, it is not this wild play of form of which the narrator is wary, but rather another concept of representation. At the close of *The Emigrants* he imagines himself standing before a photograph taken in the Litzmannstadt Ghetto by the bookkeeper Genewein, who prided himself on his celebratory documentation in color slides of Nazi organization. Three young women look across to the narrator from behind the threads of a loom: he stands on the very spot where Genewein had stood to capture his image. The one at our left fixes him with a steady and relentless gaze. They are there, it seems, as the three fates, ready to take his measure. It is the close of the volume. They stand in judgment. Has Sebald achieved anything more, anything different from Genewein, the would-be documentarian? What is a photograph? What is an image? How to assess the way in which he collects documents and makes a gesture toward preserving memory? How to think these gestures of fidelity to reality in relation to the frame-rupturing leaps of connection to which we have also been witness and to the concept of citation?

The Rings of Saturn (1995, chapter 3) offers something of an answer or, at least, a series of answers. Over and over, in any case, it poses the question of the frame in relation to a dream of fixing reality. Early on in that volume we encounter the image, reproduced in black and white and taking up a full two-page expanse, of Rembrandt's *Anatomy Lesson of Dr. Nicolaas Tulp*. At stake from a certain point of view are Cartesian claims that reduce the body to a machine or scientific diagram. Yet, in stark contrast to the rest of the vast canvas, recognized for its fidelity to reality, and in order to signal his act of compassion for the victim of state cruelty whose body is being violated, Rembrandt gives to the flayed hand a false construction. Rembrandt's purposeful, crass misrepresentation of the object of the artist's gaze, we are told, critiques the faulty vision and values of the scientific gathering. That the unfeeling onlookers portrayed there look past the body to an anatomical atlas is evidence of their moral failures. But when Sebald in turn does some cutting of his own, when he excises a piece of that full canvas and reproduces it on the following page, he flouts his act of reframing as further distortion and thereby unsettles the analysis of representation he has offered in relation to ethical conscience. While professing the thoughtful gaze, what the narrator practices is distraction.

And distraction, detour, is, of course, the path of Sebald's prose. Here in *The Rings of Saturn* one thing leads to another and we find ourselves suddenly reading Thomas Browne who finds a fixed pattern that runs through the entire natural world. His quest brings us back to the frame, this time in the form of Browne's Quincunx. The quincunx is valid everywhere: in *The Garden of Cyrus* (1658) a fifty-five-page list of things that partake of its form proves the point. The four-cornered field framing a fifth point at its center, comes to us as the ever encountered and inescapable order of things, a promise of iterable certitude. And yet, like Rembrandt's anatomy lesson, the quincunx too is charged with distraction. For Browne's thoughts, as Sebald reminds us, could not hold steady on the ever repeating pattern that seemed to account for everything. If one turns from reading Sebald to reading Browne's *The Garden of Cyrus* one finds the narrative wandering from the reassuring repetition of the enclosing quadrilateral form, to the letter *X* drawn by lines that run between the rhombus's opposing angles, wandering then again to the Roman numeral *V.* Thus Browne shifts back and forth between the frame and its undoing in the open forms of X and V. What appears to take place spatially at the core of Browne's essay, this shuttling back and forth between closed and open forms, the lozenge-shaped frame of the quincunx and the *X*s and *V*s also derived therefrom, reappears in the dedicatory letter of Browne's *Garden of Cyrus.* That is to say, the *X*, which is later so crucial in the succeeding chapters as a spatial figure, first assumes a linguistic form in a cluster of words beginning in *ex-*. As Browne chatters about the errant path of his text, he strews it with an *ex-* of a verbal order—*Excursion, Exception, Extremity,* and *Extraneous*—invoked to mark once again the break from the rhombus form that later claims to account for and enclose.

The oscillation between stable form and dispersion, which in Browne's preface is something of a mirthful dance, appears in a more somber form in Sebald's *Austerlitz* (2001, chapter 5).[15] The opening pages raise the question of the letter *A*—and not only because the narrator meets Austerlitz in Antwerp, just two of the many proper *A*-names that swarm through the pages to follow. At the dead center of the long prose text (Sebald refused to call his books novels), through a long and redemptive passage of eighty pages, *A* has a place of honor. Austerlitz, who had been brought to Wales as a small child on the *Kindertransport,* returns to his native city of Prague to seek out his past. He goes to the state archives where the archivist, Ambrosová, finds his family name in the perfectly preserved alphabetical files and directs him at once to his family apartment. There he finds his nanny, her name promising truth (Vera), who brings back his past as well his ability to both understand and speak his childhood Czech language. This is the core of the story, solid enough to convince some readers that it is a volume about recovered memory. It reminds us that the alphabet is our means for understanding, organizing knowledge, recording the spoken word, reading, and recovering the past—above all, for making good on loss.

And yet, our first encounter in *Austerlitz* with the letter *A* has none of that promise of recuperation after trauma; it is at best an inarticulate reliving of a never to be articulated pain. In the early pages of the fiction, the narrator tells of Gastone Novelli, tortured by the Nazis, who, after his liberation, immediately headed for South America to live among the native people and escape what we tend to think of as civilization. While there he compiled a dictionary of their language consisting mostly of vowels and especially of *A*-sounds. Novelli's return to his European home was far from Austerlitz's linguistic rediscovery of the mother tongue. Instead, with a technique akin to that of Aurach in *The Emigrants*, he filled canvases with the letter *A* by scratching the paint out to form a tableau of letters, spelling out a horrific scream that rose and fell in waves.

The double register of language-in-*A*s (as the path to articulated knowledge and memory as well as their disintegration) is also that of sight—the sight of the narrator to be precise. At the chronological close of the tale, though still in its opening pages, as something of a preface to the tale of Austerlitz we are about to read, the narrator discovers that the sight in his right eye, threatened by black crosshatching, is almost gone. The hatch marks that define the narrator's incapacity to see also haunt Austerlitz throughout the entire book. They echo as well the artwork of Novelli, it too a series of scratched markings. The left eye, at least for now, maintains a sense of clear sight and the narrator maintains clarity in the right eye at the edge of his field of vision. But, with the impaired eye, he can see nothing head on. The entire work evolves out of this mode of seeing and writing, shot through with intertwined strands of thoughts and images, with networks, with branchings of various sorts. We lose our sense of space and also our sense of time. The vision of recuperating a lost childhood is something of a hollow dream set at the center of a vast text that seems to know better, though we cannot be certain what.

Still, in his 1997 lectures in Switzerland, entitled "Air War and Literature," Sebald indeed seemed to know better (chapter 4). At first, at least, he held out for more than a hollow promise. If not for the recuperation of times past, Sebald called, retroactively, for the clear sight there should have been of what is presently before one, a presentation of the real circumstances in the name of truth. He expressed his moral outrage that the writers who witnessed the bombings of the German cities in World War II had failed to come to terms with, to bring into memory and onto paper what they had seen. It was their obligation as well to make the reader see. A documentary approach ("Air War" 58E, 65G), an ideal of objective truth ("Air War" 53E, 59G), in contrast to traditional aesthetics, would have been the only correct response. And yet, Sebald admits, that kind of experience cannot be grasped under such conditions and cannot be reported with precision. It is from a pseudodocumentary text of Alexander Kluge that he learns this, which, of course, gives pause. Sebald famously calls for a "synoptic artificial view" ("Air War" 26E, 33G), but the examples he gives offer no simple prism by way of which we might grasp the scene. Still, there is another artificial view begging for consideration. Sebald speaks at length of Kluge's "The Air Attack on Halberstadt on April 8, 1945" ("Der Luftangriff auf Halberstadt am 8. April 1945"). Issues of ironic amazement, intellectual steadfastness, and the challenge to learn from our past mistakes suddenly rise into view. Is epistemology still possible, can we as human beings maintain our autonomous history, or are we at a point beyond self-knowledge, which is to say more or less blind to our own experience? No answers to these questions: Sebald leaves us between possibilities, though the lectures have a dramatic ending. "Air War and Literature" closes with the famous passage from Walter Benjamin on the Angel of History. It is not that the angel, who stares as the ruins pile up before him, is the redemptive resolution to all that has gone before. The passage resembles other culminating moments of Sebald's texts: they are all citations. Moreover, just a few pages earlier we read a grudging approval of the Halberstadt photographer whose pictures, though he could not have known they would find their place there, Kluge added to his text. Is citation, then, both verbal and visual, a path to learning—is it a possible way of seeing?

Sebald turns to citation again at the close of his 1993 essay "Like Day and Night: On the Pictures of Jan Peter Tripp" (chapter 6) where citation is a medium of meditation and a path to answering questions. It was with the painter and long-time friend that Sebald had prepared, as it turned out, his final work of literature, *Unrecounted* (*Unerzählt*). That posthumous volume alternates Tripp's extraordinary images of (just) the eyes of various, often famous, people, with Sebald's haiku-like lines, which, as they had previously agreed, do not necessarily have an apparent relationship to the opposing image.

At the end of the essay on Tripp as well, Sebald poses the question of image and text. He reproduces Tripp's *Déclaration de guerre,* a large painting of two shoes on a patterned tile, and he declares it of a visual complexity not to be described in words, an exemplum, then, of the incommensurability between language and objects of sight. He poses a series of questions about the elegant footwear, as though it were a matter of actual shoes with a real-life history we are challenged to seek out. The joke is, in an essay (uncharacteristically for Sebald) riddled with jokes as it is with puzzles, that the answers materialize only when the large canvas, *Déclaration de guerre,* is cited. It is cited first by Tripp, who incorporates it into another painting. A woman now sits, her back to us, contemplating *Declaration of War* hung on the wall of what appears to be a museum space. Only when the painting is cited, when it is formally recognized as an image within an image rather than as image of real shoes, does the essay begin to narrate with ease the possible stories that explain the conundrum of the origin of the elegant pumps. That footwear, it seems, has its real-life counterpart on the feet of the woman dressed in white in the second painting. On her feet, or, rather, on one of them, is a shoe that the narrator declares "the same" as those in the picture she regards. We have found, then, the original shoes, though one is missing. Sebald has cited Tripp's citation of the declaration of war in the second, smaller painting, which he leaves untitled. But the montage of a text or image, he had reminded us earlier, compels us to look through our knowledge of texts and pictures: doing so, we find the name of the smaller canvas—*Déjà vu oder der Zwischenfall* (*Déjà vu or the Incident*). That is the question. Is the relation between the two scenes, the image of the shoes in the first painting and the image of the lady (with a dog) contemplating the image of the shoes, a repetition of what has been seen, or does it suggest an incident whose explanation requires a narrative?

Sebald obliges. First he tells the story of the woman, weary at the end of the day, who had removed the second shoe, held it in her hand, whereon it then totally vanished. In place of it (in *Déjà vu oder der Zwischenfall*) we see another, hardly identical, object at the foot of a dog who gazes out of the painting. For this incident, too, Sebald has a tale to tell: of the dog who played fetch, who, in leaps to which we have become accustomed, jumped the frame of Tripp's work, crossing the centuries, crossing the English Channel, bringing the sandal back from a masterpiece of Van Eyck hung in another museum.

Thus the last pages of the essay on Jan Peter Tripp gather together in something of a jumble, a dizzying series of questions on the work of art: as preserving life, as recording history, as a reminder of its own materiality, and yet again as a bit of a prank, or rather an elaborate joke, under the guise of commentary. This is one of the most profoundly literary performances in Sebald's works, despite its pretentions to be something else, and one of the most subtle theoretically. The essay closes with yet another set of eyes brought to the fore as Sebald, once again (as in *Rings of Saturn*), excises a piece of the canvas. The dog from the second painting (*Déjà vu . . .*), which cites and comments on the first, is ready for his close-up. He is, though we hardly take notice of him at first, the star of the show. The dog from *Déjà vu . . .* who has cavorted about, leaping in and out of artworks, takes an object from another work, another era, another country, treats it as a thing, and plops the footwear down, leaving it to us to figure out the puzzle of his sleight of the eye. With one eye, Sebald writes, the domesticated one, he looks right at us. With the other, however, he looks right through us, the spectator. So it is with Sebald's writing that we are as readers at once the spectators and also the object of scrutiny and judgment.

In short, what *Sebald's Vision* attempts to make clear is that the literary texts and the essays (in their practice) as well as the interviews (in their straightforward assertions [chapter 7]) show Sebald thinking through his writing strategies and poetics with enormous care. What follows concerns Sebald's implicit theorizations about language, literature, epistemology, and the ethical. These meditations arise out of careful attention not only to the larger gestures of the texts but also to what I have called a myopic reading. It is my hope that thereby something new jumps to the eye.

Sebald's works are referred to with short versions of their English titles. These are followed by the page numbers in the published

English translations, marked with an E, and by the page numbers in the German originals, marked with a G. The extended titles of Sebald's works, as well as that of other authors, can be found in *Works Cited*. Throughout this book English translations appear in the body of the text. The original German of the longer citations can be found in the endnotes. Modifications to the translations were made where they seemed necessary for understanding the argument.

ACKNOWLEDGMENTS

ONCE AGAIN my deepest gratitude to the Baldwin family for establishing the Birgit Baldwin professorship in Comparative Literature. It is a title which I hold with a sense of great honor and with full cognizance of their dedication both to the memory of their extraordinary daughter Birgit Baldwin and to the study of literature.

To the people at Columbia University Press who have transformed my sense of what the spirit of a publication collaboration should be: my thanks to Philip Leventhal whose strong support and dedication to my manuscript right from the beginning made all the difference; to the editors of the Literature Now series for their belief in this project, especially to Matt Hart for his great kindness and attentiveness; to Whitney Johnson who was there every step of the way with superb guidance, patience, efficiency, and grace; and to Susan Pensak who copyedited with a marvelously vigilant eye and with such devotion to detail and the style of the project.

For a remarkable year spent working on this volume (2010–2011), I wish to thank the Internationales Kolleg Morphomata, University of Cologne: both Günther Blamberger, director, and Martin Roussel in particular, but also so many other people there who welcomed every one of the fellows with such generosity of spirit.

Warmest thanks to Thomas Stachel for his highly professional, dedicated, and exceptionally intelligent work on editing and proofing my manuscript in its very last stage.

Sebald's Vision is published with the very generous assistance of the Frederick W. Hilles Publication Fund of Yale University.

My warmest thanks to Jan Peter Tripp, who so graciously granted permission to use the images he provided of his extraordinary work (chapter 6). It was a great and unique honor to meet him through our exchange. It is Tripp's work that inspired some of Sebald's most important theoretical thinking.

My gratitude to Michael Lenarz and the Jüdisches Museum Frankfurt am Main for permission to use figures 2.3 and 2.4, images of the chief accountant and also of the weavers at the ghetto of Łódź. These photographs were also gathered in the catalogue "Unser einziger Weg ist Arbeit": Das Getto in Łódź 1940–1944 (Vienna: Jüdisches Museum Frankfurt am Main and Löcker Verlag, 1990).

And I offer my heartfelt thanks to Urs Engeler, that most daring and generous of publishers. An earlier version of my reading of Sebald's "Like Day and Night" is here spread out over chapters 6 and 7 and originally appeared as "A Little Tripp" in Aris Fioretos, ed., Babel: Festschrift für Werner Hamacher (Basel: Urs Engeler, 2009), 258–67.

Thanks also to Thomas Dobrowolski of the Wylie Agency for so kindly and efficiently, with such exquisite patience, facilitating the rights to images from the major works as follows: seven images by W. G. Sebald. Copyright © The Emigrants, 1996; The Rings of Saturn, 1998; and Austerlitz, 2001 by W. G. Sebald, used by permission of the Wylie Agency, LLC on behalf of the W. G. Sebald Estate.

Permission to use their materials was also granted by

The National Gallery, London for the right to use their digital image of Jan van Eyck, The Arnolfini Portrait © The National Gallery, London;

Mauritshuis, The Hague, for permission to use their digital image of Rembrandt van Rijn (1606–1669), The Anatomy Lesson of Dr Nicolaes Tulp, 1632;

The Johns Hopkins University Press for permission to reprint the essay of chapter 2 of this volume. Copyright © 2005 by The Johns Hopkins University Press. This article was first published in MLN 119, no. 5 (2004): 905–29. Reprinted with permission by Johns Hopkins University Press;

Walter de Gruyter: some pages of chapter 5 were previously published as "Reading, Writing, Hatching," in Eva Meyer and Vivian Liska, eds., *What Does the Veil Know?* (Zurich: Voldemeer, 2009), 130–43 (http://www.degruyter.com/);

Random House of Canada Limited, which requests the following acknowledgment: excerpted from *After Nature* by W. G. Sebald. Copyright © 1988 W. G. Sebald. Copyright © 1988 Eichborn AG, Frankfurt am Main. Translation Copyright © 2002 Michael Hamburger. Translation has been published by arrangement with Hamish Hamilton, a publishing division of Penguin Books Ltd. Reprinted by permission of Vintage Canada/Alfred A. Knopf Canada, a division of Random House of Canada Limited, a Penguin Random House Company;

Penguin Random House which requests the following credit line: "As the Snow on the Alps," "Dark Night Sallies Forth," and "And if I Remained by the Outermost Sea" from AFTER NATURE by W. G. Sebald, translated by Michael Hamburger, translation copyright © 2002 by Michael Hamburger. Used by permission of Random House, an imprint and division of Random House LLC. All rights reserved.

SEBALD'S VISION

1

"LIKE THE SNOW ON THE ALPS"

After Nature

CROSSING BORDERS

WHOEVER OPENS *After Nature* (*Nach der Natur*) might well be lost. The epigraph to the first of its three poems invokes a guide, but what reader would thereby be given hope?

> *"Now go, for a single will is in us both:*
> *Thou guide, thou lord, thou master,"*
> *So I said to him; and when he had set forth*
> *I entered on the steep wild-wooded way.*[1]

Dante, led into the *Inferno* by Virgil, is taken on a wooded way (which will eventually find echoes in Sebald's poem) and follows his guide with blind abandon. That we are on the way to hell in Sebald's first major literary publication, in the first of the three poems that comprise that work, is not immediately evident. But we might be struck from the outset by its title, which cites, not the opening phrase of the poem, the customary gesture for titling a text, but, rather, its closing words: "like the snow on the Alps" (*After Nature*, 37E, 33G).[2] The poem, devoted to the sixteenth-century painter Matthaeus Grünewald, thus anticipates its own end, makes it foregone. With the phrase "like the snow on the Alps" it might also seem to celebrate nature, or at the very least its own capacity to paint therefrom (*nach der Natur*). We will see.

Like its title, the beginning of the poem asks us to think the relation of opening and closure. It is a question of how we have access to a work of art, what kind of art that is, and how it relates to those outside it.[3]

> *Whoever closes the wings*
> *of the altar in the Lindenhardt*
> *parish church and locks up*
> *the carved figures in their casing*
> *on the lefthand panel*
> *will be met by St. George.*[4]
> (AFTER NATURE 5E)[5]

To be met by the work of Matthaeus Grünewald, perhaps that of Sebald as well, one must perform a certain task. We must close the door on, withdraw from sight, certain kinds of figures. Carved and three-dimensional, to them belongs a casing or housing that guarantees fixed place. We must lock these away, with their attempts at rounded replication, and give ourselves over, rather, to what comes to meet us. We are called to an encounter—if not yet to account.

> *Foremost at the picture's edge he stands*
> *above the world by a hand's breadth*
> *and is about to step over the frame's*
> *threshold. Georgius Miles. . . .*
> (AFTER NATURE 5E)[6]

Floating just slightly above the earth, nothing fixes St. George in place—much less grounds or closes him in. Poised on the border of image and world, he is about to cross the threshold between painting and beholder. This permeability of the work of art, this crossing of borders—an interchangeability of spaces, of figures, of times—will have a crucial role to play across the parts of *After Nature* as well as in each of the four works to follow, in *The Rings of Saturn*, *Vertigo*, *The Emigrants*, and *Austerlitz*.

On the facing panel, another wanderer: the older man, St. Dionysius, is Matthaeus Grünewald's chosen protector:

> *at the centre of*
> *the Lindenhardt altar's right wing,*
> *that troubled gaze upon the youth*
> *on the other side, of the older man*
> *whom, years ago now, on a grey*
> *January morning I myself once*
> *encountered in the railway station*
> *in Bamberg. It is St. Dionysius,*
> *his cut-off head under one arm.*
> (AFTER NATURE 6–7E)[7]

If St. George is poised to enter our space, Dionysius had already done so—jumped the frame and made it to the other side. Doubly. First with his eyes, directed toward the youth on the facing panel—but, also, crossing out of the painted surface, out of the sixteenth to the twentieth century—to the Bamberg train station where the narrator had seen him years before.[8]

St. George is about to step over the threshold to us, leaving his dragon yet to be slain. St. Dionysius has already, without our knowing, entered our world. "In the midst of life [Dionysius] carries his death with him" (*After Nature* 7E, 8G) in the form of his own severed head. Perhaps it is this one face too many (the dead one with the closed eyes) of the saint that allows him to wander out of the work of art and into the everyday life of the author. Closed eyes, a death of sorts, may be the ticket to Sebald's many railway stations.

Saints George and Dionysius may wander among us. Access to Grünewald is another matter. "The face of the unknown / Grünewald emerges again and again in his work" (*After Nature* 5E, 7G) in St. George to begin with, as well as in the work of Holbein and others. In a barely disguised instance of resemblance, how can one fail to recognize also Sebald's eyes, sliding sideways in so many photos as though burdened with grief and loneliness?

Always the same
gentleness, the same burden of grief,
the same irregularity of the eyes, veiled
and sliding sideways down into loneliness.
. . .

These were strangely disguised
instances of resemblance, wrote Fraenger
whose books were burned by the fascists.
Indeed it seemed as though in such works of art
men had revered each other like brothers, and
often made monuments in each other's
image where their paths had crossed.
(*AFTER NATURE* 6)[9]

The staged coincidences, connections, similarities, the rupture from the image world to its apparent other, the temporal volt over a threshold of centuries that seems to divide the past from the present and death from life,[10] the haunting by a Holocaust never quite absent: throughout the works of Sebald, these are defining gestures—also the irregularity of eyes that cannot be ruled.

DEPICTIONS

If his face is to be found in various forms, depicted by various hands, still: "Little is known of the life of / Matthaeus Grünewald of Aschaffenburg" (*After Nature* 9E, 10G). If not the life, then might we know the works? They come to us at first indirectly, if at all (in section II of the poem) by way of "The first account of the painter / in Joachim von Sandrart's *German Academy* / of the year 1675" (*After Nature* 9E, 10G). There we read of one work, lost since the nineteenth century, and of another, looted and lost in a shipwreck, and of other paintings that Sandrart also never got to see. Nevertheless, we are asked to trust the report of Sandrart, since an image of him in the Würzburger Museum shows him at eighty-two "wide awake and with eyes uncommonly clear" (*After Nature* 9E, 10G). The clarity of the critic's eyes alongside the irregularity of the painter's: what are we to make of this?

Might we speak of the clarity of the critic's eye in the narrative of *After Nature*? There are many verbal depictions of Grünewald's images, pages on pages of them: the Lindenhardt Altar with its St. George and St. Dionysius, the fourteen auxiliary saints, Cyriax and Diocletian's epileptic daughter, the self-portrait in the Erlangen library, the transfiguration of Christ on Mount Tabor, the blind, murdered hermit on the Mainz cathedral altar panels, the self-portrait of Nithart in the Chicago Art Institute, the Sebastian panel, the Isenheim altar, the Basel Crucifixion of 1505, the temptation of St. Anthony in all its excruciating detail, all these are laid out before the mind's eye. Take the following passage, a scene from the temptation of St. Anthony, but, surely, also, the fulfilled premonition of hell announced in the epigraph.

> *Low down in the bottom-left corner*
> *cowers the body, covered with*
> *syphilitic chancres, of an inmate*
> *of the Isenheim hospital. Above it*
> *rises a two-headed and many-*
> *armed androgynous creature*
> *about to finish off the saint*
> *with a brandished jaw-bone.*
> *On the right, a stilt-legged bird-like beast*
> *which, with human arms,*
> *holds a cudgel raised up. Behind*
> *and beside this, towards the picture's centre ...*
> (AFTER NATURE 25–26)[11]

In lines set to read as poetry, a prose of belabored description keeps the words from taking flight. Is it this exaggerated clarity of eye (*After Nature* 9E, 10G) that calls for trust?

For as Sebald recounts what little is known of the life of Matthaeus Grünewald, something is profoundly amiss in the relation between the language he uses and what it is said to represent. Interspersed in the biographical narrative, and despite the occasional reassuring phrases *one sees* and *you see* ("sieht man" and "siehst du"; *After Nature* 26 & 33G), line after line struggles to reproduce the paintings of Matthaeus Grünewald and others, the spatial relations of their figures, the unimaginable colors, the emotional force.[12] We are dazzled if not blindsided by passage after passage overpacked with details, recounting the unrecountable. The irregularity of Sebald's eyes "veiled / and sliding sideways down into loneliness" (*After Nature* 6E, 7–8G), so unlike the uncommon clarity of Sandrart's vision, might have told us that. Sebald's project is not—not in any literal or conventional sense—to make us see.

And thus we do not see. In lines that would share a visual object, we sense the awkward prose gropings of someone whose vision falls short. For the textual descriptions, more often than not, rather than reproducing Grünewald's paintings and passing them on to the reader, create a sense of lack in our capacity to visualize and a no doubt naive desire to have before us what we find we are unable to properly, precisely, imagine. We inevitably turn elsewhere for these images to fill in an absence.[13] Perhaps, paradoxically, this makes *After Nature* of a piece with the prose fiction work to come. For there, too, though in very different and complex ways that are specific to each moment, image and text are no easy matter.

Still, blindness has an unpredictable role to play: at once the threat to human well-being, and also an out. It defines the force that creates our hell on earth but also, though no comfortable road to tread, the entangled path of artistic creation. For, on the one hand, Sebald writes this of nature:

> *The panic-stricken*
> *kink in the neck to be seen*
> *in all of Grünewald's subjects,*
> *exposing the throat and often turning*
> *the face towards a blinding light,*
> *is the extreme response of our bodies*
> *to the absence of balance in nature*
> *which blindly makes one experiment after another*

and like a senseless botcher
undoes the thing it has only just achieved.
(*AFTER NATURE* 27)[14]

The senseless handicraft of a mad and oblivious tinkerer; we are the botched and transient experiments of blind nature. Is this the nature of *After Nature?*

THE BLINDNESS OF ART

For there is a nature, perhaps equally blinding, to which Grünewald apprenticed himself at an early age. It is the eclipse of 1502, and the painter is no merely passive creation of nature's violence. He paints "after [this] nature," recording the catastrophic madness of the last bits of light before the moon blots out the sun.

Most probably Grünewald painted
and recalled the catastrophic incursion
of darkness, the last trace of light
flickering from beyond, after nature,
for in the year 1502

. . .

on the first of October the moon's shadow
slid over Eastern Europe from Mecklenburg
over Bohemia and the Lausitz to southern Poland,
and Grünewald, who repeatedly was in touch
with the Aschaffenburg Court Astrologer Johann Indagine,
will have travelled to see this event of the century,
awaited with great terror, the eclipse of the sun,
so will have become a witness to
the secret sickening away of the world,
in which a phantasmal encroachment of dusk
in the midst of daytime like a fainting fit
poured through the vault of the sky,
while over the banks of mist and the cold

heavy blues of the clouds
a fiery red arose, and colours
such as his eyes had not known
radiantly wandered about, never again to be
driven out of the painter's memory.
(AFTER NATURE 30)[15]

Nature, even as it wastes the world away and threatens with mental blackout, creates for the Aschaffenburg artist a palette never before, perhaps never since, seen by the human eye, thus making possible painting from nature (*nach der Natur*).

In the figures of blind Homer, Tiresias, or even Milton, the Western tradition celebrates an inner sight that has triumphed over and replaced an inferior, external gaze. In Sebald's literature the wound to sight never ceases to be linked to suffering and creation. However, it is a way of being in the world, not of rising above it. For Grünewald too: "pain had entered into the pictures" (*After Nature* 7E, 8G). We see this not only as an aesthetic motif but also as an ethical gesture of compassion in section VII of "Like the snow on the Alps." It is spring of 1525. Grünewald has returned from Windsheim and from conversations with old and dear friends, now fugitives of the law. "I know that the old coat is tearing," he says, "and I am afraid / of the ending of time" (*After Nature* 34E, 30–31G). An apocalyptic foreboding, this *Reißen*, soon to be echoed in the poem's closing lines. The last battle of the German Peasants' War approaches.

In mid-May, when Grünewald
with his carved altarpiece had
returned to Frankfurt, the grain
whitening at harvest-time,
the whetted sickle passed
through the life of an army of five thousand
in the curious battle of Frankenhausen
. . .

When Grünewald got news of this
on the 18ᵗʰ of May

he ceased to leave his house.
Yet he could hear the gouging out
of eyes that long continued
between Lake Constance and
the Thuringian Forest.
For weeks at that time he wore
a dark bandage over his face.
(*AFTER NATURE* 34–35)[16]

That the painter got news of this on the birthday of W. G. Sebald is and is not a coincidence.[17] Just one of the many barely disguised instances of resemblance that the mirroring between "Like the snow on the Alps" and "Dark Night Sallies Forth" (the final poem of the volume, devoted to Sebald himself) touches on. Like those other sixteenth-century counterfeiters of Grünewald, Sebald makes a monument to him as something of a brother. No doubt, therefore, that this interpenetration of lifetimes, already there in the opening lines, might explain that the writer as well, if only metaphorically, always wore a dark bandage over his face.

NAMING

But then again, there are also sidesteps. They are not an escape from pain, but, rather, a parallel world to the thematization of literal harm to the organ of sight. These, too, comment on both the painterly and ethical worlds. Sections III and VIII, which we have yet to touch upon, practice modes of naming and description where the silent transformations of language bring about eradication and blurriness of another order: uncertainty of the identity assured by physical sight performed in acts of language.

Section IV offers an oblique version of these concerns. It is a commonplace of Grünewald scholarship that the cloudy identity of Mathys (*After Nature* 13E, 13G), the painter of Aschaffenburg, and the signed name of the artist are a vexed issue. (It is a commonplace in reading Sebald that in his works, too, dubious identity and the ambiguities of name, Sebald, say, or Austerlitz, are at play.)[18] The varied signatures of "M.N," and "M.G. and N." testify to this. Following the work of W. K. Zülch, Sebald begins by suggesting that Mathis Nithart and Grünewald might have been one and the same.

> The reason for the signature "M.N."
> above the window-frame must be
> that the painter Mathis Nithart,
> discovered in archives but otherwise
> not identified by any works of his own,
> hid behind the name of Grünewald.
> Hence the initials M.G. and N. on the Snow
> Altar at Aschaffenburg. . . .
>
> . . .
>
> And indeed the person of Mathis Nithart
> in documents of the time so flows into
> the person of Grünewald that one
> seems to have been the life,
> then the death, too, of the other.
> (AFTER NATURE 18)[19]

Still, the ambiguity of signature is not so much the confused namings of a single person as a tale (a moving one, as Sebald tells it) "of a male friendship" (After Nature 19E, 18G).

And yet he also tells of another kind of devotion or love and another complexity of name. If very little is known of the life of Matthaeus of Aschaffenburg, his marriage, nevertheless, has a privileged place. The Jewess Enchin gives up her name to be christened in the name of St. Anna. In this way she might now be betrothed to the painter and become "die Grünewald Anna" (Nach der Natur 15). But the painter, we learn, "had more of an eye for men, / whose faces and entire physique / he executed with endless devotion" (After Nature 15–16E, 15G). Perhaps, the poem suggests, this explains why she grew quarrelsome; perhaps this is why, mad at last, she became prisoner in a hospital where she was forced to endure it all.

Still, the section begins with others, centuries earlier, with the long tradition of persecuting Jews in Frankfurt, with the massacres of two centuries, the yellow rings and gray circles they were forced to wear on their clothing to signal the danger of carnal relations with Christians, long before the incompatibility of Anna's body with that of Mathys could be sensed. The 1938 book by Zülch on Grünewald, produced in honor of Hitler's birthday, Sebald writes, bringing us to the twentieth century, could not record such a strange union.

What colors that marriage of the sixteenth century, Anna's life in Frankfurt, and section III of "Like the snow on the Alps" is the color green. Perhaps more precisely—the letters of its name, *Grüne, Grune*, which, now as a color in the spectrum, now as a part of the painter's name, appear nine times in four short pages.

> *By Grünewald's time . . .*
>
> . . .
>
> *Each night—on Sundays at four in the*
> *afternoon—they were locked up, and*
> *might not walk into any place*
> *where a green tree grew,*
> *not on the Scheidewall*
> *nor in the Ross, nor on the Römerberg*
> *or in the Avenue. In this ghetto*
> *the Jewess Enchin had been raised*
> *before, not many months preceding*
> *her marriage to Mathys Grune*
> *the painter, she was christened*
> *in the name of St. Anne.*
> (*AFTER NATURE*, 13–14)[20]

Raised in a space where no tree meets the eye, locked up in her early years (as she would be later on), Enchin is deprived of the green of trees. Her baptism as Anna, her change of name, will free her from the ghetto, and her marriage to Mathys will bring her the *Grune* so brutally denied her. Isn't this what we are to understand in the lines to follow?

> *But there is no evidence that it was he who induced*
> *this Anna, betrothed to him a year later,*

to change her religious faith.
Rather it seems that she herself
had facilitated this step
attesting great strength of will,
or desperation, by looking the painter
straight in the eyes; perhaps
at first merely in love with
his green-colored name . . .
(AFTER NATURE 14)[21]

It is a phrase, this last one, that takes one's breath away (or is it one's sight?), one that questions whether we have read correctly. That Enchin becomes Anna, the reader can take in. But the author writes here that Anna, perhaps, first fell in love with his "green-colored name." As she looks Mathys in the eye, and this more than once, she falls in love, not with the green of his eyes, nor with his eyes as those of the master artist, not with their powers of seeing, with Grünewald, inventor of hues (*After Nature* 21E, 19G). Nor is the love of Enchin/Anna for the green of the trees she has been denied that haunt the poem throughout, nor even for the green of his name. Hers is not a green open to sight, not *grün* as that which names an attribute of foliage outside language, but *Grune/Grüne* that creates green-as-name and that makes green possible. Thus Anna's sense of a green-colored-name is the counterweight to those long and loyal descriptions of the hell of St. Anthony's temptation, a language of simple denomination. Her love is a liberation of sorts, and not only from the ghetto. If this is madness, and no doubt it is, it explains, perhaps, Anna's sad captivity at the end by a society that tends to lock up such challenges to its norms of thinking, speaking, writing, being different. Perhaps this strangeness of mind is shared now and then, and at critical junctures, by "Like the snow on the Alps." To be in love with the green-colored name is to take the sensual green out of green, to think, alongside its meaning, the materiality of language—and this is neither the first nor last such instance in "Like the snow on the Alps."

We do not know much of Grünewald's life. We do know the scramble of letters and names on which a life story might be hung, the *M.,* the *N.*, the *G.*, Nithart and Grünewald, that last with its promise of green woods, were one to forget that it is a proper name. We do not know much of Grünewald's death. It is a very beautiful path, this last one (*After Nature* 32G), the path of the painter and son. And when painter and son come together in this manner, the name of Anna, left by the wayside in section III, is invoked one last time, perhaps also thereby her love for a green-colored name: "a nine-year old child, / his own, as he ponders in disbelief, / conceived in his marriage to Anna" (*After Nature* 36E, 32G). As that tale comes to an end, in this the briefest of the poem's sections, it echoes with *Grün* and *Wald*, not only with the name of the painter, Grünewald, but also its fragments. They lie here and there like the leaves of a tree scattered by the wind. They are difficult to see. We are losing the green of the trees:[22] "The air stirs the light / between the leafage of trees" (*After Nature* 36E, 32G). The breeze moves not the leaves themselves but the light between them, for they have lost the presence that might have seemed to define them. Slowly, as the shadows come, it is to us that the poem is shifting. It is we who are driven by the wind and neither the leaves nor the light. "The wind drives us into flight / like starlings at the hour when / the shadows fall." (*After Nature* 36E, 32G).

With the eclipse of light, father and son then ride together toward the workplace of art: the son as apprentice, the father to the altar at "Erbach im Odenwald."[23] "What remains to the last / is the work undertaken." (*After Nature* 36E, 32G). They journey for art and they move toward a death surrounded by incomprehension.

> *and*
> *always between the eye's glance*
> *and the raising of his brush*
> *Grünewald now covers a long journey,*
> *much more often than he used to*
> *interrupts the execution of his art*
> *for the apprenticing of his child*
> *both in the workplace and outside in the green country.*
> *What he himself learned from this is nowhere reported,*
> *only that the child at the age of fourteen*
> *for no known reason suddenly died*

and that the painter did not outlive him
for any great length of time.
(AFTER NATURE 37)[24]

Grünewald ponders the conception of this young life with astonishment (*Verwunderung, After Nature* 36E, 32G) and likely parts from it yet again with no understanding. The death of the child lies between the green/*grün* of "grünen Gelände" (green country) and the "Wald" that appears seven lines later. The disintegrating name of the painter, by way of a material practice of language, accompanies the deformation of life.

PEERING SHARPLY AHEAD

If the artist is no more, what remains to the last is the text undertaken, and also yet to come, for Sebald's poem is not yet at an end. That end, let us remember, is also its striking beginning, the title of the poem—all of which suggests that "like the snow on the Alps" is, simply, what this poem is most crucially about.

The border is crossed once again. It is we who are now called to account, commanded to see: this too is a sight without knowing.

Peer ahead sharply,
there you see in the greying of nightfall
the distant windmills turn.
The forest [Wald] recedes, truly,
so far that one cannot tell
where it once lay . . .
(AFTER NATURE 37)[25]

The evening becomes gray. We are losing the light. The wind that stirred the light between leaves and then drove us into flight like starlings, although we cannot see it, causes the windmills to turn. The painter who, three years before, wore a dark blindfold, even as he heard the gouging out of eyes (*After Nature* 35E, 31G), is no more. A trace of his name, *Wald*, with its previous promise of green remains, though not that noun's object. In this poem, which opened with Dante's "steep wild-wooded way" (*After Nature*, epigraph), "the forest recedes" ("Der Wald weicht zurück"). This loss of *Wald* is the only avowed truth we are offered: "truly," the woods (*Wald*) recede so distantly that we lose the possibility of knowing where they once lay.[26] Like the painter at the end of his days whose son died of unknown cause, we must accept that the *Wald*, like its namesake, is beyond our capacity to know: "Little is known of / the life of Matthaeus Grünewald of Aschaffenburg" (*After Nature* 9E, 10G).

Dante, whose words open *After Nature*, returns. Not only the woods of the epigraph (canto II) but also the icy scene of the last canto (XXXIV) in which the poet must look upon Dis or Lucifer.[27] It is a question in Dante as in Sebald, of looking ahead sharply. Perhaps Sebald guides us as Virgil had Dante. "The distant windmills" that turn in Sebald's lines make an appearance in *The Inferno* as well. The earlier poet mistakes Lucifer for just such a structure driven by the wind. The error in vision is accompanied by (dare one say, turns on) "Just as" ("Come" in the Italian).

> *"and therefore keep your eyes ahead,"*
> *my master said, "to see if you can spy him."*
> > *Just as, when night falls on our hemisphere*
> *or when a heavy fog is blowing thick,*
> *a windmill seems to wheel when seen far off,*
> > *so then I seemed to see that sort of structure.*
> *And next, because the wind was strong, I shrank*
> *behind my guide; there was no other shelter.*
> (DANTE, *INFERNO*, XXXIV, 2–9)

There is another hell that returns as well, from "The Temptation of St. Anthony," this time of Grünewald's and Sebald's making, in the figure of an "Eishaus."[28]

> *and the ice-house*
> *opens, and rime, into the field, traces*
> *a colourless image of Earth.*
> *So it becomes, when the optic nerve*

tears, in the still space of the air
white like the snow
on the Alps.
(AFTER NATURE 37)[29]

We have lost the power of knowing where the *Wald* lay, the last fragment of Grünewald's name ("The forest [Wald] recedes . . . / so far that
one cannot tell / where it once lay" *After Nature* 37E, 33G): other fragments of text return instead, from Sebald, from Dante, and they speak
of hell. Long gone are the colors born as the moon passes before the
sun in 1502. Apprenticing oneself to nature, while also painting "after nature" (*After Nature* 30E, 26G), one must be prepared to lose the
object of sight. But this is an eclipse of another order. We are left in
a realm devoid of sound and sight, "in the still space of the air." We
who have been asked to look ahead must come to terms with an optic
nerve severed. Perhaps the attempt to see sharply has had something
to do with that. Perhaps it is the oversharpness of sight that severs us
into a new kind of art. It has lost all color, this art: a colorless image
of earth ("farbloses Bild der Erde") drawn into the field by the frost.[30]
Perhaps this is how nature mimics itself, making an image according
to nature, creating yet another (this time faceless) of those strangely
disguised "instances of resemblance" (*After Nature* 6E, 8G).

Does the close of the poem abandon our capacity to take in the
drawing/*Zeichnen* of these previous lines? Are we no longer able to
see—even the image of the Earth made as the rime gouges its drawing into the field? Do the last four lines shift abruptly to place us in
a state of utter blindness: as when the optic nerve tears and all turns
white? If Sebald's project has never been to make us see in any conventional sense, what happens when the optic nerve tears? Everything pivots on the word *So,* and also on the term *wie* (like) two lines
later. "Might we not read *So* as an adverb suggesting "in this way":
in the way rime produces its hueless image, so things become white,
like the snow on the Alps? Does *So* mark a connection and comparison to the radical creation of image that came before (the rime tracing a colorless image of Earth into the field), or does it announce a
rupture from it, away from all delineation? If it is a connection, then

what we read tells us that nature's colorless double of itself produces a white like that we find elsewhere. It gives us the sense, however faint, of a previous image and it suggests—this is the critical issue—that any textual passage might shift what it has to say by relating to yet another. Another version, perhaps, of the crossings of borders with which the poem opened.

"Like the snow on the Alps" would not dead end, then, simply in whiteness. Sebald's threat to a vision-of-the-senses would not then exclude the possibility of signification, practiced as retrospective, and also deferred connection. A connection of pause, of distance, rather than fixed meaning, because significance of this kind, for Sebald, is free of certainty. "People always want what seem to them to be symbolic elements in a text to have single meanings. But, of course, that isn't how symbols work. If they are any good at all they are usually multivalent. They are simply there to give you a sense that there must be something of significance here at that point, but what it is and what the significance is, is entirely a different matter."[31]

"When the optic nerve / tears" (*After* Nature 37E, 33G) it is not "the promis'd end" (*After Nature* 110E, 95G), it is not the end of sight, nor is the end in sight. For one might still be compelled not only to look back at what came before, the tracing of the colorless image of the Earth, but also to look ahead, once again, as we had been commanded to do ("Späh scharf voran"). To read is to look and hear elsewhere. To write, as well. The inaugural point of Sebald's literary writing lies here.[32]

All becomes white, after all, *like the snow on the Alps*, and neither snow nor Alps is without resonance elsewhere in *After Nature*. The second poem, "And if I remained by the outermost Sea" ("Und blieb ich am äussersten Meer"), is a rather flat biographical tale of the late life of Georg Wilhelm Steller, a matter-of-fact narrative that, unlike the object of its narration, shows no remarkable energy to explore new (in this case linguistic) territory.[33] It closes with his dead body in the snow: "until . . . someone . . . / left him to lie in the snow / like a fox beaten to death" (*After Nature* 78E, 68G). At the moment of death, and in the snow, Steller becomes *like* something else. The only other instance of simile in this, the second poem of the volume, is in the earlier phrase, "like the pasture slopes of the Alps" ("wie die Triften der Alpen"; *After Nature* 70E, 61G), that also echoes "like the snow on the Alps."[34]

Steller was an explorer of Alaska: the last lines of the third and final poem of *After Nature*, a literary version of Sebald's life, will bring us, rather, to another, quite different continent, this one unexplored. Here, too, we end in snow:[35] The snow and ice mountains that tower up as the light disappears echo not only the snow but also the loss of sight and the ice house (*Eishaus*) that rises up at the end of the first poem.[36]

> and, still farther in the distance,
> towering up in dwindling light,
> the mountain ranges,
> snow-covered and ice-bound,
> of the strange, unexplored,
> African continent.
> (AFTER NATURE 116)[37]

The threefold image of snow in the closing lines of each part of *After Nature*: can we call this coincidence? And, if so, how are we to understand coincidence? Sebald had this to say of coincidence in a 1992 interview: "When disturbing coincidences arise one always has the feeling that they must mean something. But one doesn't know what" ("*Auf ungeheuer dünnem Eis*" 74).[38] However we proceed to think the answer to the question of the place of snow in each, the context of the language that variously surrounds it brings us back to the question of representation at play in our reading so far. The second and third instances of snow lie in modes of narration quite different from the closing lines of the first poem, "Like the snow on the Alps," which might seem resigned to announce a parting from the visual world.

The third of the three, "Dark night sallies forth" ("Die dunckle Nacht fahrt aus"), offers in its last lines an ekphrasis of a painting by Altdorfer.[39] Here at the close of the closing poem, the narrator tells his dream to God—that he had flown to Munich to see the battle of Alexander. The goal of his destination becomes "the vision / [not of

Sebald but] of Altdorfer" (*After Nature* 114E, 97G). The description of the artist's 1528–29 painting, titled *The Battle of Alexander,* fills the final pages. Sebald's dream takes up the vision of another of his brothers in art, a citation of sorts, and ends with snow, an echo of what happens when the optical nerve tears.

No doubt the last lines of "Like the snow on the Alps" are the panels one must open to shed light on the other two poems. Or is it the other way around? Impossible to say. Do the endings of the second and third derive at least some of their meaning as repetitions of the first? Do we understand the broader theoretical implications of the first poem only on seeing its images recapitulated in the poems to come? The precise relation between the ten lines that command us to "Look sharply ahead" and the two poems to follow will have to remain "unexplored"/"unerforscht" (*After* Nature 116E, 99G), if *erforscht* (explored, researched) were to imply a closure and completion of meaning that never takes place here. The relation between those ten lines of "Like the snow on the Alps" and their later echoes in the "snow" and "Alps" suggests that there is more to tell than mere retelling either of human events or art.[40] Perhaps the relation between the passages is like the rime and the earth it draws into. Perhaps the end of "Like the snow on the Alps" marks a sketch of signification into the open fields of the texts to come.

More clearly, the elaborate, ten-line, colorless passage that is generated (precisely because of its later echoes) acts, retrospectively, less as a scene of utter blindness than as a productive potential for making sense. It doesn't, at least not simply, become white, when the optic nerve tears. When the optic nerve tears, something else takes place, the connection to what came before in the preceding lines and the connection to what comes after in the closing lines of the poems that follow. And this, through the power of the *So* and the *like.* The gap between the endings of the three parts energizes the work into something of a theoretical windmill. Because snow and the Alps come back to haunt, they set the earliest, long passage on blindness in motion as a theorization about how significance is generated. The image of blindness makes it possible for us to see through a net of interconnections. Or is it all coincidence? Sebald, in an interview of 2001, had this to say of coincidence:

Yes, I think it's this whole business of coincidence, which is very prominent in my writing. I hope it's not obtrusive. . . . But it seems to me simply an instance that illustrates that we somehow need to make sense of our nonsensical existence. And so you meet some-body who has the same birthday—the odds are one to 365, not actu-ally all that amazing. But if you like the person, then immediately this takes on major significance. [Audience laughter.] And so we build. I think all our philosophical systems, all our systems of creed, all our constructions, even the technological ones, are built in that way, in order to make some sort of sense, which there isn't, as we all know. [Audience laughter.][41]

Once one sees that snow has its place at the end of all three poems, it is difficult to shake the sense that something significant is at stake, even if one cannot say, with smug academic certainty, and given Se-bald's somewhat unexpected irony on the subject, precisely what. Still, the call to look carefully ahead and its aftermath in the severed optic nerve, the *So*, the *wie* (like), the snow and the Alps compel us to rethink the concept of blindness and vision. Perhaps the one does not shut the other out. The "need to make sense" of such intercon-nections, though, truly, it might forever escape us, is the practice of this writer and the obligation of his reader. This is so even if the audi-ence is inevitably bound to laugh or to despair. Perhaps that is what Sebald had in mind when he said of writing "you make something out of nothing."[42] Or maybe it isn't.

2

WHAT DOES IT MEAN TO COUNT?

The Emigrants

A beautiful protocol, an exact protocol. I will write a
protocol of the sort that one doesn't experience every day.
(*KASPAR HAUSER*, WERNER HERZOG, DIR.)

Remembrance is fundamentally nothing but a citation.
("LIKE DAY AND NIGHT" 90E, 184G)

FACING THE title page of the Fischer Verlag's edition of W. G. Sebald's' *The Emigrants* (*Die Ausgewanderten: Vier lange Erzählungen*) the following blurb appears, written, no doubt, with the best of intentions, but inevitably and understandably with an eye to selling books to the German public: "With great sensitivity of feeling he describes the life stories and stories of suffering of four Jews driven from their European homeland. . . . W. G. Sebald writes in order to preserve memory. Consequently he did research and had conversations, gatherered photos and documents as well as visiting the scenes."[1]

Leave aside for the moment what it means to describe (*schildern*); discount the value of photos and documents to guarantee the worth of the accounts in question.[2] How can it be they have gotten it all wrong—and in doing so have gotten it right?—"four Jews driven from their European homeland"? Four Jews, four chapters, a full count.[3] Does it matter that Ambros Adelwarth, great uncle to the narrator, butler to a wealthy Jewish American family, long years their son's lover, was himself no Jew? Does it make a difference that Paul Bereyter, dismissed by the National Socialists as schoolteacher, because he was only "three quarters an Aryan" (*The Emigrants* 50E, 74G) and called back to serve in the motorized artillery since "the draft notice . . . was also sent to three-quarter Aryans" (*The Emigrants* 55E, 81G), was only a quarter Jew?[4] What does it mean to be a quarter Jew? What does it mean that instead of four Jews there are only two and a quarter in *The Emigrants*? And what does it mean to count like a publisher? What is a Jew, and how does one make him count?

GHOST QUARTER

From the story entitled "Dr Henry Selwyn":
Thus they turn back, the dead.
(*THE EMIGRANTS* 23E, 36G)
—

How shall we quarter them, these dead who seem to come back? Is this not what *The Emigrants* is about, the question of quartering? In a volume subtitled "Four Long Stories," Dr Henry Selwyn, Paul Bereyter, Ambros Adelwarth, and Max Aurach find,[5] perhaps, a place to reside or at least to leave their residue and gain their due—a remnant, the last that one might say about them. And yet the first that one might say about them, the epigraph to the volume's first chapter, is a call to destroy the remnant—while sparing, it seems, what Sebald calls memory (*Erinnerung*):

Destroy the remnant
Not the memory.[6]
(THE EMIGRANTS 1E, 5G)
—

Then what shelter can be offered? And are these stories not like the Jewish quarter (*Judenviertel*) that the narrator encounters in Manchester, emptied before one's arrival of their inhabitants? "Little by little my Sunday walks would take me beyond the city centre to districts in the immediate neighbourhood, such as the one-time Jewish quarter. . . . This quarter had been a centre for Manchester's large Jewish community until the inter-war years, but was given up by those who lived there who moved into the suburbs and the district had meanwhile been demolished by order of the municipality" (*The Emigrants* 157E).[7] What quarter can be given, what clemency shown, since there is no way to spare the lives of those already gone?[8]

From the story entitled "Max Aurach":
They come when night falls to search after life.
(*THE EMIGRANTS* 147E, 217G)
—

Does he fail, then, this narrator, does he fail those ghosts who inhabit the four divisions of his volume, by not bringing those seekers to life? At the moment of twilight (*im Abenddämmer*), he writes, in the afterlife, if I might shift the emphasis of the phrase *nach dem Leben*, in the wake, as well, of the day's clarity, they seek. Does he fail, this narrator, who pens himself as W. G. Sebald, Winfried Georg Maximilian Sebald, whose friends called him Max—and so shall I? For I, too, want to befriend, however belatedly, the dead. Still, they may not return to life so much as turn us ever again to them.[9]

From the story entitled "Paul Bereyter":
Again and again, from front to back and from back to front, I leafed through the
album that afternoon, and since then I have returned to it time and again, be-
cause, looking at the pictures in it, it truly seemed to me, and still does, as if the
dead were coming back or as if we were on the point of passing away into them.
(*THE EMIGRANTS* 45–46E, EMPHASIS MINE).[10]
—

Here, as Sebald's publishers promised, the "photos" gathered that will "reconstruct" "the past" (publisher's blurb). And, if they are the same "documents" we encounter in *The Emigrants*, ever again, after as before, forward and backward, we too are called on to leaf through the album Sebald leaves *us* whose pages offer the same alternatives: either the dead return *or* we must be prepared for our own *Eingehen*— our passing away into their realm of image.

There are other leaves that have the same draw—those outside the window of the narrator's new house in the opening chapter. "The trees stood scarcely fifteen meters from the house, and the play of the leaves (*Blätterspiel*) seemed so close that at times, when one looked out, one believed oneself to belong therein" (*The Emigrants* 18E, *Die Ausgewanderten* 30G).[11] What does it mean in *The Emigrants*—on looking at the photographs, on leafing through the pages—that *either* the dead return *or* we are called into their photographic abode? In what way might these be alternatives or equivalents? What is an image? What does it mean to look at an image? What is a photograph, those signature interspersions—*I* do not say documents, nor even illustrations—of Max's writing?

From the story entitled "Ambros Adelwarth":
They were silent, as the dead usually are when they appear in our dreams, and seemed somewhat downcast and dejected. . . . If I approached them, they dissolved before my very eyes, leaving behind them nothing but the vacant space they had occupied.
(*THE EMIGRANTS* 122–23E).[12]

So this is what happens when we draw close to them, when we pass too precipitously into their space.[13] This is not to say that we err if we believe ourselves "to belong therein" (*The Emigrants* 18E, 30G) or if we stand "on the point of passing away into them" (*The Emigrants* 46E, 69G). But we err if we think it easy to capture the souls of the dead, with photographs, with documents, with memories, with drawings, those souls that European mythology wisely casts as butterflies.

Perhaps this is what flits by in the mockery of the narrator's great-uncle. Aunt Fini visits Adelwarth at the mental sanitorium he has chosen for his end: "when a middle-aged man appeared, holding a white net on a pole in front of him and occasionally taking curious jumps. Uncle Adelwarth stared straight ahead, but he registered my bewilderment all the same and said: It's the butterfly man, you know. He comes round here quite often. I thought I caught a tone of mockery in the words, and so took them as a sign of . . . improvement" (*The Emigrants* 104E).[14] Adelwarth, of course, does not get better; but then, again, he was never mad.

IMAGE OF MAX

So what is it that Sebald is after? And do we not find an image of him in Max Aurach (Ferber in the English translation), the artist, prominently placed as the volume's last entry,[15] in which narrator and author seem so drawn to one another. Just as the narrator, wandering through Manchester finds a sign that guides him to Max the artist,[16] isn't Aurach the sign that might guide us to Max the writer? And what if we catch sight of him in the story of Aurach's most difficult work—a portrait of the butterfly man, the image that runs through *The Emigrants* from beginning to end? The Butterfly Man is an irrecuperable ghost from the past whose gesture, in turn, is to catch the souls of the departed and even to save the living from falling into the realm of the dead. He is the figure whose mode is unexpected recurrence and who, nevertheless, obscures the particularity and possibility of memory. A chasm of amnesia separates the artist from the actual encounter with his subject. "For what reason and how far this lagoon of remembrancelessness had spread in him had remained a riddle to him, despite his most strenuous thinking about it" (*The Emigrants* 174E, 259G). *Aus welchem Grund*, for what reason, has the lagoon of oblivion taken him over?—but, also, out of what ground? For the man with a butterfly net unsettles any sense we have of ground, in art, in reason.

"If he tried to think back to the time in question, he could not see himself again till he was back in the studio, working at a painting which took him almost a full year, dragging on with minor interruptions—the faceless portrait 'Man with a Butterfly Net.' This he considered one of his most unsatisfactory works, because in his view it conveyed not even the remotest concept of the strangeness of the apparition it referred to" (*The Emigrants* 174E).[17] No way to go back to the time in question. A lesson perhaps for the dead who return searching for life and for the living who, feeling they belong to an earlier world, are prepared to pass away into it. When Aurach tries to displace himself into the past of that encounter, chasing after the man who forever chases, he finds he has already been at work on the faceless portrait, which will prove one of his most ill-conceived works. No meeting the past here, much less the object of his art, only the rupture of memory, the long experience of failing to have met him, to draw him, to capture him in an image, as in a net. Perhaps this is why it is the strangeness of the appearance, more precisely "the apparition," and not the man himself that Aurach attempts to but cannot produce.

Max travels to the Swiss Alps "to take up there once again a trace of experience that had long been buried and which [he] had never dared disturb" (*The Emigrants* 172E, 256G). He climbs to the summit of the Grammont, as he had done with his father in 1936 (*The Emigrants* 173E, 258G), and finds himself drawn to the world below, the landscape of Lake Geneva.[18] It is, perhaps, not entirely unlike the lagoon of remembrancelessness that will soon gain ground within him. He would have fallen, it seems, become one of the dead, had not the man with the butterfly net caught him, rising up before him—"like someone who's popped out of the bloody ground" (*The Emigrants* 174E, 259G).[19] This is, after all, what his net (which pops up so unexpectedly throughout the tales) captures—less the butterfly souls of the departed than the folly of feeling "compelled to fall into them" (*The Emigrants* 174E, 259G), the simple passing away (*Eingehen*) into them (*Die Ausgewanderten* 69G). And is this not what the canvas (*Leinwand*) cannot subsequently contain—the play between catching and falling, production and destruction?

"Work on the picture of the butterfly catcher had taken more out of him than any previous painting, for when he started on it, after countless preliminary studies, he not only painted over it time and again but also, whenever the canvas could no longer withstand the continual scratching-off and re-application of paint, he destroyed it and burnt it several times" (*The Emigrants* 174E).[20] Perhaps all of Max's work is like that. Failed portraiture. The past, the person, replaced by the process of its reproduction. The "butterfly man" who is, after all, no one in particular and many in his multiplicity. A gesture toward "the picture of . . ." (*The Emigrants* 174E, 260G), then again and again painted over,[21] scratched down, reapplied, finally, yet repeatedly destroyed. This is, of course, also the way Max Sebald works, or at least his narrator, and never more so than when he writes a portrait of Max Aurach.[22]

The scene of production, his "manner of working" (*The Emigrants* 162E, 239G), is less the canvas than what falls away from it, drawn, it seems, by the same seductive force of gravity against which and in the name of which the Man with the Butterfly Net pops out of the bloody ground.

> Since he applied the paint thickly, and then repeatedly scratched it off the canvas as his work proceeded, the floor was covered with a largely hardened and encrusted deposit of droppings, mixed with coal dust, several centimetres thick at the centre and thinning out towards the outer edges, in places resembling the flow of lava. This, said Ferber, was the true product of his continuing endeavours and the most palpable proof of his failure. It had always been of the greatest importance to him . . . that nothing should change at his place of work . . . and that nothing further should be added but the debris generated by painting and the dust that continuously fell and which, as he was coming to realize, he loved more than anything else in the world.
> (*THE EMIGRANTS* 161E)[23]

Aurach's failures are thus his success.

Art does not capture a lost object. It is not in search of times past, it is neither testimony, nor recovered memory—at least not only, not simply. It takes place when matter, the charcoal sticks Max uses up as he draws, the paint scratched off from the canvas, the coal dust that falls from the "continual wiping of that which is drawn" (*The Emigrants* 162E, 239G), "when the matter, little by little, dissolves into nothing" (*The Emigrants* 161E, 238G)" or almost nothing. His work "was in reality nothing but a steady production of dust, which never ceased except at night" *The Emigrants* 162E, 239G).[24]

BUTTERFLY WORK

And yet, this is no doubt too precipitous. We cannot leave it there, on the floor, under the easel of what the narrator calls Aurach's study of destruction (*The Emigrants* 180E, 269G). Let us rethink this production of dust. Aurach, on seeing the narrator after a hiatus of many years, has this to say: "There is neither a past nor a future. At least, not for me. The fragmentary images of memory by which I am haunted have the character of compulsory ideas" (*The Emigrants* 181E, 270G).[25] For Aurach there is neither past nor future, rather, memory's fragmentary and compulsive images: remnants that come home to spook not only Aurach but the entire text of *The Emigrants*, crossing the borders of its four stories, disrupting the frames of the four portraits, making strange leaps and fissures, running through the text like the butterfly man, popping up here and there out of its bloody ground.

"Dust production," then, but as *Bestäubung*,[26] as cross-pollination —what, say, a butterfly might accomplish as it flits erratically from flower to flower—here a cross-pollination of memory's fragmentary images from one chapter to another; such are the ghosts of *The Emigrants*. There is a kinship here with the haunting reappearance of snow in *After Nature* and the many other gestures we traced there, the crossings of borders or instances of resemblance and interrelation, that teach us to read otherwise. Perhaps this explains why Max's portraits, belonging to no individual, can have no face, no definitive identity: their greatest achievement is their refusal to portray, won by long labors of obliteration.[27] The butterfly chaser, the mountain scene overlooking the land beneath, the landscape of Lake Geneva, unbound to the particularity of singular identity: like the dead, they are ever returning to us.

We find these same revenants flit through the first of the stories.[28] The narrator and Clara join Dr Henry Selwyn and his friend Edward Ellis for dinner. The scene is set, like others as well, with blind mirrors, flickering lights, and uncertain images. "High on the walls mirrors with blind patches were hung, multiplying the flickering of the fire and letting unsteady images appear in them" (*The Emigrants* 12E, 21G).

The foreigners who grew up in the mountains are asked their impression "of England, and particularly of the flat expanse of the county of Norfolk" (*The Emigrants* 12E, 21–22G). No need to delineate, really, since the unsteady images, a flickering of who is who and where is where, have already transformed the flatland of Norfolk into the Alps. "The light of the west still lay on the horizon, though, with mountains of cloud whose snowy formations reminded me of the loftiest alpine massifs" (*The Emigrants* 13E, 22G). "Dusk fell" (*The Emigrants* 12E, 22G). It is, as always in *The Emigrants*, the hour of ghosting.

Like Aurach after him, in the pages that follow, it is of the Alps that Selwyn will speak, and this, too, is a tale of falling. Bern, 1913, and Selwyn is "more and more addicted to mountain climbing" (*The Emigrants* 13E, 23G)—addicted as well to the friendship of his alpine guide: "Nothing fell so hard upon me . . . as the departure of Johannes Naegeli" (*The Emigrants* 14E, 24G). This is a loss soon to be

FIGURE 2.1 Glacier. Copyright © W. G. Sebald. Reprinted by permission of the Wylie Agency, LLC (*The Emigrants* 14).

FIGURE 2.2 Newspaper. Copyright © W. G. Sebald. Reprinted by permission of the Wylie Agency, LLC (*The Emigrants* 22).

doubled when, a few months later, Naegeli, in an accident, falls "into a crevasse in the Aare glacier" (*The Emigrants* 15E, 24G). Selwyn is left in "a deep depression" during which it was as if he "was buried under snow and ice" (*The Emigrants* 15E, 25G). Here Sebald places a photo of the glacial scene: it is duplicated, more or less, at the close of the chapter, though, in a second incarnation. A man has popped up in the originally deserted snowscape: his back to us, he poses faceless. He offers us the shoe he extends behind him.

Between these twin images,[29] like the covers of a slim volume, like the placement of the photographs in the first edition of *After Nature*, we find the story of Dr. Selwyn's life, the home in Lithuania that he must leave behind, his childhood in London, a failed marriage, the

Heimweh that subsequently overwhelms him, his suicide. Before that life and after, as preface and afterword, the mountain scenes that flicker in all their multiplicity. Not least the passage that closes the chapter in which the second photo appears as a critical document. It is July 1986. The narrator takes the train from Zurich to Lausanne. "As the train slowed to cross the Aare bridge, approaching Berne, I gazed way beyond the city to the chain of mountains of the Oberland. . . . Three quarters of an hour later, not wanting to miss the landscape around Lake Geneva, which never fails to astound me as it opens out, I was just laying aside a Lausanne paper I'd bought in Zurich when my eye was caught by a report that said the remains of the Bernese alpine guide Johannes Naegeli, missing since summer 1914, had been released by the Oberaar glacier, seventy-two years later. Thus they turn back, the dead" (*The Emigrants* 23E).[30]

How *do* they come back, these dead? —unhoped for, unsuspected, less in body than in letters, less in the landscape of their disappearance, which the narrator is bent on *not* missing, than in the scriptscape of the newsprint that actually catches his eye, the tale of a "guide disparu,"[31] the documentation of a repeated image that now calls on us to consider the remains of Naegeli as a pun on the dead man's name. "Sometimes . . . they come out of the ice and lie on the border of the moraine, a small heap of polished bones, and a pair of hobnailed [*genagelter*] boots" (*The Emigrants* 23E, 36–37G, emphasis mine.)

SLIDE SHOWS

A few pages before this alpine tale, the narrator and Clara, that vague promise of light and clarity, attend a slide show presented by Selwyn and his friend Edward Ellis (Edwin Elliott in the English translation). They revisit the mountains of Crete on a wood-framed screen that finds its appropriate place, before the mirror.[32] "Once or twice, Edwin was to be seen with his field glasses and a container for botanical specimens, or Dr Selwyn in knee-length shorts, with a shoulder bag and butterfly net. One of the shots resembled, even in detail, a photograph of Nabokov in the mountains above Gstaad that I had clipped from a Swiss magazine a few days before" (*The Emigrants* 15–16E, 26G).[33]

As the narrator says of another butterfly man, we have "not even the remotest impression of the strangeness of the apparition" (*The Emigrants* 174E, 260G)—all the more so when one returns to the pages that precede it. Between the photograph dustcovers that enclose Selwyn's life story, alongside that tale that begins in the Alps and ends in the pages of a Swiss newspaper, other mountains come flickering to us in a manner so natural (or is it so artful?) we forget their origin. With Nabokov on the scene, the mountains of Crete slide to those of the Alps, and again, soon, to those of the Caucasus. The Greek, the Western European, and the Asian are as interchangeable as the names Selwyn gives his old horses: Hippolytus, Humphrey, Herschel, the last a version of Hersch and Henry in a study of the letter *H*.[34]

Aurach's Grammont, Naegeli's Oberaar, Nabokov's Gstaad are reflected miragelike, in the view from the heights around the Lasithi plateau in Crete that Selwyn wishes to share. It is a view that cannot but strike the onlooker at Selwyn's dinner party, and, all the more so, the reader. "To the south, lofty Mount Spathi, two thousand metres high, towered above the plateau, like a mirage beyond the flood of light. . . . We sat looking at this picture for a long time in silence too, so long that the glass in the slide shattered and a dark crack fissured across the screen. That view[ing] of the Lasithi plateau, held so long till it shattered, impressed itself deeply on me at the time, yet I forgot it for a considerable time thereafter" (*The Emigrants* 17E).[35]

The image that trembles lightly on the screen now bursts (*zerspringt*) its frame: it breaks not only the glass of the slide but sends that crack—perhaps not unlike the fissure into which Nageli has fallen—to the wood-framed screen on which the image is projected, the deep impression of which shatters, in turn, the view of the narrator. He is left like Aurach before that other white canvas in a state of remembrancelessness (*Erinnerungslosigkeit*; *Die Ausgewanderten* 259G). Whereas Aurach sets about to re-produce the lost figure (of the Butterfly Man), the narrator's vision of the scene is brought to life once again—not by a return of the windmills of Lasithi but by a dream force outside him, another landscape that dreams him involuntarily back to Lasithi. It comes to him, if not under the pale green veil (*Die Ausgewanderten* 26G) of Crete, then overcast by another sort of film. "It was not until a few years afterwards that [the view] returned to me, in a London cinema, as I followed a conversation between Kaspar Hauser and his teacher, Daumer. . . . Kaspar . . . was distinguishing for the first time between dream and reality, beginning his account with the words: Ja, it dreamed me. I dreamed about the Caucasus" (*The Emigrants* 17E, translation somewhat forced).[36]

Not *es träumte mir*[37]—for Kaspar, it seems, is both dreamer and the dreamed. "The camera then moved from right to left, in a sweeping arc, offering a panoramic view of a plateau ringed by mountains, a plateau with a distinctly Indian look to it, with pagoda-like towers and temples . . . in a pulsing dazzle of light, that kept reminding me of the sails of those wind pumps of Lasithi, which in reality I have still not seen to this day" (*The Emigrants* 17–18E, 29G).

Into *The Emigrants* Sebald inscribes Kaspar Hauser, a narrative, we are repeatedly told, that leaves unsolved the enigma of origin.[38] He substitutes instead the gestures of *Bestäubung* (cross-pollination), returning the narrator only by way of a film to Lasithi, which in reality he has never seen. This takes place by bursting and fragmenting the frame of narration among various narrators, realities, views, viewers, and images.

It seems we've been at the flicks, the motion pictures. The flickering on the movie screen that disturbs the images of Kaspar's Caucasus dream is that of the unsteady images that Sebald's narrator, too, insists on.[39] It returns once more, as Kaspar lies dying. His final act is that of narration: a story, as Kaspar tells it, of which he knows the beginning but not the end. A caravan passes through a desert, that is surrounded, of course, you will have guessed it, by mountains, even if the mountains are declared, for this is the point of his fragment: to be *nur eure Einbildung*. The mountains are a question of imagination.

The caravan approaches the spectator: human figures, camel legs, seem to graze the focal point of the lens and step out this, our, side of the screen, bursting the bounds, violating the rules, of the cinematic contract. The same violation—to the point of madness—takes place in Cosmo Solomon's retelling of a scene from the film *Dr. Mabuse, the Gambler*. It is the spectacle staged by a hypnotist who produces "a collective hallucination in his audience" (*The Emigrants* 97E, 141G): a caravan passes from the mirage of an oasis onstage out into the audience, drawing Solomon with it as it leaves the hall. Kaspar is right: his story has no end and has no limit. It steps into Sebald's narrative, here in the story of Henry Selwyn, there in that of Ambros Adelwarth, and again in that of Max Aurach.

It oversteps the border of the final chapter as well. In the story of Max Aurach, narrator and painter sit in the flickering light of the Wadi Halfa café.

> The Wadi Halfa was lit by flickering, glaringly bright neon light . . . and when I think back on our meetings in Trafford Park, it is invariably in that same place that I see Ferber, always sitting in front of a fresco painted by an unknown hand that showed a caravan moving forward from the remotest depths of the picture, across a wavy ridge of dunes, straight towards the beholder. Because the painter lacked the necessary skill, and the perspective he had chosen was a difficult one, both the human figures and the beasts of burden were slightly distorted so that . . . the scene looked like a mirage, quivering in the heat and light. And especially on days when Ferber had been working in charcoal, and the fine powdery dust had given his skin a metallic sheen, he seemed to have just emerged from the desert scene, *or* to belong in it.
>
> (*THE EMIGRANTS* 164E, EMPHASIS MINE)[40]

And have we not come full circle—to our question of how to quarter the dead? Difficult to say if Aurach has come out of the desert image [*Wüstenbild*],[41] or whether, though denizen of this side, he nevertheless belongs within. Hovering between, or perhaps straddling both at once, in this flickering light it's hard to tell. He is neither saved by the markings that create the picture nor sent back to the unskilled fresco of unknown hand. But this his portrait tells us: Aurach becomes his own work of art: his fate, perhaps, that of the photographer whom he finds in a similar fix, in the pages of yet another newspaper.

> But anyway, he went on . . . the darkening of his skin reminded him of an article he had recently read in the paper about silver poison-

ing, the symptoms of which were not uncommon among professional photographers. According to the article, the British Medical
Association's archives contained the description of an extreme case
of silver poisoning; in the 1930s there was a photographic lab assistant in Manchester whose body had absorbed so much silver in
the course of a lengthy professional life that he had become a kind
of photographic plate, which was apparent in the fact . . . that the
man's face and hands turned blue in strong light, or, as one might
say, developed.
(*THE EMIGRANTS* 164–65E)[42]

A martyr of sorts to his art of photography. That long practice of taking in silver. What does it mean to take in silver? And where does Sebald stand in all this? What does he develop? What his narrator tells
is surely no "beautiful protocol, [no] exact protocol," but he develops
"a protocol of the sort that one doesn't experience every day." Such
writing leaves its subject and subjects, the author too, an enigma,
even if, by the light of publication, in the many documents and photographs, their memories may *seem* preserved.

The uncertainty of the light in which that leaves them all hardly
escapes the narrator. It is the final pages of *The Emigrants.* He returns from visiting the ash-gray Aurach who, so close to death,
has a voice like the rustling of dried up leaves (*The Emigrants* 231E,
345–46G) that recalls, in another incarnation, the leaves outside the
narrator's window. In a room he has taken in the Manchester Hotel where Aurach has also resided—an act of solidarity, perhaps?
certainly not identity—in that room the Polish industrial center of
Łódź, once known as the Polish Manchester (*The Emigrants* 235–36E,
352G), comes to him. Manchester—Łódź—or, as the Nazis renamed
it, Litzmannstadt, a name that hints at the entangled web into which
we have already entered.[43]

In the narrator's imagination, then: "On those flats [of an infinitely
deep stage], which in truth did not exist, I saw, one by one, pictures
from an exhibition that I had seen in Frankfurt the year before.[44] They
were colour photographs, tinted with a greenish-blue or reddish-
brown, of the Litzmannstadt ghetto that was established in 1940 in
the Polish industrial centre of Łódź, once known as *polski Manczester*"

FIGURE 2.3 Litzmannstadt Ghetto—chief accountant. By permission
of the Jüdisches Museum Frankfurt am Main.

-(*The Emigrants* 235–36E, 352G). Something of a second slide show,
you see, whose relation to the first should be preserved. A color slide
show out of memory and imagination. "The photographs, which had
been discovered in 1987 in a small wooden suitcase, carefully sorted
and inscribed, in an antique dealer's shop in Vienna, had been taken
for the purpose of remembrance by a book-keeper and financial expert named Genewein . . . who was himself in one of the pictures,
counting money" (*The Emigrants* 236E, 352–53G).

The ghetto's chief accountant, bookkeeper, financial expert,
"counter of money" (*Geldzähler*), and, as history judged him later (if
not the courts), embezzler and thief of the worst order.[45] Genewein
obsessively documents the ghetto in almost four hundred color
slides—to celebrate the Nazi sense of "organization." "The photographer had also recorded the exemplary organization within the
ghetto: the postal system, the police, the courtroom . . . the laying
out of the dead, and the burial ground" (*The Emigrants* 236E, 354G.)
He celebrates no less, and perhaps above all, what he regarded as his
own cutting-edge photographic experimentation.

The last of these photographs, imaginary slides (*Lichtbilder*), fixes the narrator's gaze. It is a question of how to frame all these documents, a question, you see it now, no doubt, of another screen and another frame, this time, and out of time, the frame of a loom.

"Behind the perpendicular frame of a loom sit three young women, perhaps aged twenty. . . . Who the young women are I do not know. The light falls on them from the window in the background, so I cannot make out their eyes clearly, but I sense that all three of them are looking across at me, since I am standing on the very spot where Genewein the accountant stood with his camera" (*The Emigrants* 237E).[46] Sebald places his narrator, himself, of course, too, on the spot—on the spot where the accountant, the *Rechnungsführer,* had stood, that keeper of books and financial expert, who was so good at taking in silver and no doubt knew all too well how to count by quarters.[47]

At stake are the names of the weaving young women, how they are woven together: with one another, with their German analogues,[48] and what the shift from the individual to the abstract mythological frame might signify. Also what it might mean, as the publisher has it,

FIGURE 2.4 Litzmannstadt Ghetto—weavers. By permission
of the Jüdisches Museum Frankfurt am Main.

to preserve memory, to collect photos and documents (see the opening lines of this chapter). "The young woman in the middle is blonde and has the air of a bride about her. The weaver to her left has inclined her head a little to one side, whilst the woman on her right is looking at me with so steady and relentless a gaze that I cannot meet it for long. I wonder what the three women's names were—Roza, Lusia,[49] and Lea, or Nona, Decuma and Morta, the daughters of night, with spindle, thread and scissors" (*The Emigrants* 237E).[50] At the close of 350 pages the narrator stands in the place of Genewein. He is no longer, necessarily, like the besilvered Manchester photographer, a martyr to his art. He does not take a picture so much as await his fate.

We cannot count on him. *The Emigrants* does not and cannot save Henry Selwyn, nor Max Aurach, nor the quarter of Paul Bereyter that is Jewish, nor the one-and-three-quarters gentiles whose fates are just as tragic.[51] The dead cannot come back, nor can one go to them, whatever the temptation. Still in strong light (*bei starkem Lichteinfall*), something *develops*, even though we may have lost the negative— even though we may know neither the original story nor its end for sure.[52] The interwovenness of all four, better still, their *Bestäubung*,[53] their cross-pollination, the way in which anything can rupture into anything else, challenges a politics based on identity and bursts the gazes (of author, narrator, reader) that have been held fast: a liberation of sorts that shatters the frame and keeps alive the resistance— the resistance to thinking in terms of bio-logical definition, believing it might yet mean something to count as a Jew.

3

FRAMES AND EXCURSIONS

Rings of Saturn

An extensive, disorderly, incoherent web.
(RINGS OF SATURN 275E, 326G)

The Rings of Saturn consist of ice crystals and probably
meteorite dust particles describing circular orbits around the
planet's equator. In all likelihood these are fragments of a former
moon that was too close to the planet and was destroyed by its
tidal effect (→Roche limit).   *Brockhaus Encyclopaedia*
(RINGS OF SATURN FRONT MATTER)

FRAME 1. THE WINDOW ON THE PAST

LIKE ALL those who set out to set down a memoir, Sebald's narrator in the opening pages of *The Rings of Saturn* (*Die Ringe des Saturn. Eine Englische Wallfahrt*) is torn. He is both at the end and at the beginning of his journeys.[1] He is at the end of the pilgrimage of the subtitle,[2] in the world of the living, and at the beginning of another journey, in that of writing. It is the passage between these worlds that counts and which will also turn out to be a matter of life and death.[3] It is impossible to inhabit this space between life and its representation, all the more so since fixed place as well as the concept of habitation will ultimately prove beside the point in *Rings of Saturn*. Let us just say that the narrator is in limbo. If the opening chapter is about anything, it is about this.

What would it mean to get a window on what Sebald is up to? Not long into the volume, we are offered a seduction. It comes to us as a citation in strikingly large letters and in the style of print called Fraktur. Is it here that Sebald talks straight with us, or as one used to say in German: *mit uns Fraktur redet?*

> ### Ich bin der Anfang und das End
> ### und gelte
> ### an allen Orthen
>
> *I am the beginning and the end and am valid in all places.*
> (*RINGS OF SATURN* 35G, 23E)

Could this tell us something about the structure of *The Rings*? In the *Continuatio* of Grimmelshausen's *The Adventures of Simplicissimus Teutsch* (*Der Abentheurliche Simplicissimus Teutsch*), this scriptural fragment holds the secret to making mute things speak.[4] Are these lines, by way of their analogy with the beginning and closing chapters of the volume ("I am the beginning and the end"), the key that opens up the entire work? Perhaps parts 1 and 10 (Sebald called them parts rather than chapters) as they encircle the inner core of the story, drawn to it by something of a gravitational pull, are what we are pressed to understand.[5] Perhaps they are the fragmentary rings of *The Rings of Saturn*. What kind of validity or worth (*Geltung*) is at stake here? Does it hold water? Or, like the urns at the close of part I, only ashes.

The narrator sets out on his journey. The walking tour is to still an emptiness left by the production of a major piece of writing—even while embracing the desolation of East Anglia and collecting the materials for the next.[6] The narrator had written himself empty and now gathers new experience to fill that void. He is left a year later in a state of paralysis, both physical and mental, a kind of cocoon out of which, after several transmigrations, he will have to emerge to spin his yarn anew. "Perhaps it was because of this that, a year to the day after I began my journey, I was taken into hospital in Norwich, the provincial main city, in a state of almost total immobility, where I then, at least in thoughts, began the writing down of the pages that follow" (*Rings of Saturn* 3–4E, 11–12G). Caught in a double memory of freedom and paralyzing horror (*Rings of Saturn* 3E, 11G),[7] the narrator begins to fill the pages we are about to read: still, it is not on paper that he writes but in the frail medium of his thoughts. Somewhere between the written word and the experience it claims to have fixed in place we encounter the first of the mesmerizing images that string us along for some three hundred pages: a photograph of his hospital window "strangely [hung] with a black net" (*Rings of Saturn* 4E, 13G).

What the narrator remembers at this point is not what he saw in East Anglia but a *Vorstellung*, a picturing to himself:

"I still remember precisely how, upon being admitted to that hospital room on the eighth floor, I became overwhelmed by imagining that the Suffolk expanses I had wandered through the previous summer had now shrunk once and for all to a single blind and deaf point" (*Rings of Saturn* 4E, 12G). At play here are neither the circumstances of past experience outside the window that will lead him to write the text nor the text itself which he is destined to produce. Replacing the vast expanses of Suffolk of which we are soon to read (and replacing as well any thought of their notation) is a blind and senseless single point that eradicates all Cartesian conceptualization of space. And in place of that blind and senseless point (how could one figure it after all?)—this image. Is this the shape of things to come—the perspective from which he and we will be forced to see?

Fearing that the reality of his past has disappeared forever, the narrator makes a short journey before giving us the longer one of parts II–IX. He slides from his hospital bed and makes his way to the wall on all fours: a prelude to all sixes. He draws himself up to the window and leans against the glass. What follows is what he perceives only in his mind's eye. For before we discover what he actually sees, or fails to, we read of where he turns his thoughts, however involuntarily. "I stood leaning against the glass pane and I *could not help* thinking of the scene in which poor Gregor, his little legs trembling, climbs the armchair and looks out of his room, with cloudy recollection (so the

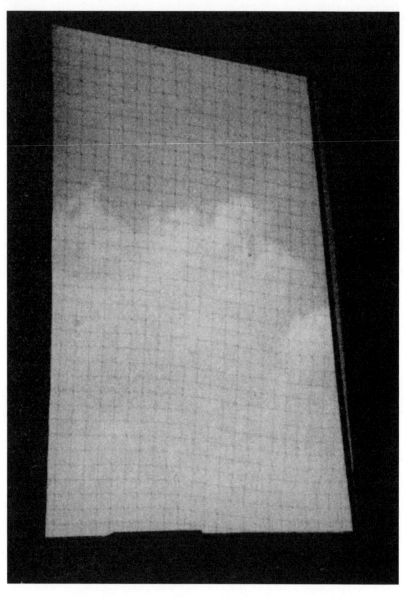

FIGURE 3.1   Hospital window with net. Copyright © W. G. Sebald. Reprinted
by permission of the Wylie Agency, LLC (*Rings of Saturn* 4).

narrative goes), of the sense of liberation that gazing out of the window had formerly given him. And *just as* Gregor's dim eyes no longer recognized the quiet Charlottenstraße . . . *so* it seemed to me" (*Rings of Saturn* 5E, emphasis mine).[8] Whatever window we have on Sebald's writing, we are told, it goes by way of involuntary thought and brings us to the question of metamorphosis. What befalls the narrator is "exactly like [that which befell] Gregor,"[9] who, like the narrator of *The Rings of Saturn*, has been transformed into another figure whose reality (*Wirklichkeit*) has disappeared forever. For Sebald's narrator, as for Gregor, what he encounters through his window seems completely strange (*Rings of Saturn* 5E, 13G).[10]

The point of this meditation on *The Rings of Saturn*, which, it is hoped, is not entirely blind and deaf to its object is the following: in what way might the encounter with the strange passages, images, and citations of part I, and even a further meandering in the texts of Thomas Browne and Grimmelshausen, allow us to theorize about representation and epistemology as it operates at the core of the text?

THE INTERLUDE OF DEATH

Part I is set between the wanderings through the county of Suffolk and the written text (parts II–X) that accounts for them. The first frame in *Rings of Saturn* is that of the hospital window hung with netting. It is the threshold between inside and out, between walking and paralysis, between experience and writing, and marks a state of mind in which the past has been shrunk to a single point. The narrator is between lived life and the written page, and his thoughts gravitate to those who have passed on in the interlude between his pilgrimage in Suffolk and the completion of his literary work. He himself is once again in limbo, in between, neither quite alive nor dead, neither conscious nor unconscious. Involuntary thought, in Sebald, drives the tale, and does so with none of the apparent ease of Proust's *mémoire involuntaire:* it ruptures the narrator from one identity to another and from one place to the next. This is the compelling force we must come to terms with on this English pilgrimage. Along the way, what the narrator is also compelled to think of is death.

"Today when I begin to write a fair copy of my notes, more than a year after my discharge from the hospital, I *am compelled to think of*" ("kommt mir zwangsläufig der Gedanke"; *Rings of Saturn* 5E, 14G, emphasis mine), he will go on to write. That said, the narrative hovers over the deaths of two colleagues who, precisely between the narrator's hospitalization with its impending mental write-down (*Niederschrift*) and the actual writing of his current work, passed over to the other side. The space that *The Rings of Saturn* occupies is a passage on the way to death. The closing lines of the volume will make this evident as they turn to another traveler: the soul of the dead as it leaves its body behind.

But for now the narrator's story takes its new departure from the unfathomable passing of Michael Parkinson and their mutual colleague, Janine Dakyns, who followed soon after.[11] Parkinson, like the narrator, made long walking tours (*Rings of Saturn* 6E, 15G). Dakyns, like the narrator, created a simulacrum in paper of such experiences. Her ever expanding "paper universe" (*Rings of Saturn* 8E, 18G) prefigures the dizzying interpolation of landscapes to come. What begins as a walk in the English countryside, what starts in Suffolk with the modest and local distances between empty villages, sweeps us, before we are done, to Waterloo, to the Balkans, to the Congo and to China, and even to the outer reaches of our solar system—all of which, of course, thus creates another paper universe or, at least, another universe on paper, this time Sebald's.

In this hiatus between the narrator's lived experience and his written text, Parkinson and Dakyns leave the land of the living. Thus begins Sebald's elaborate game of hopscotch played on the names of the dead.[12] As in the children's game, going over the edge brings in a change of players. Much of *The Rings of Saturn* moves by way of these guidelines: it skips, with the barest of warnings, from third-person description to first-person narration and back again, while shifting as well among narrators.[13]

The writerly path of (often) involuntary thought does in the speaking subject and, just as abruptly, does in the subject matter about which the narrative speaks. Nowhere is this more evident than at the beginning of the first chapter. Enlightenment (*Aufklärung*) and explanation are what the rest of the chapter is about: or rather the uneasy juxtapositions among mind, body, science, truth, perspective, art, language, representation, meaning, and, of course, death.[14] What follows feels as inevitable as it is stupefyingly unpredictable: a dash through Thomas Browne, Rembrandt, Descartes, Grimmelshausen, and Borges. If there is anything drawing this chaos together, it is the attempts and announced failures of representing an order that strove for perfection (*Rings of Saturn* 9E, 19G). For each of these figures, though never definitively, makes multiple and often conflicting claims to ordering our perception of the world.

The narrator leaves the Norwich hospital on a somewhat mad quest in search of Thomas Browne's skull only to find that it has gone astray. "It was Janine who referred me to the surgeon Anthony Batty Shaw . . . when soon after my discharge from hospital I began my enquiries about Thomas Browne, who had practiced as a doctor in Norwich in the seventeenth century and had left a number of writings that defy all comparison. I had at that time come upon an entry in the *Encyclopaedia Britannica* in which it was said that Browne's skull was kept in the museum of the Norfolk & Norwich Hospital" (*Rings of Saturn* 9E, 19G). The narrator has left the hospital. Dakyns, who always knew how to locate right away "whatever she was seeking, among her papers, in her books or in her head" (*Rings of Saturn* 9E, 19G), also knows a guide to the wandering head of Thomas Browne. Anthony Batty Shaw, (Sebald inscribes his name three times, lest we overlook the joke), brought him the desired explanation (*Rings of Saturn* 10E, 20G). After decades of exhibition at the hospital for the "purpose of medical demonstration" and the enlightenment of the public, Browne's head had been returned to its original grave. The *Encyclopaedia Britannica* insists it should, in the narrator's moment of crisis, have been there in the museum of the hospital "where [he himself] had until recently lain" (*Rings of Saturn* 9–10E, 19G). "Thomas Browne came into the world in London on the 19th of October, 1605 as the son of a silk merchant" (*Rings of Saturn*, 11E, 21G), a trade in which, we are given to understand, he, like so many other figures to follow, is somehow entangled. Silk is a thread in *The Rings of Saturn* that runs from the first chapter to last, from the birth of Thomas Browne to the closing lines and the image of the dead on their last journey.[15]

FRAME 2. REMBRANDT'S ANATOMY LESSON

Eight lines later, almost before we know it, Sebald has Browne in Amsterdam. The man whose skull was destined to spend decades on show in a "cabinet of horrors" (*Rings of Saturn* 10E, 20G) was himself, at a tender age, a spectator at a somewhat gruesome anatomical performance. It is 1632 and an "important date in the calendar" of a society that imagines itself stepping forth "out of the dark into the light" (*Rings of Saturn* 12E, 22G). Sebald has found another way to get inside Browne's head. As the narrator casts his own light on the event, Rembrandt paints the enormous *Anatomy Lesson of Dr. Nicolaas Tulp* and Browne, we read, is in the audience. "Although it is nowhere clearly substantiated, it is more than likely that the announcement of this dissection did not escape Browne and that he was present at the spectacular event, which Rembrandt captured in his painting of the Guild of Surgeons" (*Rings of Saturn* 12E, 22G). Just why the narrator wishes to place Browne here, through a reasoning that is neither clear (*eindeutig*) nor, for that matter, made convincingly probable (*wahrscheinlich*) is something we might only conjecture.[16] Onto this scene of scientific enlightenment, which is coincidentally a scene of artistic production, Sebald grafts his ethical questions. What does Rembrandt show us?[17] What is the subject of the painting? With whom does the artist identify? At stake is the relationship between different modes of representation and the assumption of an ethical stance.

It all depends on how one frames it. The spectacle (*Schauspiel*; *Die Ringe des Saturn* 22G) was intended to demonstrate a courageous drive to scientific research ([*Forschungsdrang*] *der neuen Wissenschaft*; *Die Ringe des Saturn* 22G), yet something else is also at play: a judgment by the narrator of those engaged in the performance. In the dissection of the body of Aris Kindt, hung no doubt for his crimes of theft, we also witness, the narrator tells us, the archaic ritual of tormenting the flesh even beyond the moment of death. The narrator places us, himself as well, precisely in that audience: "we are standing precisely where, in his time, those who were present at the dissection in the Waaggebouw stood, and we believe that we see what they saw then: in the foreground, the greenish, prone body of Aris Kindt, with his neck

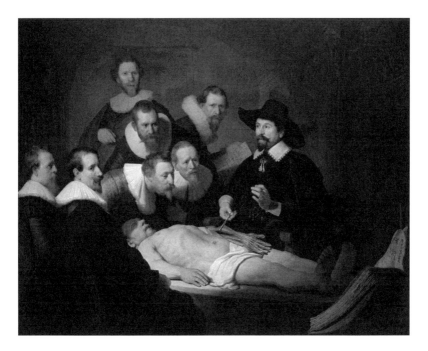

FIGURE 3.2 Rembrandt van Rijn (1606–1669), *The Anatomy Lesson of Dr Nicolaes Tulp*, 1632. *Mauritshuis, The Hague.*

broken and his chest risen terribly in rigor mortis" (*Rings of Saturn* 13E, 23G). What they and we presumably witness is precisely what the surgeons, dressed up for the ritual in their best threads, apparently fail to see: the body of Aris Kindt.

"And yet it is debatable whether anyone ever saw that body in truth, since the art of anatomy, then in its infancy, was not least a way of making the reprobate body invisible. It is significant that the gazes of the colleagues of Doctor Tulp are not directed to this body as such, rather they go just past it to the opened anatomical atlas" (*Rings of Saturn* 13E).[18] What draws them is not the man, whose body their glances overlook, but the image in an anatomical atlas propped open at his feet. In the science of anatomy the condemned man disappears. It is replaced by a schema, a diagram, to which the human has been reduced (*ein Schema des Menschen; Die Ringe des Saturn* 23G).

How to take into account, if not disentangle, some of the many strands of Sebald's claims: the perspective of the surgeons in the painting—what they see and what they overlook? The ethical stakes involve substituting schematic scientific representation for the individual human being. The commentary on Descartes, whom the narrator presumes to put there alongside Browne (*Rings of Saturn* 13E, 26G) makes the narrator's position on this quite clear.

> the gazes of the colleagues of Doctor Tulp are not directed to this body as such, rather they go just past it to the opened anatomical atlas in which the appalling corporeality is reduced to a diagram, a schematic plan of the human being, such as envisaged by the enthusiastic amateur anatomist René Descartes, who was also, so it is said, present that January morning in the Waaggebouw. In his philosophical investigations, which form one of the principal chapters of the history of subjection, Descartes teaches that one should disregard the flesh, which is beyond our comprehension, and attend to the machine within, to what can fully be understood, be made wholly useful for work, and, in the event of any fault, either repaired or discarded.
>
> (*RINGS OF SATURN* 13E)[19]

In presumed contrast to this is Rembrandt, the artist: the general audience of the Waaggebouw, and "we," alongside the narrator in the Mauritshuis, are called upon to take our stand from the same perspective. And if it is questionable whether the surgeons "ever saw that body in truth" (*Rings of Saturn* 13E, 23G), that cannot be the case for Rembrandt, given his much praised proximity to reality (*Wirklichkeitsnähe*; *Rings of Saturn* 16E, 26G). What is the truth, then, that Rembrandt has to offer? How does he present it? What is the logic by which Rembrandt's mode of representation can claim the position of a true perception? What allows him and thus us to achieve what the surgeons fail to? "It is with him, the victim, and not the Guild that gave Rembrandt his commission, that the painter identifies. His gaze alone is free of Cartesian rigidity. He alone sees that greenish annihilated body, and he alone sees the shadow in the half-open mouth and over the dead man's eyes" (*Rings of Saturn* 17E, 27G). The surgeons fail to see the victim. This is what Rembrandt shows us. He does so, not simply by representing the reality of the corpse before him, the green body, its mouth and eyes cast in shadows: Rembrandt does so as well through a purposefully crass misrepresentation of the dissected left arm. Rather than copying what is before his eyes, the reality of the tormented "incomprehensible flesh" (*Rings of Saturn* 13E, 26G), he cuts into his canvas a (no doubt true) copy of what the scientists stare at in the anatomical atlas, the diagram, the schema.

To the strange exclusion of the body which is nevertheless open to contemplation, there is a correspondence with the fact that the much-praised verisimilitude of Rembrandt's pictures proves on closer examination to be more apparent than real.
(*RINGS OF SATURN* 16E)[20]

Now this hand is most peculiar. It is not only grotesquely out of proportion compared with the hand closer to us, but it is also anatomically the wrong way round: the exposed tendons, which ought to be those of the left palm, given the position of the thumb, are in fact those of the back of the right hand. In other words, what we are faced with is a purely academic transposition from the anatomical atlas, evidently without further reflection, that turns this otherwise true-to-life painting (if one may so express it) into a crass false construction at the exact center point of its meaning, where the incisions are made.
(*RINGS OF SATURN* 16–17E)[21]

This is not a lapse in the Dutch master's capacity to copy reality, but rather an intentional rupture (*Durchbrechung*) of the composition.[22] It is precisely by cutting the misshapen hand (*unförmige Hand*; *Rings of Saturn* 17E, 27G) out of the atlas and into his otherwise mimetic painting that Rembrandt reveals his identification with the victim rather than with the other figures portrayed. Rembrandt shows that the scientists do not see, not by reproducing the violence to Kindt's hand correctly, but by abandoning his own talents of proximity to reality and reproducing their misperception. He incorporates it into the scene by bypassing the body for its schema, thus committing their error once again.[23] The perspective of Rembrandt, then, is not the moralizing, judgmental voice of the narrator, but an ironic juxtaposition of two modes of recording and thinking that which is seen.

And is this violation of realistic representation not what Sebald does to us in turn? The narrator tells us what to think, how to interpret. The false construction (*Fehlkonstruktion*) that Rembrandt cuts into his painting, no doubt from the atlas of anatomy at Aris Kindt's feet, shows the wrong hand and the wrong tendons. That this is possibly an error on Rembrandt's part is out of the question. Misrepresentation on the part of the master can only be intentional, for he knows how to reproduce reality if he knows anything at all. Sebald too, for just a few years later, in lectures entitled "Air War and Literature" ("Luftkrieg und Literatur"), he gives explicit instructions on how literature should go about mirroring reality. In *The Rings of Saturn* the narrator offers us a schema that brings us to identify with his own savage indignation. All eyes, he tells us go right past the body of the victim to the figurations of enlightenment at his feet, substituting an Enlightenment, diagrammatic form of truth for the actual body at hand, a body they, in truth, have never taken into account. That none of the guild members looks at the body is perhaps what we too can observe. But if we look with care, it is hardly that all of the gazes go just past the victim to the anatomical atlas. Of the eight witnesses that Rembrandt paints, five have their eyes wandering in all different directions: at best three seem to look at the book in the lower right of the two-page reproduction (*Rings of Saturn* 14–15E, 24–25G).

Tulp looks off to our left, suggesting that his audience is, after all, there and not where, as Sebald's narrator had suggested, Rembrandt, Browne, Descartes, and we are located. The two highest figures at the back stare more or less in our direction, as though they expected something (better) from us. The two figures on the left seem to split their attention: one looks at Tulp, the other at something slightly outside the frame to his right. Their communal attention then is distracted, sent off in almost all possible directions that a convincing portrayal of their eyes will allow.[24] The narrator nevertheless imposes a schema on the image (all eyes are on the anatomical atlas) to bring him to the moral certainty we would no doubt like to share. Can we be as certain about his intentions as he claims to be about Rembrandt's?

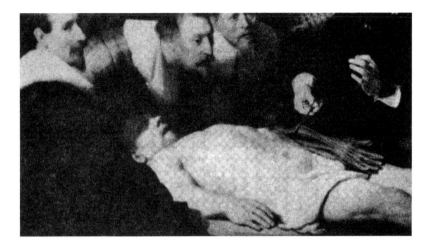

FIGURE 3.3 Rembrandt van Rijn, *The Anatomy Lesson of Dr Nicolaes Tulp*, 1632. *Mauritshuis, The Hague.* Detail as in W. G. Sebald (*Rings of Saturn* 16).

When Sebald cuts out a piece of that canvas to reproduce what he calls its center of meaning (*Bedeutungszentrum*; *Rings of Saturn* 16E, 27G), the shift in frame brings about a shift in perspective.[25] It moves the center of the full painting (the point at which the diagonals of the regular quadrilateral intersect) both down and a bit to the left. This only emphasizes the narrator's own crass misconstruction, his *Fehlkonstruktion* of a description. At best, now, only one of the three heads portrayed there seems to look toward the feet of the thief where the anatomical diagram would lie. What seemed intentional gaze becomes distraction: the disrupted lines of view caught up in the mistaken lines of tendons.

What if Sebald's *The Rings of Saturn* moves by offering us the same halting reminders? Distraction overlaps with all determinations of the intentional glance. What we read is not a simple warning against Enlightenment diagrammatics, against the brutality of the Cartesian grid that threatens Rembrandt's proximity to reality,[26] nor is it simply a matter of crass and intentional misrepresentation. Loss of form accompanies all assertion of certainty. An overall cloudiness in perception means we fail to read any sign that haze might engulf, which may or may not be reason for melancholy.

The narrator first erases the distraction of the guild of surgeons by turning all their eyes to the book at Kindt's feet, only to intensify it in his own act of excision. He does this in order to first tell us a tale in which Enlightenment science betrays human individuality by replacing it with the diagram and by treating the human body as a machine. He tells of Rembrandt's intentional misrepresentation of the dissected arm within the painting to make a moral point, by himself misrepresenting the painting in his own textual description and then dissecting the painting once again to exaggerate his false construction.

If the narrator finds this impossible to confess directly, if he insists on knowing the perspective of Rembrandt, he at least tells us that Browne's point of view, and thus ours presumably, is hardly as certain as he had originally insisted (*Rings of Saturn* 13E, 23G). What has taken place is rather a matter of unfixable perspective: "From what perspective Thomas Browne, if, as I believe, he in fact found himself among the onlookers in the anatomy theater in Amsterdam, followed the dissection and what he saw, of that there is no clue" (*Rings of Saturn* 17E, 27G). Just as Sebald unsettles our perspective, so it is impossible to locate that of Browne or even to be sure if he was there at all. There is no *Anhaltspunkt*, no clue, no ground, no fixed point from which we might gain perspective, no way to be certain how Browne might have regarded it all, but also no stop to the movement of Sebald's always soon-to-be-other writing.

MIST AND FOG

The claims to truth on the part of the narrator are a game of smoke and mirrors. This becomes obvious immediately thereafter when we read of Thomas Browne's sense of "mist" and "fog" and of the narrator's own experiences under the surgical knife. "Perhaps it was the white mist, as Browne maintains in a later note about the great fog that lay over large parts of England and Holland on the 27th of November 1674, that rises from within a body opened presently after death, and which during our lifetime, so he adds in the same stroke, clouds our brain when asleep and dreaming. I still recall how my own consciousness was veiled by the same sort of fog as I lay in my hospital room on the eighth floor once more after surgery late in the evening" (*Rings of Saturn* 17E).[27] What is this mist and fog that arises from an opened body—a haze that can overtake both England and Holland at one time?[28] Did it fog the mind in 1632 in the amphitheater of the Waaggebouw as it did in November of 1674, according to the writings of Browne? Does it account for the fogginess of mind that the narrator's operation brings about in August of 1993? How is the narrator's mind (*Bewusstsein*), overhung "with such veils of mist," to be thought in relation to his hospital window, which was hung with a black netting, in a book where hanging in various forms haunts us from the beginning to the very last lines?

Still, for the narrator, the opening of whose own body might also be supposed to have released such haze into his world, there is also a certain, if temporary, high (*Rings of Saturn* 19E, 30G). It allows him to reach the heights from which Sebald so famously narrates in critical moments, heights he soon associates with the rhetorical flights of Browne's prose, a feeling of levitation that rides on citation, overflowing metaphors, and analogies. "Under the wonderful influence of the painkillers coursing through me, I felt, in my iron-framed bed, like a balloonist floating weightless amidst the mountainous clouds towering on every side" (*Rings of Saturn* 17E, 28G).

Brought back down to earth from his heights, he becomes once again aware of his body ("I became aware again of my body, the insensate (*tauben*) foot"; *Rings of Saturn* 18E, 29G) and gazes once again through his hospital window. He reads what he sees there and misreads it: "I saw a vapour trail, as though of its own power, cross the piece of the heavens framed by my window. At the time I took that white trail for a good omen, but now, as I look back, I fear it was the beginning of a fissure that has since riven my life. The aircraft at the tip of the trail was as invisible as the passengers inside it. The invisibility and intangibility of that which moves us remained in the end an unfathomable enigma for Thomas Browne too, who saw our world as no more than a shadow image of another one" (*Rings of Saturn* 18E).[29] And for us, in turn, what moves the text of Sebald remains unseeable, ungraspable, and an insoluble enigma. The rhythm of heights and depths, of sight and shadows,[30] of representation and its (sometimes intentional) failure is that of the entire first chapter. It marks the complex interweaving of the Enlightenment and its ironization, of scientific schemas and their disruption in the lesson of Dr. Tulp. We revisit it again in Browne's ups and downs with respect to order, in Grimmelshausen's tale of Baldanders, which the narrator is soon to tell, and in the search for meaning with which the chapter will close. The trace of vapor seen through the hospital window is attributable to no visible machine. We must think *Maschine* here not only as the airplane gliding by but also as the machine of Descartes. Nor is any human presence within that machine graspable.

FRAME 3. THOMAS BROWNE'S QUINCUNX

No matter how we devote ourselves to the order of things (Sebald tells us) Browne tells us, the sense of what is actually laid out within them eludes our grasp. "We study the order of things, says Browne, but we cannot grasp their innermost essence. And because it is so, we may write our philosophy only in small letters, using the shorthand and contracted forms of transient Nature, on which alone a reflection of eternity lies" (*Rings of Saturn* 19E, 30G). Browne himself is unable to grasp the world around us. Only "isolated lights in the abyss of ignorance" (*Rings of Saturn* 19E, 30G) come to us, which is also the case with *The Rings of Saturn*.

What that pale reflection of nature has to offer us, in all its astonishing multiplicity and variety, is a pattern—a single form that Browne will claim runs through all of organic life and inorganic nature,[31] through that which is created by humans and that which they merely encounter, through the entire cosmos. It may read like utter nonsense, but there is nevertheless something reassuring about this expansive claim: a consistency of form that (as Grimmelshausen puts it) is valid everywhere (*Rings of Saturn* 23E, 35G).

Sebald devotes a mere half-page to his list of Browne's quincuncial examples, whereas Browne rages on for fifty-five pages. Over five chapters, he creates a surrealistic space for the encounter of the most outrageously anomalous animals, plants, objects, and structures, all of which share the form of the quincunx. Their radical incompatibility is at odds with the claim of their all-encompassing form.

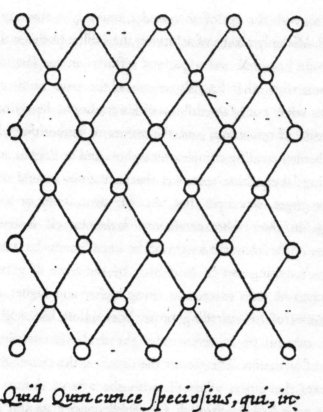

FIGURE 3.4 Quincunx. Copyright © W. G. Sebald. Reprinted by permission
of the Wylie Agency, LLC (*Rings of Saturn* 20).

Perhaps caught too long in the quincuncial funhouse, the reader
understands that this is the point in *The Rings of Saturn* where much
comes together. The quincunx is shorthand for a form that haunts
from beginning to end—and always at critical moments. We find this
grid, this net, the reticulations, these criss-crossed patterns throughout: the hospital window hung with quadrilateral-patterned netting

along with the fear that the expanses of Suffolk have been reduced to a single point; the canvas of Rembrandt, with its striations of muscles and tendons, its "center of meaning" always a bit displaced; the weaver's loom toward the close of the volume, a frame, we read, to which all humans are bound, and the writer most of all (*Rings of Saturn* 282E, 334G).[32]

We begin to grasp the quincunx as "the order of things" though we do not yet grasp precisely what is laid out therein (*Rings of Saturn* 19E, 30G). It is a pattern whose regularity is demonstrable everywhere, Browne tells us, as well as always in question, forever confirmed and disturbed in each of its evocations. Browne's "presentation [*Vorstellung*] [of] the endless mutations of Nature, which go far beyond any rational limit [*Vernunftgrenze*], or the chimaeras produced by our own thinking" (*Rings of Saturn* 22E, 34G) send us in all directions in the natural, fabricated, and imagined worlds. With that in mind, we might pretend to organize Sebald's text as well. Still his prose moves in a flight pattern much more like that of a bat or moth than the neatly articulated meshing hung over the institutional window—or even the *Maschine* that crosses it—while seeming to leave a readable, heavenly sign (*Rings of Saturn* 29G).

Despite his monomaniacal preoccupation with the quincunx, Thomas Browne is often diverted from its reassuring regularity of isomorphic lines, as the narrator writes: "Thomas Browne too was often distracted from his investigations into the isomorphic line of the quincunx by his inquisitive tracking of singular phenomena, and by work on a comprehensive pathology (*Rings of Saturn* 22E, 33G). Deflection takes place when Browne moves away from the regular and repeated quincuncial form. He does this on the one hand, as the narrator suggests here, by following his curiosity with respect to the singular or pathological, thereby leaving the quincunx aside.

But moves of distraction of another, less apparent, order are also performed in *The Garden of Cyrus*, not only as a shift in content, away from the five-pointed figure, not only because Browne talks of something else.[33] There is a concept of distraction already embedded within the multiple nature of the quincunx itself. For *quincunx* as Browne uses it, serves to name not only the form of the trees, four arranged in the form of a lozenge which contains a fifth at its center, but also the figure for the Roman numeral five (*V*), the double of which forms the letter *X,* the *decussation* that runs through the field of the rhombus.[34]

> That is the rows and orders so handsomely disposed; or five trees so set together, that a regular angularity, and through prospect, was left on every side. Owing this name not only unto the Quintuple number of Trees, but the figure declaring that number, which being doubled at the angle, makes up the letter X, that is the Emphatical decussation, or fundamentall figure. . . . Wherein the *decussis* is made within a longilaterall square, with opposite angles, acute and obtuse at the intersection; and so upon progression making a *Rhombus* or Lozenge figuration.
> (*GARDEN OF CYRUS* 194–95)[35]

The Quincunx is a figure of inclusion and exclusion at once: it calls up not only the enclosing layout of the trees (the rhomboid form that encloses the fifth tree) but also the open figure for their number, the Roman numeral *V* and the decussation (or *X*) formed by mounting that *V* on its double, which has been rotated 180 degrees. "Of this Quincuncial Ordination the Ancients practised much, discoursed little; and the Moderns have nothing enlarged; which he that more nearly considereth, in the form of its square *Rhombus*, and decussation, with the several commodities, mysteries, parallelismes, and resemblances, both in Art and Nature, shall easily discern the elegancy of this order" (*Garden of Cyrus* 197). No wonder the Ancients practiced much and discoursed little while the Moderns have remained silent on the matter. The noun Quincunx challenges easy presumptions about discourse. It moves unsettlingly among the "parallelismes, and resemblances": from bodily nature (the five trees that form a field and its content) abruptly to the abstracted figuration, not of the natural objects (the trees), but to the arbitrary figuration of their number, the *V,* which when doubled into a second figure forms the cross. The *X* and the *V* exclude not only the trees of a natural, embodied world, but also any thought of the original rhombus.[36] The lozenge of which Browne writes is the enclosed field (*Garden of Cyrus* 193) of the garden, whereas the *X* is a figure of dispersal and, in more ways than one, excludes any sense of containment. Anyone who has read Sebald's prose, say parts 2–9 of *The Rings of Saturn,* recognizes the experience of being abruptly ruptured away from the prose's subject matter, with a sense of fragmentation, toward something else not yet assimilated.

Something of this back and forth between framing and its undoing, between representation and its radical abstraction, was at work in the earlier scenes of *The Rings of Saturn*: between the hospital window of the narrator and the point to which the expanses of Suffolk may have shrunk (*Rings of Saturn* 4E, 12G); between the full painting of Rembrandt's *Anatomy Lesson of Dr. Nicolaas Tulp* and its elusive, excised center of meaning (*Rings of Saturn* 16E, 27G). The narrator accuses the guild members, within the frame of the painter's work, of valorizing a schematization of the natural, brought about by their strange exclusion of the body of Adriaan Adriaanszoon that has been made open to view.[37] And yet, we discover, their gazes are dispersed in all directions, all the more so when Sebald dissects the canvas in turn. This takes place, it is difficult to miss, in the grouping of figures in the full painting, which also suggests a decussation.

EXPELLED FROM *THE GARDEN OF CYRUS*

This shuttling between a field of enclosure, of inclusion, and the act of exclusion is also the veiled and witty point of much of Browne's "Epistle Dedicatory," a text Sebald leaves out of *The Rings of Saturn.* For the style of Browne's writing, his diction, his wordplay, draw together the linguistic and epistemological stakes as he challenges conventional modes of knowledge. Here, as Browne introduces his "garden," we read an act of scriptural abstraction: the plentiful puns on the terms for gardens and plant life dispel the tangible content. In the central passage of his dedication Browne explains the point of his text. He writes no "herbal," no conventional treatise on plants, no simple lists of names and properties. Nor does he pretend to "multiply Vegetable Divisions by [adding] Quincunxial and Reticulate Plants" (*Garden of Cyrus* 187): that would simply enlarge the past attempts at taxonomy that might have hoped to take everything into account.[38] For the quincuncial is not yet another, definable category of vegetable life that may be thought within the confines of already established modes of classifying plants. It is not an area for study, not a circumscribable object open to scientific observation: the quincuncial rather resembles the vapor trail that cuts across the narrator's window. "The Field of Knowledge hath been so traced, it is hard to spring any Thing new. Of old Things we write something new, if Truth may receive addition" (*Garden of Cyrus* 188),

"Field" (*Garden of Cyrus* 188), "spring" (*Garden of Cyrus* 188):[39] the language of the garden invades Browne's writing in metaphorical play. Of old things he writes something new by transgressing their seemingly natural meanings. Still, to the "Field of Knowledge" as conceptually imagined by others, Browne has no "Thing new" to add. The quincunx form is like no traditional parameter to pigeonhole a new category of plant life. Browne has no new thing to add to an already organized field of science, but he is able to undo the perimeters of those fields of "old Things" that claim to embody knowledge, and he thereby transforms both the conception of physically containable Cartesian space and also the concept of knowledge. Browne doesn't add yet another division to the old ways of organizing thought: rather he writes something new "of old Things" that cuts across and breaks open the divisions of the old manner of thinking. The quincunx is valid in all places.

Perhaps this is why the pages that follow in the dedication are playfully peppered not only with the subject matter of exception but also, within a single page, eight instances of words that set forth with *ex-*. It's as though the decussations of which we have yet to read in *The Garden of Cyrus* have already broken out of their proper, rhomboid walls. It is as though they have invaded the conceptualization of the piece of writing that means to contain them. "*Ex*ample," "*ex*cursion,"

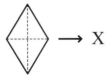

FIGURE 3.5

"*exception*," "*extremity*," and "*extraneous*" (*Garden of Cyrus* 188–89) are called to explain the "*Ex*cellency of this [quincuncial] Order" (*Garden of Cyrus* 188, emphases all mine).

Were we to contain what is at stake in this passage in simplified terms, we might say that Browne simply explains here the errant course of his treatise. He defends its lists of examples, which are to the point on the one hand, and he also shifts to apparently extraneous ex-ceptions. This digression (*Ablenkung*) from the investigation of isomorphic lines inevitably takes place when Browne's curiosity follows individual phenomena; thoughts branch out here and there as Sebald pretends offhandedly to suggest. The distractions from the isomorphic lines of the quincunx, as *The Rings of Saturn* puts it, Browne's linguistic and epistemological practice, is of a piece with Sebald's literary practice of meandering. In the physical form of the Quincunx it is impossible to distinguish any single point on Browne's diagram that seems to establish the position of the lines in a field of enclosure (as one of the four points of the diamond shape) from the point at the center of the next field over.[40] Like the quadruped traces that move crosswise over one another (*Rings of Saturn* 20E, 32G), like the movement of the narrator on all fours, half on his belly, half sideways, toward the hospital window (*Rings of Saturn* 4E, 13G), Browne's thinking, his writing, also his content move erratically by way of example and exception, contained order and the extraneous.[41] "It is hard to spring any Thing new," he writes, no doubt because the path to what he proposes as new is precisely a spring. "If Truth may receive addition," he adds—which of course it may not. Browne's treatise neither multiples ("We pretend not to multiply Vegetable Divisions"; *Garden of Cyrus* 187), nor does it add. It may offer a "Multiplicity of writing" (*Garden of Cyrus* 188) but we are warned to "expect herein no Mathematical Truths" (*Garden of Cyrus* 188). In *The Garden of Cyrus* "bye and barren Themes are best fitted for Invention" (*Garden of Cyrus* 188), themes that turn in a side direction, moving away from the main purpose, by the way, incidentally. Browne refuses to contain his powers of invention or even to follow on the paths of past writers except when he takes wide liberties darting from the direct path of truth as his example. "Subjects so often discoursed confine the Imagination, and fix our Conceptions unto the Notions of

Forewriters. Beside, such Discourses allow Excursions, and venially admit of collateral Truths, though at some distance from their Principals. Wherein if we sometimes take wide liberty, we are not single, but err by great Example" (*Garden of Cyrus* 188). The reader is to be presented, therefore, with only the single diagram we have already cited ("We have not affrighted the common reader with any other Diagrams, than of itself"; *Garden of Cyrus* 188), and it is a diagram that fails to follow the path of Sebald's (and Browne's) description.[42] No perfectly rigorous diagram. No mathematical truths. No "U Finitas" (rules without exceptions) in Browne's "Garden Discourse" (*Garden of Cyrus* 189). "We range into extraneous Things, and many Parts of Art and Nature" (*Garden of Cyrus* 189). We burst the enclosed quadrilateral for a myriad of "collateral Truths" (*Garden of Cyrus* 188).[43]

No wonder Browne moves to close his treatise with the lines that Sebald (though not quite precisely) cites: "thus with a fine turn of phrase and image, he concludes his treatise—the constellation of the Hyades, the Quincunx of Heaven, is already sinking beneath the horizon, and *so it is time to close the five ports of knowledge.* We are unwilling to spin out our waking thoughts into the phantasms of sleep; making cables of cobwebs and wildernesses of handsome groves" (*Rings of Saturn* 21E).[44]

The constellation of the Hyades, shaped like the Roman numeral *V,* sinks behind the horizon. It is neither the *X* of the decussation, which brought distraction and dispersal, nor the *X* of ex-ample and also ex-cursion, the ex-traneous, ex-ception, ex-tremity (*Garden of Cyrus* 188–89) on which Browne so insists. A broken piece of a decussation, the *V* leaves the once enclosed field wide open and doubles as a figure for the five ports of human knowledge. It is by way of those five ports, of course, that Browne has invented his text. Sebald too. That is to say, the work subtitled "the Quincunciall, Lozenge, or

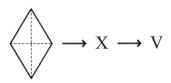

FIGURE 3.6

Net-work Plantations of the Ancients" (*Garden of Cyrus* 185) has the quincuncial five points or ports of human knowledge (the senses) as the imaginative origin of the work.[45] If human consciousness, what we might be content to conceive of as the point of departure for both scientific observation and writing, is thus woven in here as yet another example into the ubiquitous forms of the quincunx, it is also then subject to all the unsettling movements of which we have read. "The five ports of [human] knowledge" do not stand outside the quincunx as unchanging and rational powers of observation. We need to rethink, then, what it means to read.

Browne is forever "unwilling to spin out [his] thoughts into the phantasmes of sleep" (*Rings of Saturn* 21E, 32G). With that refusal he seems to be preserving his text from the chaos of dreams: the pattern of a handsome grove, no doubt quincuncial, must not be turned into a chaotic wilderness: and cobwebs, he writes as well, must not be granted the stability and strength of the cable ("making cables of cobwebs and wildernesses of handsome groves"; *Rings of Saturn* 21E, 32G). The narrator leaves us with his balanced indecision between cobwebs and the planned patterns of the ancient plantations, between fragile and sticky interrelation (that might, on contact, ensnare us) and established pattern.

FRAME 4. BALDANDERS' FRAKTUR

With this sense of bewilderment and order, the narrator of Sebald's text leaves Browne behind, soon to turn to another figure.[46] It is, after all, always one frenetic thing after another in Sebald that moves the text. The insignia for Browne was the quincunx diagram, that for Grimmelshausen, as Sebald goes on, is a citation from *Der Abentheurliche Simplicissimus Teutsch und Continuatio des abentheurlichen Simplicissimi* (a title variously translated, most recently as *The Adventures of Simplicius Simplicissimus*). The inscription that Baldanders writes for Simplicius is as attractive as the quincunx, for once again we have a written figure that seems all-inclusive, that seems to account for everything. It was from this point, the citation from Grimmelshausen, that we set out. Like the quincunx in Browne's *The*

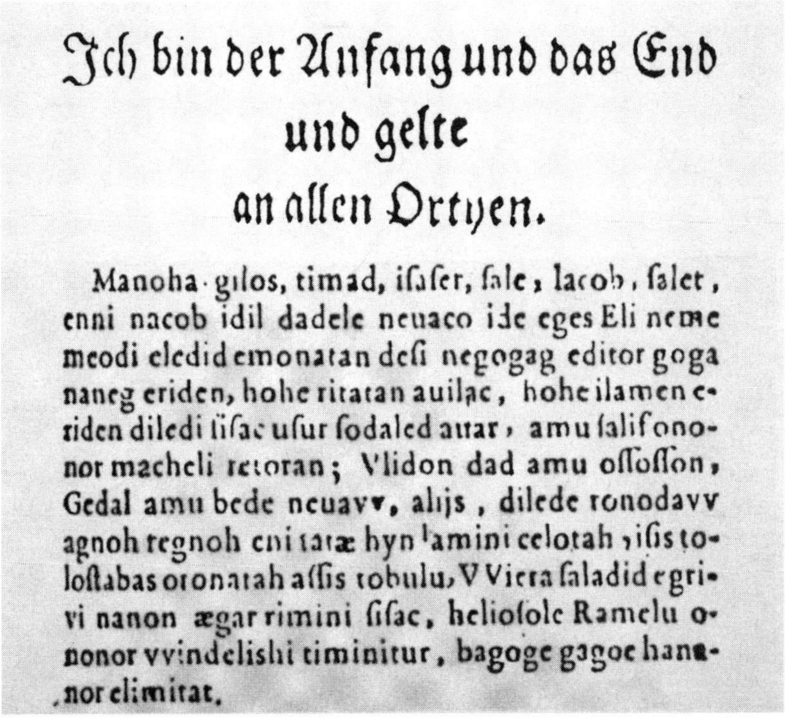

Ich bin der Anfang und das End
und gelte
an allen Ortyen.

Manoha· gilos, timad, ifafer, fale, lacob, falet,
enni nacob idil dadele neuaco ide eges Eli neme
meodi eledidemonatan defi negogag editor goga
naneg eriden, hohe ritatan auilac, hohe ilamen e-
riden diledi fifac ufur fodaled auar, amu falifono-
nor macheli retoran; Vlidon dad amu offoffon,
Gedal amu bede neuavv, alijs, dilede ronodavv
agnoh regnoh cni tatæ hyn 'amini celotah, ifis to-
loftabas oronatah affis tobulu, V Viera faladid egri-
vi nanon ægar rimini fifac, heliofole Ramelu o-
nonor vvindelishi timinitur, bagoge gagoe hane-
.nor elimitat.

FIGURE 3.7 Baldanders' riddle. Copyright © W. G. Sebald. Reprinted by
permission of the Wylie Agency, LLC (*Rings of Saturn* 23).

Garden of Cyrus, Baldanders' inscription conjures up a knowledge
that will be valid everywhere.

To be sure, we have shifted from the spatial and fixed diagram of
Browne to a linear and linguistic text. Its decoding depends, however,
in locating its critical spatial points, in this case the beginnings and
ends of each word. In a remarkable essay on Sebald's *The Rings of Saturn,* Bianca Theisen reminds us where the solution lies:

Method and result of the decoding process are not revealed to the
reader. Only a later episode retrospectively casts light on how to
crack the code. Baldanders' initial sentence, "Ich bin der Anfang
und das End und gelte an allen Ortyen" (. . . "I am the beginning
and the end, and I am valid everywhere"), a reference to St. John's

apocalypse, offers the instruction for decoding the secret message by taking the first and the last letter of each word in sequence. The deciphered text then reads:

You may yourself imagine how each thing fared and then discourse about it and believe whatever seems like the truth, then you have what your foolish curiosity desires.

Magst dir selbst einbilden vvie es Einem ieden ding ergangen hernach einen discurs daraus formirn Vund dauon Glauben vvas der vvahrheit aehnlich ist so hastu VVAs dein naerrischer uovvitz begehret.[47]

A warning about verisimilitudes of truth, the passage takes us on a journey that begins by promising a truth that is everywhere valid and culminates by mocking curiosity and gullibility as well as a certain foolishness. It ironizes being taken in by a written text that might seem to solve the riddle of its own ultimate meaning. It reduces that text—which we are called upon to read by making it into a reticulated form, not unlike the quincunx, as we highlight the first and last letters of each word—to a single blank and senseless point.

Baldanders, Sebald's narrator tells us, declares himself to have been, unbeknownst to Simplicius, with him at all times and on every day of his life (*Rings of Saturn* 23E, 34G).[48] But there is a wider frame to this joke that Sebald chooses to exclude as he glosses the passage in Grimmelshausen. Baldanders arrives as an answer of sorts to the insoluble riddle of Browne: "The invisibility and ungraspability of that which moves us remained an ultimately unfathomable riddle for Thomas Browne too" (*Rings of Saturn* 18E, 29G). Baldanders, whose name means "soon other," appears as that which itself endlessly changes, but also as that which, in a literal sense moves us. Baldanders is the force that makes all people, and most especially Simplicius, continually change: "you never noticed me, despite the fact that I made you more than other people, now big, now small, now rich, now poor, now high, now low, now jolly, now sad, now bad, now good, in sum now one way, now another" (*Simplicissimus* 506). Baldanders is both the object that refuses to hold still before our eyes (he is *bald anders*, "soon other") as well as the force that makes the beholder change. "Inconstancy is his residence" (*Simplicissimus* 507) as Simplicius puts it, though not his point of perspective. That is the point, of course, that there is no fixed point with respect to Baldanders.[49] There is no "with respect to," since there is no "him" there whom we might apprehend or comprehend, and no identifiable, observing "I," for that matter, from which one might observe him.

This is something the reader might have noticed from the very first encounter of Simplicius with Baldanders. Sebald (whose name uncannily echoes the *bald* of Baldanders) writes that Baldanders is first seen "as a stone sculpture lying in a forest, resembling a Germanic hero of old" (*Rings of Saturn* 23E, 34G). Grimmelshausen had more to say. Simplicius, in an act of frivolous self-reflection, wanders in the woods in order to listen to his own idle thoughts. There he finds an artful and natural life-sized stone image (*Bildnuß*; *Simplicissimus* 505), we read. But Simplicius, as a man of curiosity, wishes to see and know more: "whether I couldn't see more of his foundation, didn't become aware of anything of the sort, rather then I found a lever which a woodcutter had left, took it up and stood near the statue to turn it over in order to see how it was made on the other side; but hardly had I placed the lever under the neck and begun to lift when it began of itself to move and to say: 'Leave me in peace, I am Baldanders.'"[50] Simplicius is in something of an Archimedean predicament; he seeks a lever capable of moving that on which he himself, at least in a metaphorical way, has his ground. He wants to see the "Fundament" of Baldanders, the figure that changes rapidly and who is forever responsible for the transformations in Simplicius himself. There is no way to see how Baldanders as a fixed figure is made from the other side, the other side which is always other.

In carrying out his quixotic task, Simplicius brings the dumb object to speech.[51] In response to Baldanders' description of himself as the force of perpetual transformation, Simplicius asks if he is good for anything else. "Oh, yes, Baldanders answered, I can teach [people] an art whereby they can talk with all things that are dumb by nature, like chairs and benches, kettles and bowls" (*Simplicissimus* 506). The art that Baldanders teaches is that of bringing to speech things that are dumb by nature, say, a life-sized figure one might find in the woods, just when one wishes to give air to one's own thoughts. And it is an art that leaves nothing still and in place. Is this not what Baldanders does for us with respect to his enigmatic, fractured text, transforming its silent unreadability into speech that is valid in all places, once we learn the secret of the "beginning and the end"? He brings to humans, moreover, the capacity to speak with chairs and benches, pots and bowls. The apparently random examples of chairs and benches, pots and bowls, set us up for another spill. Pots and bowls make us capable of containing and giving shape to what would otherwise resist form. Chairs and benches are objects that support and give shape to the human frame. They are in a sense our temporary fundament or perhaps that which hides our other, back side. Baldanders brings to speech our capacity to consciously give form (perhaps our language, as tool), but also brings to speech that which gives *us* shape and serves as our own fundament. For want of a better name, we are tempted to call this too "language," in which we are produced in ever changing linguistic acts that mark our fundament as the inability to ever stay the same or maintain our own shape. This second conception of language is like having a lever (*Hebel*) with which we try to turn ourselves over. It is like Simplicius, who turns from his own thoughts and tries to turn over the life-sized statue, which, it turns out, is itself always changing form, has no fundament, and is what in turn keeps Simplicius himself perpetually in a state of change.

Sebald wisely leaves all that unglossed, unsaid, unread. Perhaps it hits too close to home. Instead he closes his passage on Baldanders with an account of his further transformations.

Then, before the very eyes of Simplicius, Baldanders changes into a scribe who writes these lines,

Ich bin der Anfang und das End

. . .

And then

into a mighty oak, a sow, a sausage, a piece of excrement, a field of clover, a white flower, a mulberry tree, and a silk carpet. Much as in this continuous process of consuming and being consumed, nothing endures, in Thomas Browne's view.

(*RINGS OF SATURN* 23E)[52]

The oak tree produces the acorns; the acorns are eaten by the sow who in turn is made into a bratwurst; the bratwurst results in the excrement that no doubt fertilizes the field and the white-flowered mulberry trees; the mulberry trees feed the silkworms, the threads of whose cocoons are woven into silk carpets. Sebald leaves it here. Grimmelshausen does not. Simplicius continues, "until he changes himself finally again into human figures and changes these often" (*Simplicissimus* 507). Baldanders brings the dead to life. He brings to life the dead stone as which Simplicius first finds him and also the silk carpet as the list of his transformations returns us to living human figures. The narrator of *The Rings of Saturn*, too, brings the dead to life (Browne, Conrad, Casement, Chateaubriand, among others), but in the passage just cited he ultimately cuts the thread of transformation and dead-ends in woven silk. He is ever on his way to death. Part 1 of the *Rings* and part 10, not to mention the disastrous histories of destruction in the intervening pages, seem hell-bent on nothing else.

A SCRAP OF SILK

As the first part comes to a close, we are at the end of the line. The narrator turns to Browne's *Hydriotaphia, Urne-Buriall* (1658), in which he goes on about "the rites we enact when one from our midst sets out on his last journey" (*Rings of Saturn* 25E, 37G). It is a question of the sepulchral urns found in a field in Norfolk. The thin-walled earthen containers have miraculously survived undamaged with their ash and bone remains of the dead and a dizzying, seemingly arbitrary array of "things protected from the passing of time" (*Rings of Saturn* 26E, 38G). Still, perhaps the most amazing piece is not, as the narrator would have it, a completely perfect drinking glass but another object that shares none of the sense of bright transparency, none of the sense of wholeness and potential for containing, none of that sense of escape from destruction attributed to the glass. "The most marvelous item, however, is a drinking glass, so bright it might have been newly blown. For Browne, things of this kind, protected from the passing of time, are symbols of the indestructibility of the human soul assured by Scripture. . . . Browne [searches] among that which escaped annihilation for any sign of the mysterious capacity for transmigration he has so often observed in caterpillars and moths. That purple piece of silk he refers to, from the urn of Patroclus—what does it mean?" (*Rings of Saturn* 26E).[53] How shall we fathom the transmigration of the caterpillars and moths that crawl and flutter so often in and out of *The Rings*? What kind of a symbol or emblem for the indestructability of the human soul is the *Bombyx mori*, killed for its thousand feet of silk before emerging from its cocoon? And what can a scrap of silk possibly signify?[54]

This is the question: it is posed to the reader, abruptly. A question of meaning. If the transparent, undamaged drinking glass is a "symbol of the indestructability of the human soul assured by Scripture" (*Rings of Saturn* 26E), how to understand the meaning of the tattered, woven silk from the urn of Patroclus? This is a rhetorical question—and not only because no answer is truly expected. It stages the uncertainty of meaning which is followed by the blank between chapters. One feels, nevertheless, compelled to respond. Are the chapters that follow a response of sorts to this provocation?

In parts II–IX silk is something of a *roter Faden*, a thread traceable through the entire English pilgrimage as well as the many digressions that interrupt its recounting.[55] Every reader of *The Rings of Saturn* is sure she is onto something here.[56] And yet, as it runs through these many pages, "silk" brings with it, at each instance, a shock of mild surprise. It is the kind of surprise one experiences with involuntary thought. It is perhaps not unlike the myriad coincidences of dates that haunt not only this book but *Austerlitz* as well. It brings about a discomfort of puzzlement alongside the comfort of recognition into which we are lulled. It enacts the arbitrary and erratic eruption of an apparently meaningful but always elusive symbol. For silk, as it sporadically tears through the contexts of different passages, neither stitches nor weaves together. It opens, each time anew, the question of what its distracting reappearances might possibly come to mean. It might almost give us the sense, like the net-covered hospital window, of everything shrunk together into a single blind and senseless point.

FRAME 5. THE FORBIDDEN FRAMES OF THE DEAD

What separates us from the next world is not more than a piece of silk.
(*AUSTERLITZ*, 54E, 84G)

After all the transmigrations of the intervening pages, "Part X" (which echoes the *X*, Browne's decussation, as a figure of distraction) returns us to the silken thread of the story on which everything hangs. It is that thread, once again, which intermittently seems to connect everything in between the opening and closing of Sebald's volume. Is it this chapter that will take up the scrap of silk (*Fetzchen Seide*) found in the urn of Patroclus? It presents what some readers might long for: simple linear histories with beginnings and ends, the life of the *Bombyx mori* (the silkworm), and the history of silk production in the West. That history culminates, as we know it must in Sebald, in the Nazi concentration camps. More than that, as the narrator turns to an unfindable passage, the closing lines might seem to answer the question that was posed and left hanging since the outset: "What does it all mean?"

> And Thomas Browne, who as the son of a silk merchant may well have had an eye for it, remarks, in some passage or other of his text *Pseudodoxia Epidemica* that I can no longer find, that in the Holland of his time it was customary, in the house of someone who had died, to drape silk mourning crepe over all the mirrors and all pictures on which landscapes, people or the fruits of the field were to be seen, so that the soul leaving the body would not be distracted (*abgelenkt*) on its final journey, either by the sight of itself or by that of its home (*Heimat*) soon to be lost forever.
> (*RINGS OF SATURN* 296E)[57]

Thomas Browne would have had an eye for this, for it is, once again, a question of silk—still this time not as a thread one might follow, nor as a torn fragment in the burial urn of a pagan warrior, but as silk threads interwoven to form a veil.[58] Perhaps not an answer to the question of meaning after all, so much as a repetition of an image, that might make the past incompleteness seem whole. In Holland, the home of Rembrandt, when out of their midst someone prepared to set out on his last journey (*Rings of Saturn* 25E, 37G), a journey from which the soul must not be diverted or distracted, the mirrors and paintings were draped with silk.

The end of the pilgrimage through Suffolk is the beginning of this other journey, this time and space of the dead. Still something haunts of the places we have been and the things we have seen in the past chapters. Landscapes, people, fruits of the field and the image of the traveler who reports his experience: what if not these are the scenes of the walk through the English countryside? The mourning crepe veils all that has come to pass in *The Rings of Saturn* and also the reflection of the figure who has narrated. It veils, that is, what *The Rings of Saturn* might in its simplicity seem to be: the representation as in paintings of the places described and the self-representation as in a mirror of the narrator who tells the tale.

Hung over the paintings and mirrors, the woven mesh returns us as well to the forms and frames of the opening pages. It is not a question of a thread that brings us back to the same, of a continuity out of which we might make clear sense of it all. It doesn't give us more perfect knowledge of the past passages. Nor does this passage fix one exact form valid in all places, as a center of meaning that will escape the tendency to shift. It does not decode the frame or many frames of the text into a neatly expressible aphorism or image. Still the mourning crepe hung over the paintings and mirrors echoes not only Patroclus's scrap of silk but also the earlier frames: the hospital window hung with net, Rembrandt's painting in which the strands of tendons and sinews alongside the corpse of a hanged man lie at the "center of (its) meaning," the reticulated lines of Browne's quincunx diagram, and the grid created by Baldanders' text once the first and last letters are marked. It fulfills the narrator's initial fear: that a net-draped frame might deny access to any view beyond it.

We have not come full circle. That is not the point. The soul leaving the body that clothed it (*Rings of Saturn* 296E, 350G), this last journey, might just as well be read as a continuation of the journey that we have been following, but now from the other side. *The Rings of Saturn* opens in the hospital between a past experience and the not yet written text that might represent and fix it in place. It is perhaps with this in mind that Claudia Albes so convincingly and suggestively speaks of that first image of the book, the piece of sky framed by the narrator's hospital window (*Rings of Saturn* 4E, 12G), as a picture puzzle (*Vexierbild*) between the signified and signifier, the clouds and what might be seen as the scene of signification, the squared paper of a writing block.[59]

Still there is something disturbing when one looks more precisely at the irregularity of those lines, a waviness that suggests the three-dimensionality of an almost imperceptible weave not of threads but of printed strips of fabric. It's as though the weave, which is said to hang over and behind the window (as a black net), sits, rather, in place of the pane. Instead of giving access *through* the interstices of the threads to the realm of the narrator's past experience, the veil, the apparent reality behind it, and the image one might make of them are inextricably bound up with one another. It's as though there were no gap that lies between window and net, and perhaps no observable gap, for that matter, between the gazing eye inside the window that attempts to look out at its object. Object and image along with the veil or net have collapsed, we are tempted to say, citing Sebald (*Rings of Saturn* 4E, 12G), into a single deaf and blind point. A strange formulation, this notion of a point that is both deaf and blind—though inevitably we understand it by shifting the failure of sense perception over to the observer. For there is no point here—no Cartesian plane, for that matter—in the irregular weave of imaged strips: no Cartesian space in which a coordinate system can rule. The narrator's attacks on Descartes would seem to affirm that. Isn't this the lesson of those other systems that offer themselves as the key to knowledge? Baldanders teaches us to read, to satisfy our curiosity, by making a grid of his riddle—only to find a solution that reveals us as thorough fools? And isn't this the performance of the quincunx, an omnipresent grid whose fixed structure is repeatedly exceeded? Thomas Browne might have had an eye for it, the narrator writes.

EXCURSION

Thomas Browne might have had an eye for the woven silk cast over the frame of representation, the narrator writes. Celan, too, would have had an eye for this image, Celan, who haunts Sebald's work, despite the marked silences surrounding his name.[60] One might claim, then, that here, and perhaps therefore almost from the outset of *The Rings of Saturn*, Sebald has truly learned to see with the eyes of a Jew. On contemplating that image of the net-hung window (which was linked to imagining that the narrator's experience had been reduced to a single blind spot), one might be set involuntarily thinking of the scene in Celan's famous "Conversation in the Mountains" ("Gespräch im Gebirg"). Two Jews come together. Perhaps not even two Jews so much as the figuration of just enough difference between voices to make language possible. Theirs is a peculiar kind of talk, especially given the natural surroundings. As in *The Rings of Saturn,* the act of seeing is bound up with the possibility of naming, writing, talking.[61]

There in the mountains, there in the face of a nature waiting to be named and celebrated, another order of seeing and speaking transpires. "So it was quiet, quiet, up there in the mountains. It wasn't quiet for long, because when one Jew comes along and meets another, then keeping silent is soon over, even in the mountains. Because the Jew and Nature, that's two very different things, as always, even today, even here."[62] Jews and Nature are not to be thought as one. How to describe their way of seeing? Yet that is not the question. Rather how to perform this way of seeing, which is not a connection across a vectored distance of observer and observed? For the lines that follow go first in one direction and then change course.

So there they stand, first cousins, on the left is Turk's-cap in bloom, blooming wild, blooming like nowhere, and on the right, there's some rampion, and Dianthus superbus, the superb pink, growing not far off. But they, the cousins, they have, God help us, no eyes. More precisely, they've got eyes, even they, but there is a veil hanging in front, not in front, no, behind, a movable veil; no sooner does an image go in than it remains hanging in the web, and already there is a thread on the spot, which spins, spins itself around the image, a veil-thread; spins itself around the image and produces a child with it, half image and half veil.

Poor Turk's-cap, poor rampion! . . . they are tongue and mouth, these two, as before, and in their eyes hangs the veil and you, you poor things, you're not there and are not blooming, you are not present.

(CELAN,"CONVERSATION IN THE MOUNTAINS" 397–98)[63]

These are no organs of sight in any recognizable sense. One must re-envision the eye—first with a veil that hangs in front. Then, no, rather a veil that hangs behind. No, rather a movable veil in the eyes ("und in den Augen hängt ihnen der Schleier"), entangling thread and image, veil and eye.[64] The spatial sense of in front and behind loses its certainty—loses its certainty as surely as the temporal before and after dissolves. "No sooner does an image go in than it remains hanging in the web, and already there is a thread on the spot." In front of, behind, before and after, no longer. The veil, which cannot be fixed in space, is viewed along with the image as the child (*Kind*) of its own production. Woven web, thread, veil-thread, image: (*Geweb, Faden, Schleierfaden, Bild*): they are bound together in a progeny that leaves the Turk's Cap and Rampion, remnants of a natural order, objects of a potential, conventional representation, beside the point.

Woven web, thread, veil-thread, image: though they are not the same in "Conversation in the Mountains" and in Sebald's image of the hospital window; still, the two scenes are perhaps first cousins. Sebald's window might be envisioned as a picture puzzle that marks both an outside and inside, something that is represented and the means through which that representation or cognition takes place. But isn't there also a far more vexing insistence that, in front and behind the eye and what it perceives cannot be disentangled from one another? An insistence, then, on all that the networks of *The Rings of Saturn*, both spatial and temporal, have come to perform.[65]

The mourning crepe over the paintings and mirrors is the final performance of the net cast over the frame of all we might see. It calls to mind not only the hospital window but also the Cartesian coordinate system, with its failed schematization, in Rembrandt's anatomy lesson. It brings us back to the isomorphic lines of Browne's quincunx whose enclosures were at play with gestures of exclusion. It returns us to the grid that solves Baldanders' riddle, a grid formed from the first and last letters of its otherwise nonsensical words, which chides the reader who searches for truth. The woven piece of silk in the house of someone who has passed away is cast over the frame of a reality or past lived experience (landscapes, people, fruits of the field) that was destined to be transferred and written down in Sebald's text. But not only that. The silk, we read in the closing lines, is, more precisely, cast over the already accomplished representation (*Bilder,* "images," "pictures") of scenes very like all that has come to pass in the previous hundreds of pages and over any potential reflection of its narrator. Like the scrap of silk in the urn of Patroclus, once again that woven piece of silk poses the question "What does it mean?" (*Rings of Saturn* 26E, 39G). With this in view, he who tells of the traces of destruction (*Rings of Saturn* 3E, 11G), that traveler in limbo between life and death, is sent off on his final journey. Whether, now silenced, excommunicated, he sets out in the name of a foregone damnation or in the name of a newly imagined mode of salvation that *The Rings of Saturn* might have brought about, will forever remain to be seen.

4

TOWARD AN EPISTEMOLOGY
OF CITATION

"Air War and Literature"

Hardly anything in any way describable happened.
<small>("AIR WAR" 20E, "LUFTKRIEG" 27G)</small>

FIVE YEARS after the first publication of *The Emigrants* in 1992, Sebald gives a series of lectures entitled "Air War and Literature" ("Luftkrieg und Literatur"). *The Emigrants* closed with the judgment of Genewein, the would-be documentarian of the Łódź Ghetto who imagined, no doubt, he was fixing reality in place. "Air War and Literature," as it opens, demands an aesthetic (or anti-aesthetic) that turns that suspicion of the documentary on its head. It sets us up for a theory and practice of "concrete memory." Representation is clearly called upon to serve reality. Still, the shift from the earlier prose fiction to the "Air War" lectures is no symmetrical displacement, no difference as extreme or easy to grasp as that between night and day. It is no move, say, from the frivolities of art to the gravity of history. Sebald's ultimate refusal to be the vehicle of a déjà vu, the writer's fundamental skepticism by the end of the lectures with regard to what has been seen, establishes a kinship between his commentary on German postwar literature and his earlier literary publication. And yet this is hardly evident at the outset of those lectures.

In 1997 Sebald holds forth from the other side of the German border, from that no-man's-land of what is, from a certain geopolitical viewpoint, regarded as Swiss neutrality. With his two lectures delivered in Zurich, Sebald drops something of a bomb. What he ostensibly speaks of is literature—literature of a particular historical place and time. "Air War and Literature" castigates the failure of a generation of German writers "for their incapacity to record and *bring into our memory* that which they had seen" ("Air War" xE, 7G, emphasis mine). He dreams of a language of immediacy that unproblematically names the experience of the observer, which then, somewhat magically, might become that of the reader as well. Sebald writes of an aesthetic imperative arising out of a "moral imperative" ("Air War" 51E, 58G), imposed, in turn, by the particular object to be portrayed: in this case the utter destruction of the German cities by the Allied bombing attacks in the late years of World War II. But here, already, lies something of the well-recognized scandal of his text. The author of those genre-bending volumes about (and yet not always quite about) the Holocaust—*The Emigrants* (*Die Ausgewanderten*, 1992) and *Austerlitz* (2001), to name those now most familiar to Sebald's audience, came to Switzerland in the name of another, the other victim. It is no longer the murdered and expatriated victims of European history and the Third Reich in the thirties and forties, both Jews and non-Jews, but those who by choice or fate remained on German soil. What would they, could they, have to say for themselves, of themselves? How does their speech or silence relate to their particular political and (thus) moral position and to the more generalizable situation of trauma?

This is a text of accusation and judgment, written from the perspective of a writer who knows what's what and knows what's right. His essay seems a matter of verbal retribution against those who failed to live up to their ethico-literary responsibilities to give the facts and nothing but the facts.[1] A year later, in an interview with James Wood, Sebald casts judgment on just this kind of writing. "I think that fiction writing, which does not acknowledge the uncertainty of the narrator himself, is a form of imposture and which I find very, very difficult to take. Any form of authorial writing, where the narrator sets himself up as stagehand and director and judge and executor in a text, I find somehow unacceptable."² And on December 6, 2001, interviewed on KCRW, speaking of the horrors of the Nazi period and in the spirit of such works as *The Emigrants* and *Austerlitz*, Sebald says: "The only way in which one can approach these things . . . is obliquely, tangentially, by reference rather than by direct confrontation."³ Is "Air War and Literature," then, in its moral certainty "a form of imposture"? Would the texts Sebald calls for, retrospectively, also be "somehow unacceptable," if one takes Sebald at his word?

Over and over Sebald insists that what he is looking for is "the presentation (*Darstellung*) of the real circumstances" ("Air War" ixE, 7G). It is difficult, almost impossible, he tells us, to get even a halfway adequate picture or idea (*Vorstellung*) of the extent of the devastation of the German cities. It was as though the Germans had entered into a tacit understanding that the true state of the moral and material destruction was not to be described, when what was surely called for was a steady gaze at reality ("Air War" 51E, 57G). And yet, Sebald has to admit, not everyone was capable of that steady gaze. This too was a large part of the devastation: it took with it the human capacity to understand. Faced with "the unmistakable signs of a catastrophe engulfing the whole country, it was not always simple *to bring into one's sense of experience* anything exact about the kind and extent of the destruction. . . . The need to know (*wissen*) was contradicted by the tendency to close one's senses (*Sinne*). [Stories circulated] that exceeded every capacity to comprehend" ("Air War" 23E, "Luftkrieg" 30G, emphasis mine). The sense experiences of the survivors seem to have left them unaffected: "Apparently [the experiences] didn't *penetrate into the sensorium* of those survivors who were there. . . ." and they subsequently tended to act "truly as though nothing had happened" ("Air War" 5E, 13G emphasis mine).⁴

But what would a steady gaze at reality have brought forth? How should the real circumstances have been presented? If, as Alexander Kluge, cited by Sebald, says, what happened "never became a publicly readable cipher" ("Air War" 4E, 12G), how would a factual text have read? Sebald opens "Air War and Literature" with a page of statistics about the bombings and concludes: "but what in truth all that meant—we do not know" ("Air War" 4E, 11G). Statistics teach us next

to nothing. On the contrary, Sebald comments, those documenta-
tions that did appear were compilations, untouched, it seems, by
their subject matter, and served first and foremost "to sanitize or get
rid of a kind of knowledge that was incompatible with normal understanding," nor did those who compiled such data "understand the as-
tounding faculty for self-anesthesia (*Selbstanästhesierung*) of a community that, apparently, came out of a war of annihilation without
any psychological damage to speak of" ("Air War" 11E, 19G).

Sebald demands a language that closely follows upon the events
of destruction and brings them into our memory, brings them "into
[our sense of] experience" ("Air War" 23E, 30G), which "carries [them]
over the threshold of the national consciousness" ("Air War" 11E,
19G). But the Germans, as he tells it, rather than bringing their (sometimes non)experience of destruction to language and consciousness,
rather than practicing a linguistic economy of representation or recapitulation, instead raced headlong into the business of remaking
the German economy. They substituted the production of the future-
looking "economic miracle" of the postwar years for the past as a
way to forget it. "This total destruction appears thus, not as a horrific end of a collective aberration, but, so to speak, as the first step of
the successful rebuilding" ("Air War" 6E, 14G). "After the devastation
brought about by the enemy in war," the rebuilding of the country
made possible "the second liquidation of their own previous history"
("Air War" 7E, 16G) and made any remembrance (*Rückerinnerung*, literally, "remembering back") impossible. The new progress, with all
the weight that term will take on at the end of the essay as it turns to
Benjamin, replaces and obliterates the past.

Sebald calls for a language that makes one see. It is in this regard
that he complains of Arno Schmidt's prose in *Scenes from the Life of
a Faun* (*Aus dem Leben eines Fauns*): "however, I at least, when I read
a passage like the following one, nowhere *see* that which it is supposedly about: life in the terrible moment of its disintegration" ("Air
War" 57E, 64G, emphasis mine). How then does one look destruction in the eye, close up? Perhaps he is going about this all wrong.
Perhaps, after all, it is too much to expect that the Germans could
mark their own demise. Recapitulation would be an open admission
of defeat. Perhaps there is another perspective, one from which Se-

bald's "natural history of destruction" might better be written,[5] a perspective from which he on occasion narrates in his other works.[6] The
fourth chapter of *The Emigrants*, the chapter on the artist Max Aurach
(Ferber in the English translation), for example, opens with the narrator's first trip to England, which follows on his decision to make
England his home. The long description of the narrator's twenty-two-
hour night flight from Kloten to the British city of Manchester, written from a "bird's-eye view," is a passage strangely and anomalously
haunted by the language of air war.

> I gazed down lost in wonder at the network of lights . . . their sodium
> orange the first sign that from now on I would be living in another
> world. . . . Looping around in one more curve, the roar of the en-
> gines steadily increasing, the plane set a course across open coun-
> try. By now, we should have been able to make out the sprawling
> mass of Manchester, yet one could see nothing but a faint glimmer,
> *as if from a fire almost suffocated in ash.* A blanket of fog . . . covered
> the city . . . inhabited by millions of souls, dead and alive.
> (*THE EMIGRANTS* 149–50E, EMPHASIS MINE)[7]

In "Air War and Literature" Sebald, who, in other works, takes
pleasure in narrating from above, will retell the affair also from the
point of view of the British who fly, of course, in the opposite direction. What does this mean? Is it the bombers setting off from Great
Britain who can accomplish what Sebald's compatriots could not? If
what happened to those on the ground, as Sebald sometimes insists,
"must, of necessity, have led to an overload and paralysis of the capacity to think and feel" ("Air War" 25E, 33G), are the reports of the
perpetrators such that they can complete the work that the victims
could not? "The reports of individual eyewitnesses are therefore only
of limited worth and are in need of a supplement by way of what can
be inferred with a synoptic, artificial view" ("Air War" 25–26E, 33G). Is
it the Allied bombers who can provide this artificial, not to say artistic, gaze?

From the beginning of Sebald's description of their flights, that
seems not to be the case. Like the narrator of *The Emigrants*, what
the Brits experience is first darkness and then lights, but no light is

shed on understanding their experience. "'Now, right before us . . . lies darkness and Germany,'" followed by a "'wall of search lights, in hundreds, in cones and clusters. It's a wall of light with very few breaks and behind that wall is a pool of fiercer light, glowing red and green and blue, and over that pool myriads of flares hanging in the sky. That's the city itself!'" ("Air War" 20–21E, 28G). Hard, if not impossible, then, to distinguish the city before and after the air raid that will set it further in flames. "'We are running straight into the most gigantic display of soundless fireworks in the world and here we go to drop our bombs on Berlin'" ("Air War" 21E, 29G). Nor does the sense of hearing contribute to what fails to be fully experienced. "'It's going to be quite soundless . . . , the roar of our aircraft is drowning everything else'" ("Air War" 21E, 28–29G). This is what Sebald calls the *Vorspiel*, the prelude, the soundless overture to the musical piece, the prologue in the theater of war, followed by nothing more: "Everything happens too quickly" ("Air War" 21E, 29G), for "hardly anything in any way describable happened" ("Air War" 20E, 27G).

Disappointment, then, for those who might have hoped for "reality content" or "insight into the event from some superior point of view" ("Air War" 20E, 27G). And yet, one has to admit, that this was, nevertheless, a God's-eye point of view. The name the allies gave to the raids on Hamburg in midsummer of 1943 says just that: "'Operation Gomorrah'" ("Air War" 26E, 33G). Hamburg was to be eradicated like the biblical city of Gomorrah whose sinful ways brought down on it the wrath of God. What does it tell us about the air war that those who dropped the bombs saw themselves as God or, at modest best, as his representatives?

Perhaps it is often so that those who rain down violence on their enemies do so in the name of an angry God, even when it is not quite explicit.[8] No doubt this is why Kasack (who, according to Sebald, fails in the "presentation of the real"), in a passage Sebald dismisses as an excuse for mythologizing, chooses to see the allied forces as Indra, the Hindu god not only of war but also of weather. "As if at the prompting of Indra, whose cruelty in destruction surpasses the demonic powers, they rose, the teeming messengers of death, to destroy the halls and houses of the great cities in murderous wars, a hundred times stronger than ever before, striking like the apocalypse" ("Air War" 48E, "Luftkrieg" 55G).

War comes in the name of God and retribution.⁹ Sebald speaks of this in a November 1997 interview with Andrea Köhler:

> The most neutral form of mythology in this connection would prob-ably be the idea (*Vorstellung*) that it is a matter of an act of divine intervention for which fire and water were always the central instru-ments. Bloodless violence from above in the biblical sense, then. But even that, I believe, in this connection can in no way be main-tained for us out of the history of experience.
>
> The narrator in my texts renounces every interpretation. He doesn't make use of the possibilities of explanation; he indicates that people once thought in this or that manner. With respect to himself, I believe I can say that he has no answer to this form of radi-cal contingency. He is at a loss with respect to it, can only describe how it appeared, how it came to be.¹⁰

This too is a part, but only a part, of the story of the Allied bombings. Whose story? On first reading, those who are certain where the guilt lies might almost miss it, in disbelief: what the Germans tended to feel, according to Sebald, was less a sense of shame for the crimes of the Third Reich than a sense of disgrace and ignominy (*Schande*) for having themselves experienced such degradation. He writes of the "unparalleled national humiliation" ("Air War" viiiE, 6G) and of the life among the ruins as "an existence experienced as disgraceful" ("Air War" 36E, 43G). "The darkest aspects of the closing act of the destruction, experienced by the vast majority of the German popu-lation, remained such a shameful family secret encumbered with a kind of taboo that one could not perhaps even confess it to oneself." ("Air War" 10E, 17–18G)¹¹

From the British point of view, however, this is "the so-called *moral bombing*" ("Air War" 24E, 31G). Churchill, convinced by "Sir Ar-thur Harris (Commander in Chief of Bomber Command)" was cer-tain "that now, as he said, a higher poetic justice was at work, 'that those who have loosed these horrors upon mankind will now in their homes and persons feel the shattering strokes of just retribution'" ("Air War" 18–19E, 26G). But it is also possible, we read, that many of those affected by the air raids also felt that "the great firestorms, despite their grim but impotent fury about the obvious insanity, [were] a just punishment, even . . . an act of retribution of a higher power" ("Air War" 14E, 21G).

It may be a question of a higher power here, a power explicitly experienced as a force of "retribution," yet however "high" this power may be, it seems, it never grants access to a viewpoint from which the experience of the air raids can be seen and put to paper, concretely, with the clarity demanded by Sebald. It is, rather, the point of view of a retributive enemy that reports from an extremely "narrow, one-sided, or eccentric perspective" ("Air War" 20E, 27G), giving itself over to what Sebald calls "blindness to experience" ("Air War" 20E, 27G).

If, as Churchill insists, a certain "poetic justice" is at work, this is not only because of a morality of payback but also because the conditions of possibility of writing, a certain poetics, is at stake. Sebald admits early on that neither those on the ground nor those in the air could bring the events into their sense of experience. Still, he circles back to his retrospective demand for a new way of writing. "It was supposed to be a question [in Zurich] of lectures on poetics" ("Air War" viiiE, 5G).[12] Ultimately at stake is style, a new "literary method" ("Air War" 58E, 65G), the definition of what might constitute a literature that lives up to the task of the moral imperative of the particular historical moment. It is a question of a new aesthetics,[13] one that might find its exemplum, as Sebald repeatedly writes, in the works, or at least in some passages from the works of Nossack, an aesthetics that would leave the abstract and the imaginary behind for a "concrete-documentary character" ("Air War" 58E, 65G).[14] "In the documentary approach . . . postwar German literature really comes into its own and begins with its serious study of material that would be incommensurable with traditional aesthetics" ("Air War" 58–59E, 65G).

The battle that Sebald launches is that of an ideal of truth over and against an aesthetic or pseudoaesthetic. To be sure, Sebald concedes that even within the work of Nossack such moments are perhaps unsustainable, that they appear only as individual instances of successful reportage ("Air War" 52E, 59G). Nevertheless, "the ideal of truth inherent in its entirely unpretentious objectivity, at least over long passages, proves itself in the face of total destruction the only legitimate reason for continuing to produce literature. Conversely, the production of aesthetic or pseudoaesthetic effects from the ruins of an annihilated world is a process by which literature withdraws from its justification" ("Air War" 53E).[15]

Still, it is difficult to pin down the rules for this an-aesthetic poetics. And one might wonder how one should think the relation between the anesthetic Sebald demands here and the anesthesis of the population that he condemns, or at least bemoans, elsewhere ("Air War" 11E, 19G). This will be a writing without pretension and without pretense, like that of Nossack who was the only "writer at the time who undertook the attempt to write down what he had actually seen in the most unveiled form possible" ("Air War" 51E, 57G). It is a language, therefore, that will not *produce (herstellen)* effects so much as reveal hardly a slip, hardly a difference, between immediate observation and its expression in language. This is the search for a language that speaks the world, as Roland Barthes once suggested.[16]

To be sure, once again, for those ordinary citizens, this was a challenge. What language did they have at their disposal and what was its effect on those listening and judging its authenticity? Sebald takes as his expert on these matters an American military psychologist who speaks of his conversations after the war with those who had survived in "The Air Raid on Halberstadt on 8 April 1945" ("Air War" 24E, 31G). He does this not without a certain self-irony, for this is a character from a pseudodocumentary text of Alexander Kluge, who, along with Nossack, is the figure Sebald most praises in this otherwise judgmental essay. According to the psychologist:

"the population, although obviously possessed of an innate storytelling skill, [had] lost the psychic power of memory, precisely within the confines of the ruined areas of the city." Even if, in the case of this opinion ascribed to an allegedly real person, it is a question of one of Kluge's famous pseudo-documentary devices, it is certainly accurate in identifying the syndrome, for the accounts of those who escaped with nothing but their lives do generally have something discontinuous about them, a curiously erratic quality so much at

variance with normal instances of recollection that it easily has the appearance of invention and rumor mongering.
("AIR WAR" 24E)[17]

The authentic speech of those who survived, or rather the inauthentic speech of those who were actually on the scene and witness to it, gives the sense of something made up, of cheap sensationalism and trashy literature. It is the discontinuity of their speech, its erratic quality, that creates this effect.

"Normal" remembrance, presumably, then, must present itself as a continuity. Sebald first seeks in the speech of those who will bear witness something akin to the continuous language of a "normal" memory. But when he fails to find it there, he goes on to ask how one can trust what one hears.[18] "The apparently unimpaired normal speech that went on functioning as usual in most of the eyewitness reports casts doubt on the authenticity of the experiences they preserved" ("Air War" 25E, 32G). For the other side of their reports is that they are all too continuous, the tale made whole, "covered up and neutralized" ("Air War" 25E, 32G) by clichéd turns of phrase. "But the somehow or other false sense of the eyewitness report arises also out of the stereotypical turns of phrases which they often made use of. The reality of total destruction, incomprehensible in its extreme contingency, pales behind appropriate formulations" ("Air War" 24–25E, 32G).

Convinced that those who managed to save themselves were necessarily unable to think and feel (25E, 33G), Sebald questions the worth of *any* mode in which they might come to speech: the discontinuous, erratic qualities that stand in contrast to so-called normal perspectives of memory ("Air War" 24E, 31–32G); "stereotypical turns of phrase" ("Air War" 25E, 32G) that cover and neutralize what happened; and even, "the ongoing functioning of normal speech" ("Air War" 25E, 32G) are all suspect.[19] The eyewitness, despite Sebald's repeatedly uttered disappointment, cannot possibly fulfill his demands.

What is Sebald looking for? It is a matter of bringing "something concrete to paper" ("Air War" 30E, 37G), of "concrete memory" ("Air War" 52E, 59G) that puts aside "aesthetic or pseudo-aesthetic effects" ("Air War" 53E, 59G), of the "concrete-documentary" (*konkret-dokumentarischen*; "Air War" 58E, 65G), of images that offer a very concrete form ("Air War" 38E, 46G),[20] of "prosaic sobriety" ("Air War" 57E, 63G) and sheer facts ("Air War" 51E, 57G): "the season of the year, the weather, the observer's viewpoint" ("Air War" 51E, 57G). Not the art of abstraction and metaphysical swindle ("Air War" 50E, 56G). Not the imaginary ("Air War" 58E, 65G). How might we then envision this ideal text in which eyewitness reports are, as Sebald deems necessary, supplemented by a synoptic, artificial view? ("Air War" 25–26 E, 33G). And how are we to understand the term *synoptic?*

The passage in "Air War and Literature" that has, rightfully, caught the eye of Sebald's readers in this regard tells of the July 1943 air raids over Hamburg. No longer speaking of what must be done, Sebald, presumably, practices, in this long description of the fire bombings and their aftermath, the prose that failed most of the postwar writers. Todd Samuel Presner painstakingly follows the passage move for move as it shifts back and forth between what he calls the "global" and the "local" perspectives, the aerial view of those who dropped the bombs and the ground perspective of the victims and the survivors.[21]

Despite Sebald's protests to the contrary (he dismisses at least the "abstract-imaginary"; "Air War" 58E, 65G), Presner sees that, in fits and starts, Sebald finds his way to the domain of the real and historical by way of the imaginary and the fictional. Moreover, Presner writes of a multiplicity of possible synoptic views. Whereas one is inclined to read Sebald as counterposing a single, commanding view to that of the limited perspective of the individual ("The accounts of individual eyewitnesses . . . need to be supplemented by what a synoptic and artificial view reveals"; "Air War" 25–26E, 33G), for Presner, synopsis is not necessarily the comprehensive depiction of a single large field of vision from a single point in time or a single point of view (what Sebald calls "a comprehensive image of the world of ruins"; "Air War" 48E, 54G), but rather the "multiplicity of intersecting perspectives."[22]

Moreover, some of Sebald's gestures within the Hamburg passage were condemned or dismissed earlier in his essay: the extensive statistical material, for example, about which, early on, we were told: "What in truth all that meant, we do not know" ("Air War" 4E, 11G).

We might extend this and say that something of what Presner ascribes to Sebald's passage on the firebombing of Hamburg applies
as well to much of Sebald's essay, which on a grander scale performs
something of a fitful dance among what he calls for and what he performs. Sebald insists, for example, that he welcomes the artificial,
but not art precisely. The practice of art must be set aside. The moral
imperative for at least *one* writer (Sebald writes of Nossack here) to
note down what happened in Hamburg on that night in July leads
to a far-reaching abdication of the practice of art. A report is given in
a dispassionate mode of speech as "of a horrific event out of prehistoric times" ("Air War" 52E, "Luftkrieg" 58G).[23]

What does it mean that Nossack displaces the story he is about
to tell outside of historical times,[24] to a time, by definition, of which
no written record could possibly have been preserved? Sebald retells
Nossack's tale: "In this bombproof cellar a group of people is charred
because the doors got stuck and the stored coal in the adjacent space
burnt. *Thus it happened*.[25] 'They had all fled into the middle of the cellar away from the hot walls. There they were found crowded together.
They were bloated by the heat'" ("Air War" 52E, 58G, emphasis mine).

This is Nossack's prehistoric story, a piece of reported history that
receives the approval of Sebald in the form of an almost transparent
film of iteration: "Thus it happened," he adds. But just when we have
finally, it seems, escaped art, found the matter-of-fact, the prosaic
sobriety in all its horror, Sebald sees something else in the text besides its concrete content: "The tone in which this is reported here is
that of the messenger in [classical] tragedy. Nossack knows that such
messengers are often strung up. Built into his memorandum about
the fall of Hamburg is the parable about a man who insists that he
must tell it *as it was* and who is struck dead by his auditors for having
spread a deathly chill" ("Air War" 52E, emphasis mine).[26] Everything
here is uncannily off kilter. The exemplum of concrete documentation, of a language that adheres to its substance and avoids literature,
is imbued with a tone that makes its author (and Sebald in turn) into
the figure of the messenger in classical tragedy, a genre that dili-
gently keeps immediate violence out of sight. What was simple report now seems staged. No longer the speech of a man telling it like
it is (not only Nossack, but also Sebald with his "Thus it happened"),

his speech becomes the *parable* of the man who claims he must do so.[27] He is hung or struck dead by his listeners for this, for the spreading of a deathly chill. This is a bizarre turn of phrase in relation to a tale of intensive heat and being burned to death; perhaps evidence after all that recording and bringing into experience ("Air War" 23E, 30G) what Nossack has seen is no guarantee for communicating that experience. "Concrete memory" ("Air War" 52E, 59G) is dangerous, and it is the teller of truths, the writer, who is at risk and becomes the new victim, indeed martyr, of violence at the hands of his audience.

This is not necessarily the case in the several of Sebald's own more or less exemplary, pedagogical passages, there to teach us what he is about. Taking the phrase from Solly Zuckerman, to whom we will return, Sebald opens his second lecture in Zurich by asking "How ought such a *natural history of destruction* to begin?" ("Air War" 33E, 40G, emphasis mine). He continues with a long passage written in both the third person and the impersonal "one" that describes the parasites, the rats, the flies; then suddenly we encounter this:

> *We find ourselves* in the necropolis of a foreign, incomprehensible people (*Volk*), torn from its civil existence and history, thrown back to the evolutionary stage of nomadic gatherers. *Let us imagine* "the charred ruins of the city, a dark and jagged silhouette far away beyond the Schreber gardens, . . . towering above the railway embankment" [a footnote tells us this is a citation from Böll], and in front of them a landscape of low mounds of rubble the color of cement . . . a single human being poking around in the detritus [another note tells us this is from Nossack], a tram stop in the middle of nowhere, people emerging suddenly and, as Böll writes, apparently out of nowhere, as if they had sprung from the gray hills, "invisibly, inaudibly . . . out of this plane of nothingness, . . . ghosts whose path and goal could not be recognized. . . ." [Yet another note refers us to Böll] *Let us travel with them back* into the city in which they live, through the streets in which the heaps of rubble reach up to the second floor of burnt-out facades. *We see people* who have lit small fires in the open (as though they are in the jungle, writes Nossack). . . . The *fatherland* must have looked something like that in the year 1945.
> ("AIR WAR" 36–37E, EMPHASIS MINE)[28]

Here, too, Sebald offers an exemplum of the prose he wished to read. It couldn't be more different from the report of the Hamburg firebombing. No statistics, no aerial views. A first person, if plural, narrative, everything from ground zero, though it too, so the asides insist, pieced together from a number of sources. Thrown once again into the prehistorical, we enter a textual realm in which it is no longer, or rather not simply, a question of a third-person narration. We find ourselves there, as narrator, reader, and eyewitness of a "people" (*Volk*) at first foreign, then, moving somewhat closer, of a scene we can nevertheless imagine (*Stellen wir uns also vor . . .*), if only from a distance, and thereafter we are even bidden to join ourselves to these incomprehensible people ("Let us travel with them"). The narration closes with the startling phrase, which, though written from the long perspective of a half-century later, still shifts us abruptly into the mindset of the victims ("The *fatherland* must have looked something like that in the year 1945")—speaking of Germany as the *Vaterland*. To whom, of what, is Sebald writing? As in the Hamburg passage, we are lost in a jumble of narrative modes,[29] the citations of Nossack and Böll, the paraphrases of both these authors, the third-person descriptions, the voice of Sebald's narrator, the apparent "we" that takes over, and then the shock as Sebald speaks of the *fatherland*. One tries to imagine the faces of the Zurich audience thus addressed, their response to the invitation to be taken up by and into the viewpoint of the traumatized but still loyally nationalist postwar German citizenry.[30]

THE PRACTICE OF CITATION

So how are we to come to terms with what Sebald is about here? The repeated rants demanding concrete factuality simply do not hold as he flits in and out of different perspectives. Nor do we find here the supplement to the flawed "reports of individual eye-witnesses" ("Air War" 25E, 33G), the "synoptic view," if by that we were to understand a single God's-eye view, stable and certain in its all-encompassing powers. Sebald himself seems to understand that such a perspective inevitably leads to a mythification that repeats the structure of fascist ideology.[31] Thus of Kasack's *Die Stadt hinter dem Strom* (*The City Beyond the River*) he goes on to say: "The choice of words and terminology in passages such as this, which are not rare in Kasack's epic, shows with alarming clarity that the secret language supposedly cultivated by the internal emigration was to a high degree identical with the code of the Fascist intellectual world" ("Air War" 49–50E, 56G). But there are, as we have seen, other synoptic views that in their multiplicity hold a place of honor in Sebald's essay, if one is to understand *syn-opsis*, as Presner suggests, as a seeing together from several standpoints.[32]

In the third, retrospective, section of "Air War and Literature,"[33] one finds a meditative interlude that might have some relation to the puzzling concept of synopsis in its limited sense: it seems at first to be posed as a counterweight to the perspective of the individual. Here neither the immediacy of individual experience nor a god's synoptic view holds sway. At the outset Sebald exempts himself from any possible role as witness. "At the end of the war I was just one year old, so I can hardly have preserved any impressions of that period of destruction based on real experiences" ("Air War" 71E, 76–77G).[34] Three pages later it is the eye of God he questions: "As for the air raids on Sonthofen, I remember at the age of fourteen or fifteen having asked the parson who taught religious education at the Oberstdorf gymnasium how one could reconcile our ideas of divine providence with the fact that in this attack neither the barracks nor the Hitler-Burg but rather, in place of them so to speak, the parish church and the hospital church were destroyed, but can no longer remember the response that I got then" ("Air War" 75E).[35] Truth to tell, the single synoptic view, say of the bombers over Sonthofen, which one is tempted to conflate with God's providence (*Vorsehung*), his plan, his seeing in advance, is either too shortsighted or too farsighted and, in any case, misses its mark.

Neither a narrator's privileged eye nor that of God prevails. Solly Zuckerman understood this well. A witness to the immediate aftermath of the bombings, he was unable to write his "Natural History of Destruction" as promised and planned: after decades only a shorthand for what might have been written remains to him, the few lines that he offers read as an eradication of deictic human immediacy. The passage remembers the ruins of the human capacity to point definitively toward the *thus it must have been*; it also speaks of the ruins into which the dreams of theological certainty have fallen. "All that he had in his mind was the image of the black cathedral rising up in the middle of the stone desert and the image of a severed finger which he had found on a heap of rubble" ("Air War" 32E, 39G).

And isn't it here that the moral integrity of Sebald is to be found, in the admission, after all, that the historical certainties he sought are best left to the unsteady vision of a narrative that, precisely in its truncated imprecisions, jumbled juxtapositions, and wanderings might draw us in?[36] For, in between the impossible perspectives of direct observation and the all-encompassing, distant glance, Sebald finds his place. It is not a position of immediate experience, nor even of approximately accurate recall. He can "no longer remember" ("Air War" 75E, 80G) what happened. He tells rather of mediated experiences of the war that he was born too late to know: of the photos and films of the war, and of the shadows it cast, of the horrors he did not and could not have seen directly. He tells how he finds, everywhere he travels, traces of the German violence of murder and deportation, the memorial tablets that commemorate the deported and those who were killed, even in the most out-of-the-way villages. It is in Corsica that he comes upon something else, a painting in a church that had also hung over his parents' bed. "What I also . . . saw in Corsica— if I may be permitted a digression—, was the picture from my parents' bedroom . . . showing Christ . . . before his passion . . . sitting in the Garden of Gethsemane. . . . This same picture had hung over my parents' conjugal bed for many years" ("Air War" 73E, "Luftkrieg" 78–79G). Sebald, it seems, was conceived under the sign of this image, which has its double in Corsica, where signs of another kind speak of deportation and death in the camps. He begs us to allow him this digression, this wandering of language from the topic at hand. For the task he had posed to the postwar writers, to stick tenaciously to their immediate topic, is, no doubt, a hopeless one. "Such are the abysses of history. Everything lies all jumbled up in them, and when you look down into them, you feel dizzy and full of dread" ("Air War" 74E, 79– 80G).[37] He begs us to allow the digression, because it just could be that there are other, more critical perspectives of history, which, after all, are best trusted neither to the eye of the immediate witness nor to that of the inevitably judgmental and retributive gods.

This question of what can and cannot be won from a higher or superordinate view is a difficult one throughout the essay. Particularly so at the end of part 2, the close of the lectures given in Zurich— what one might therefore choose to regard as the synoptic, if most puzzling, moment of the lectures. Sebald turns to a description of the city of Halberstadt after the air raids of 1945. "Kluge gazes down here on the field of destruction, both in the literal and metaphorical sense" (and here Sebald uses the same term he had for the perspective of the British bombers) "from a super-ordinate point of view" ("Air War" 67E, 73G). He gazes down in the literal sense as Kluge reports what he sees, what he hears, what he smells, as he "registers the facts" ("Air War" 67E, 73G); in the metaphorical sense as he goes on to tell what more abstract lessons he has learned from such bouts of observation. Sebald cites Kluge: "After a few days, *beaten tracks* begin to run over the areas piled high with rubble and the streets obliterated by the ruins, *which in a casual way connect to* the earlier *networks of paths.*" ("Air War" 67E, 73G emphasis mine).[38]

Sebald will go on to equate Kluge's view with that of Benjamin's angel of history. Much is at stake in this very difficult segue, how Kluge reads the scene of destruction, both literally and metaphorically, how one reads Sebald's take on Kluge, how one reads Benjamin's angel, and whether we are to take Kluge and the angel as metaphorical for Sebald's narrator. The passage, as it continues, reads:[39]

> The ironic amazement with which he registers the facts allows him to maintain the distance which is indispensable for all cognition. Yet the suspicion stirs even in Kluge, that most enlightened of writers, that we are unable to learn from the misfortunes we bring on ourselves, that we cannot be taught and that we will continue along the *beaten tracks which in a casual way connect to the old networks of paths*. For all Kluge's intellectual steadfastness, therefore, his gaze at the destruction of his hometown is also the gaze frozen in horror of the angel of history, of whom Walter Benjamin said. . . .
> ("AIR WAR" 67E, EMPHASIS MINE)[40]

Of the British bombers and their superior perspective, Sebald had written that it is "rather a disappointment to anyone expecting it to provide insight into the event from some superior viewpoint"

("Air War" 20E, 27G). Here, too, such expectations might come to disappointment. Those who bombed the cities both saw and heard too little: Kluge and the angel have, no doubt, seen and heard too much.

Sebald ascribes to Kluge an ironic amazement (*ironische Verwunderung*) with which he registers the facts. Once again, no doubt, the antidote or complement to immediate experience. And this irony, he tells us, makes it possible to maintain the indispensable distance necessary for all cognition. Is the view from an ironic distance the same as knowledge, then? Does Kluge offer us something beyond factual knowledge? Or is it simply that both Kluge's ironic astonishment, on the one hand, and his knowledge gleaned from observation, on the other, cannot dispense with distance? For, his enlightened state notwithstanding, as the passage continues, Kluge is haunted not by a certainty (such as might be associated with the cold reportage, say, of resident observers) but by a suspicion, and herein lie the fruits of the metaphorical gaze. What he suspects (at least according to Sebald) is that we cannot learn from those misfortunes we bring upon ourselves, that we are condemned to continue on paths that connect to our old ways. It is this that triggers Sebald's comment that Kluge's glance is that of the angel of history, frozen in horror—and this, we read "aller intellektuellen Unentwegtheit zum Trotz" ("For all Kluge's intellectual steadfastness" as Anthea Bell translates it). Still the term Sebald chooses to mark that intellectual constancy, a constancy in turn bound, no doubt, to the possibility of cognition, is odd indeed. *Unentwegtheit*, literally, is the condition of not being drawn away from the path and incorporates the term for "path" (*Weg*) that, just a line earlier, referred to the old networks of paths (*Wegverbindungen*) from which the victims of the bombings are unable to turn, an indication of their and our incapacity to learn. Surreptitiously, then, conventional intellectual endeavor, which, *unentwegt*, in its search for fixed knowledge refuses to deviate from *the* path, is allied with the inability to head out in a new direction. Despite his intellectual constancy (*Unentwegtheit*), despite his refusal to leave the comfortable path, or perhaps because of that constancy, Kluge's glance is like that of the angel. Willingly or not, his gaze, distant and ironic just a few lines before, is now frozen in horror.

More precisely, what Sebald writes is that Kluge's gaze is *also* the view of the angel of history, frozen in horror. This does not simply equate Kluge's view with that of the angel, but tells us, rather, that Kluge's view is at least double. On the one hand, his is a gaze that includes all the aspects of his engagement with the destruction of Halberstadt that precede the announcement of his relation to the angel in the passage: irony, the distance prerequisite to cognition, intellectual steadfastness, *Unentwegtheit.* *Also*, in addition (*auch*), his is the gaze of the angel of history. To make this clear we need first to back up, take a look at all that Sebald has been trying to do for pages in describing Kluge's "The Air Raid on Halberstadt on 8 April 1945" ("Der Luftangriff auf Halberstadt am 8. April 1945").

We need then to return to the final pages of the Zurich lectures to continue to place its details in perspective. At stake is not only how Kluge views the scene but also how we read. Do we read Sebald's essay in its progression to its last citation from Benjamin's "On the Concept of History" like a locomotive arriving at its final destination? Is it here, having followed the path of the argument step by step, never deviating from it, with intellectual constancy, that we can imagine ourselves as having arrived on familiar ground? Should we also attempt a superordinate perspective, this time on Sebald's reading of Kluge, with all the irony we must, or at least should, have learned necessary to the act of viewing? And is that irony not like Benjamin's call for the "emergency brake" as one travels on the locomotive of Marx's revolution? "Marx says—revolutions are the locomotives of world history. But perhaps it is entirely different. Perhaps revolutions are the grasp of the human race traveling in this train for the emergency brake."[41] Mustn't we at least learn to situate the interruption of progress that marks both Benjamin's dialectical image and also the itinerary of the revolution for Benjamin—which is certainly not either the movement face forward of the train or face backward of the angel? Benjamin likens that seductive notion of progress in Marx's conception of revolution not only to the left but also to fascism in the theses on the philosophy of history. "One reason fascism has a chance is that, in the name of progress, its opponents treat it as a historical norm."[42]

If Benjamin's ironic relation to progress is such, we need to take the long view, not simply read "Air War and Literature" for a sense of the path, for its sense of progress and its culmination point: the angel of history, which is not what either Sebald or Kluge is finally getting at. We need to double back and read as well with an eye to what came before, and even for what appears elsewhere, say in the essay "Between History and Natural History: On the Literary Description of Total Destruction" ("Zwischen Geschichte und Naturgeschichte – Über die literarische Beschreibung totaler Zerstörung"), an essay that covers similar terrain in *Campo Santo*, though somewhat differently.[43] We need to try to take in the other gestures, however beside the point they may seem once we read what functions as a conclusion of "Air War and Literature."

Otherwise one misses the point—and it is a pivotal one—of epistemology and its relation to Sebald's moral imperative. It has always been a question of learning. Long before the summary of Kluge's superordinated vision over Halberstadt, Sebald had been concerned with how we react to overwhelming violence and what we might learn from it. For implicit throughout the Zurich lectures is the question one cannot help but pose to oneself as reader: why does Sebald insist there was a moral obligation to record what took place? Is there perhaps a glimmer of hope that something might be learned? If so, learning is not that at which you arrive, one day, definitively.

What Kluge and Sebald in turn note is "individuals and groups . . . unable to assess the real degree of danger and unable to deviate from their usual socially dictated roles" (*Campo Santo* 89E, 94G; see also the almost identical "Air War" 63E, 69G). And yet, even though no "'practicable emergency measures [could be devised] except with tomorrow's brains'" (*Campo Santo* 89E, 94G; see also the almost identical "Air War" 63E, 69G), this does not render the study of history useless. On the contrary: a "retrospective learning process," Sebald writes, is the "raison d'être of Kluge's text" (*Campo Santo* 90E, 95G; "Air War" 63E, 69G). Is it that the writings of Kluge and Sebald might teach us then to think with tomorrow's brains? Might we learn from their admonitions some three and six decades after the fact? Sebald writes:

Despite the ironic style, the perspective suggested here of an alternative historical outcome, possible in specific circumstances, is a serious call to work for the future in defiance of all calculations of probability. Precisely Kluge's detailed description of the social organization of disaster, which is programmed by the ever-accompanying [*mitgeschleppten*] and ever-intensifying error of history, comprises the conjecture that a proper understanding of the catastrophes we are always setting off sets into play the first prerequisite for the social organization of happiness.

("AIR WAR" 64E; SEE ALSO THE SLIGHTLY VARIANT *CAMPO SANTO* 90-91E)[44]

To be sure, Sebald undercuts this conjecture (hope in *Campo Santo*) by way of Kluge's extended description of the "administrative apathy" (*Campo Santo* 87E, 92G) of those who bring about destruction. Once the machinery is in gear for a campaign of obliteration, they too are unable to change their behavior and pull back, even in the face of meaningless military objectives recognized as such. They are driven by the "dynamic of technological warfare" (*Campo Santo* 86E, 91G), itself an inexorable and irrational machine. From the point of view of the British military: once the production of bombs and the training of pilots (which included training them not to think) were in place, "it *had* to happen in the end" ("Air War" 65E, 71G). And thus Kluge's citation of Marx beneath the photograph of the ruined city of Halberstadt with pointed italics. Human consciousness is determined by the history of industry. "We see how the history of *industry* and the now *objective* existence of industry have become the *open* book of *human consciousness*, human *psychology* perceived in sensory terms" ("Air War" 66E, 72G).

Sebald is uncertain, then, whether the retrospective learning process (*Campo Santo* 90E, 95G) justifies "the abstract principle of hope" (*Campo Santo* 91E, 96G) that will always defy "all calculations of probability" ("Air War" 64E, 70G; *Campo Santo* 90–91E, 95G). Everything hinges on what Sebald, after Brecht, speaks of as human "autonomy." "This divergence, for which 'tomorrow's brains' can never compensate, proves Brecht's dictum that human beings learn as much from catastrophes as the guinea pig learns about biology, which in turn shows that the level of *autonomy* of mankind in the face of the real or potential destruction that it has caused is no greater in the history of the species than the autonomy of the rodent in the scientist's cage" (*Campo Santo* 89–90E, emphasis mine).[45]

Thus Sebald rehearses a series of scenes from Kluge's account of the destruction of Halberstadt ("Air War" 61–63E, 67–69G). Here too human autonomy falters in the name of a steadfastness (*Unentwegtheit*) loyal to the old order. We read the story of Frau Schrader who "attempts to somehow or other create order" (*Campo Santo* 88E, 92G), to clear the rubble after the bombing at the Capitol Cinema in time for the two o'clock matinee. We read of the irrationality of soldiers ordered to dig up and sort out the corpses, to no known purpose; of two women on watch in a tower, unable or unwilling to abandon their positions even as the bombs fall (*Campo Santo* 87–89E, 93G; "Air War" 61–63E, 67–69G); and of a photographer who insists on recording "'his hometown in its hour of misfortune'" ("Air War" 61E, 67G). Like the others, he blindly follows his professional instincts.

It is a question here, as in what preceded it, of opening up "the view (Aussicht) in the abyss of a mind armed against everything" ("Air War" 60E, 67G). That the human psyche becomes a geological site here is no accidental fall into metaphorical language. For, Sebald continues, "The informative value (*Aufklärungswert*) of such authentic documents (*Fundstücke*), before which all fiction pales, also determines the character of Alexander Kluge's archaeological work on the slag-heaps of our collective existence" ("Air War" 60E, 67G). Kluge's perspective wavers between an ironic registration of the facts and the resultant knowledge that we cannot learn; it waivers between enlightened intellectual steadfastness and a suspension and suspicion, with respect to that knowledge, that such constancy just won't do, precisely because of its stable certainty, because that certainty, it too, shares the tendency of survivors of trauma to stick to the old ways. Therefore, like Benjamin's angel, Kluge too is driven by forces beyond his control. The slide is radical from the exalted and seemingly controlled position at the beginning of the passage, where Kluge as postwar writer is at a distance, and an ironic one at that, able to register not only facts but also what ostensibly seems to be the hard-won insights of a thinker who also knows the impossibility of learning, to that of the angel of history whose passive movement shifts horizontally and at the level of the ground. "It seems likely that only [Kluge's] preoccupation with this didactic business enables him to not give in further to the temptation of offering an interpretation of recent historical events *purely* in terms of natural history" (*Campo Santo* 95E, 100G, emphasis mine). If Kluge's gaze is also that of the angel of history, giving in to the temptation of the fall into natural history is still an open possibility. The same might be said of Sebald, for in *Campo Santo* the connection between the threat of reversion to natural history and Kluge's observations of mankind's inevitable return to its former ways (the link of the new paths to the old) is quite explicit.[46]

> The reversion of human life to the primitive, starting with the fact that, as Böll remembered later, "this state began with a nation rummaging in the trash," is a sign that collective catastrophe marks the point where history threatens to revert to natural history. [Here Sebald notes his source as Böll, *Frankfurter Vorlesungen*, 83]. . . . There is not much comfort . . . in the fact that in Nossack's account the city, now reduced to a desert of stone, soon begins to stir, that beaten tracks appear across the rubble, linking up—as Kluge remarks— "in a casual way with earlier networks of paths," for it is not yet certain whether the surviving remnants of the population will emerge from this regressive phase of evolution as the dominant species, or whether that species will be the rats or the flies swarming everywhere in the city, instead.
> (*CAMPO SANTO* 80-81E)[47]

It is a question of epistemology in its relation to natural history. What if humans do not emerge as the dominant species? What if history were no longer ours? What if human autonomy, what we so long thought of as a chosen course of human events, as progressive even, however misguided, were, at a certain tipping point, to dissolve into natural history? In "Air War and Literature," just after giving us the image of Halberstadt in ruins, Sebald writes: "This is the history of industry as the open book of human thought and feeling—can materialistic epistemology or any other such theory be maintained in the face of such destruction. Or is the destruction not, rather, irrefutable proof that the catastrophes which develop, so to speak, in our hands and seem to break out suddenly are a kind of experiment, anticipating the point at which we shall drop out of what we have thought for so long to be our *autonomous* history and back into the history of nature?" ("Air War" 66E, emphasis mine).[48]

Isn't this what is at stake in the closing pages of the Zurich lectures in the seeming slide from Kluge's ironic detachment and registration of facts to his similarity to the angel of history?[49] For Sebald asks us whether materialistic epistemology, or any other epistemology for that matter, can possibly be maintained in the face of such destruction. It is a question of what and how we know and whether we are being driven beyond the point of determining our own history—also beyond the point of self-knowledge.

And that question remains a question in "Air War and Literature." As the title of the essay in *Campo Santo* makes evident, we lie "Between [*Zwischen*] History and Natural History." This in-between is the place of the literary description of total destruction.[50] It is this point and possible point of no return that Sebald's essay practices, over which it repeatedly hovers. When he writes of Kluge's descriptions of the social organization of disaster, this includes a proper understanding of what is necessary for the social organization of happiness, which in turn is undercut by the inevitability of disaster in the dynamic of technological warfare ("Air War" 64E, 70G; *Campo Santo* 86–87E, 90–91G). That in-between is, moreover, at play when Sebald writes of Kluge's ironic gaze and registration of facts as *also* that of the angel of history.

This is and this is not progress. Neither, precisely. For if we, with Kluge, have achieved anything, it is the knowledge that we cannot progress, that the people of Halberstadt, and we too, always revert to our old paths. We learn that learning is not possible and that epistemological triumph is simultaneous with epistemological disaster; that the position of human autonomy is *also*, or immediately implies, a loss of autonomy as history threatens to give way to natural history before the eyes of the angel of history.

> For all Kluge's intellectual steadfastness, therefore, his gaze at the destruction of his hometown is also the gaze frozen in horror of the angel of history, of whom Walter Benjamin said that, with his eyes torn open, he sees "one single catastrophe which keeps piling

rubble upon rubble and hurls it in front of his feet. He would like
to stay, awaken the dead, make whole what has been smashed. But
a storm is blowing from Paradise and it has got caught in his wings
and is so strong that the angel can no longer close them. This storm
relentlessly drives him into the future to which his back is turned,
while the pile of rubble before him grows skyward. What we call
progress is this storm.
("AIR WAR" 67–68E)[51]

The angel of history makes no escape from what Benjamin calls ho-
mogeneous empty time. He is driven by one of its myths: progress.
Our own blindness names it such. Precisely in that the angel is driven
by what "we call progress" it is impossible for it to figure as Benjamin's dialectical image, which has an entirely different temporality.[52]
"The dialectical image is an image that emerges suddenly, in a flash.
What has been is to be held fast—as an image flashing up in the now
of its recognizability. The rescue that is carried out by these means—
and only by these—can operate solely for the sake of what in the next
moment is already irretrievably lost."[53] The angel, rather, has lost all
autonomy: all good intentions to the contrary (he would like to lin-
ger longer, waken the dead, and put what has been shattered back
together), he is driven inexorably away from the past toward a future
to which his back is turned. For Benjamin, for Kluge, for Sebald, progress of this sort is certainly no goal.

Still, something like what we mistakenly might tend to call progress is afoot in Sebald's and Kluge's text. Let us return to the unknown photographer who documents the destruction of Halberstadt. Although he performs precisely what Sebald has called for, a
steady gaze at reality that presents the real circumstances, Sebald
condemns him for merely following his professional instincts. "The
unknown photographer intercepted by a military patrol who claims
that 'he wanted to record the burning city, his own home town, in
its hour of misfortune' resembles Frau Schrader in following his professional instincts." ("Air War" 61E, 67–68G). But Sebald redeems this
act of instinct, precisely because the photographs have come to light
in Kluge's "The Air Raid on Halberstadt on 8 April 1945." "His intention of documenting even the very end does not appear absurd only

because his pictures, which Kluge added to his text, have come to us, which, according to what was foreseeable by him at the time, could hardly have been expected" (*Air War* 61E, 68G). What transforms the work of instinct and misplaced intention is Kluge's incorporation of the photographer's work, or is it rather, more precisely, the fact that they, the photographs, "have come to us"? It is only thus that any escape from the absurd takes place. The autonomy of Kluge here, we might note, is almost lost to that of the preserved images. Redemption, if it is one, comes, then, through no intentional gesture of the photographer himself but because the images have come to us and because Kluge has added them to his text.

No reader of Sebald, a collector if ever there was one, can miss the import of this gesture; for Sebald's texts (like Benjamin's) are shot through, well known, if not notorious, for apparent acts of citation, paraphrase, and reproduction of visual materials.[54] Such citation, of course, sidesteps the problems facing the survivors of trauma. It is not a question of bringing *into* memory ("Air War" xE , 7G) or *into* experience ("Air War" 23E 30G)[55] that which one has lived firsthand so much as the addition of found text and image into similar materials, say the images of the Halberstadt photographer into Kluge's work or the textual and visual materials of Kluge into Sebald's work. Citation of sorts certainly marks the shift from the literal observation of the field of destruction in Kluge's text to the metaphorization of that literal scene. That is, it is citation that makes such knowledge as is offered there possible. The citation from Kluge: "After a few days, *beaten tracks [Trampelpfade]* begin to run over the areas piled high with rubble and the streets obliterated by the ruins, *which in a casual way connect to the earlier networks of paths [die auf legere Weise an frühere Wegverbindungen anknüpfen]*" ("Air War" 67E, 73G, emphasis mine). To which Sebald adds the observation, by way of an unmarked citation, that Kluge suspected "that we are unable to learn from the misfortunes we bring on ourselves, that we cannot be taught, and that we will continue along the *beaten tracks which in a casual way connect to the old networks of paths [Trampelpfaden, die auf legere Weise an die alten Wegverbindungen anknüpfen]*" (*Air War* 67E, 73G, emphasis mine). The rewriting of Kluge's passage,[56] the incorporation into the second passage, written by Sebald, marks the shift from Kluge's literal observation of the rubble to what Sebald offers as Kluge's metaphorical generalization. Citation, apparently the least problematic registration of sense perception into text, entails the doubling of text and image into that which is also text and image. Might it be a path of learning and therefore something akin to progress? In this particular instance the citational act teaches that learning is impossible and the result is a collapse of distinction between the observer and observed, between Kluge's ironic observation of the survivors at Halberstadt and his own not quite exalted position of learning that we cannot learn.

The performance of Sebald's citation of Kluge is immediately followed, of course, by the incorporation of Benjamin's lines on the Angel of History who neither maintains an ironic distance nor learns much of anything. And yet there is perhaps something to be said for this. Sebald closes "Air War and Literature" with a citation. This would be unremarkable if it were not a gesture he repeats elsewhere and often in his major works. *Austerlitz* closes with a long passage from *Heshel's Kingdom*, a paraphrase so close to Dan Jacobson's text that it borders on plagiarism. *Rings of Saturn* closes with "some passage or other that I can no longer find of [Thomas Browne's] text" *Pseudodoxia Epidemica. Schwindel. Gefühle.* closes, similarly, with "words that return to me as an echo that had almost faded away— fragments from the account of the great Fire of London," words ascribed to Samuel Pepys" (*Vertigo* 262E; *Schwindel. Gefühle* 287G). All of these tell of death and devastation and each of them speaks through the words of another. They are written, then, neither from a superordinate position nor are they the reports of immediate perception so insisted on at the outset of "Air War and Literature."[57] They may speak of scenes akin to natural destruction, they "[mark] the point where history *threatens* to revert to natural history" (*Campo Santo* 80E, 85G, emphasis mine), but they do not complete that movement. Like the images of the Halberstadt photographer, in coming to us they might conceivably shed their absurdity. This is the space that W. G. Sebald so indecisively marks out for himself, and yet not quite for himself, as he (all but) abdicates both the autonomy of the individual writer and the autonomy of human history. It is unclear whether we will be able to learn from him, but perhaps, to cite Peter Szondi writing of Benjamin, he *might* give us hope in the past.

5

A IS FOR AUSTERLITZ

*The most self-evident territory had become a point of reference
more incomprehensible even than the most foreign region. The
homeland was now for him the paradigm of irreality.*
("VERLORENES LAND" 141)

A question mark and a capital A for Austerlitz.
(*AUSTERLITZ* 117E, 174G)

A IS FOR Austerlitz. We need to start at the beginning. *A* is for Austerlitz and so many other names besides: for Agáta Austerlizová,[1] his mother, and for Tereza Ambrosová,[2] the archivist who brings him back to her, almost. *A* is for the family name of Maximilian Aychenwald, his father. We need to start at the beginning of an alphabet in which it is established that *B* follows *A,* as assuredly as beta its alpha, and as certainly as Buchenwald follows Aychenwald.[3] We need to take as our point of departure those signs on which we depend to read, an alphabet that phonetically encodes and recapitulates the spoken word and promises other far-reaching powers of ordering as well. We need to relearn our A, B, Cs, to return to childhood, to bring it back from the shadows, to relive even earlier

moments in which speaking began or at least to the time of an origi-
nary mother tongue, however squirrely that grasp of language might
be. Isn't this the point of W. G. Sebald's book, as some of his readers
insist: an account of "recovered memory" that retells the life story of
Jacques Austerlitz?[4]

Better to start with this. Better to start from point A, ground oneself in a sense of progress, even though our first outright encounter
with that letter completely sidesteps Jacques Austerlitz, the focal
point of the story. For we read, rather, of another Holocaust victim.
Tortured by the Nazis at Breendonk, at the close of the war he chose
to shuffle the letters of his patronym, Mayer, to shake his Austrian
homeland and become Jean Améry.[5] And we read of Claude Simon's
Le Jardin des plantes in which the similarly tortured Gastone Novelli
tries to forget the so-called civilized beings of Europe by living with a
South American tribe:

> To the best of his ability [he] compiled a dictionary of their lan-
> guage, consisting almost entirely of vowels, particularly the sound
> *A* in countless variations of intonation and emphasis. Later Novelli
> returned to his native land and began to paint pictures. His main
> subject, depicted again and again in different forms and composi-
> tions . . . was the letter *A* which he scratched in . . . in rows crowd-
> ing closely together and above one another, always the same and yet
> never repeating themselves, rising and falling in waves like a long-
> drawn-out scream.
> AAAAAAAAAAAAAAAAAAAAAAAAAAAAAAAAAA
> AAAAAAAAAAAAAAAAAAAAAAAAAAAAAAAAAA
> AAAAAAAAAAAAAAAAAAAAAAAAAAAAAAAAAAA
> (*AUSTERLITZ*, 27E)[6]

Novelli tries to remember or rather to register that nightmare of his
pain. But what does it mean to paint a picture, to form an image? How
shall we understand the scarcely readable ciphers, huddled together,
always and yet never the same, in paintings that, rather than layering
color, violently gouge a series of *A*s into an inarticulate scream?

PRAGUE

Still, Sebald's story does and does not belong to Novelli, to Simon, to Améry. Let us forget this byway of the errant alphabet that destroys memory as it also creates it. *A* is for Austerlitz. On first hearing that name, his name, in April of 1949 at the age of fifteen, Austerlitz says that in relation to the word *Austerlitz* he couldn't imagine anything (*Austerlitz* 67E, 102G). "I couldn't think how the name would be spelled, and read the strange, it seemed to me secret password three or four times, syllable by syllable, before I looked up and asked: excuse me , Sir, but what does it mean?" (*Austerlitz* 68E, 104G).

Unlike the long drawn-out scream of Novelli's *A*s, it means that Austerlitz has found the password to his childhood, that, spelling the name, one can spell out the past. It means, as he has always suspected, that "my name alone . . . ought to have put me on the track of my origins" (*Austerlitz* 44E, 68G).[7] For, in rapid succession, many years later, as the culmination of a year-long crisis in relation to language, in a bookstore presided over by Penelope Peacefull (*Austerlitz* 140–42E, 207–9G), a voice on the radio speaks to him of the *Kindertransport* and of "PRAGUE." With no trouble to speak of, this Odysseus,[8] who up till now could simply have traveled with an unknown destination and for an unpredictable period of time, suddenly leaves the British Isles and makes his way directly home: only two pages later, at the state archives in Prague, the dead center of Sebald's meandering text, he tells Tereza Ambrosová that he has come to the conjecture that he had been brought to Great Britain with the Kindertransport; that he believes "that I had left Prague at the age of four and a half, in the months just before the war broke out, on one of the so-called children's transports departing from the city at the time, and I had therefore come to consult the archives in the hope of seeking out, with their addresses from the registers, people of my surname living here between 1934 and 1939, who could not have been very numerous" (*Austerlitz* 147E).[9] To which Ambrosová replies—in a fairy-tale-like *no sooner said than done*—"that the registers of those living in Prague at the time in question had been preserved complete, that Austerlitz was indeed one of the more unusual surnames, so she thought there could be no particular difficulties in finding me the entries I wanted by midday tomorrow" (*Austerlitz* 148E).[10] All thanks to the archive and its alphabet.[11] Six pages later, Jacques Austerlitz finds himself at the door of his childhood apartment in conversation with Vera, who had cared for him in his earliest years.[12]

And at this, surely the most touching, most critically emotional moment of the book, Vera's first words are "Jacquot . . . est-ce que c'est vraiment toi?" ("Jacquot . . . is it really you?" *Austerlitz* 153E, 224G). How can one not hear here the echo of that other Jaco: the ash-gray parrot that his school friend Gerald so often took out of his cardboard sarcophagus? He too, like his namesake, with "a whitish face, as one might imagine, marked by deep grief," he too having lived his life out in Welsh exile, imitating "most fondly of all . . . the voices of children" and who, like Austerlitz, had reached the great age of his sixties (*Austerlitz* 82–83E, 125–26G).[13]

Over eighty pages Vera retells Austerlitz's past, says Austerlitz. It comes to us in a rhythm of said-said, said Vera, said Austerlitz.[14] And during that parroting, at once marked by the distancing of a triple narration: said Vera, said Austerlitz (said the narrator), and the apparently unproblematic path of verbal repetition, almost all at once, miraculously, not only memory returns but also the mother tongue. For just as Vera speaks of how they would shift from French to Czech at the evening meal, just in the middle of this remark: "Vera herself, quite involuntarily, had changed from one language to the other, and I, who had not for a moment thought that Czech could mean anything to me . . . now understood almost everything Vera said, like a deaf man whose hearing has been miraculously restored" (*Austerlitz* 155E).[15]

The wonder of understanding is that of the reader as well. Eighty pages of clarity in a text which, for reasons we have yet to trace, has not always been easy to follow, in which our own powers of recapitulation are rendered precarious. Suddenly, here, a chronological laying out of events: how Agáta met Maximilian; how Vera came to care for her Jacquot; how, one after another, Maximilian, Jacques, and Agáta were forced to leave Prague; and how Vera was left behind to remember. A retracing of social as well as family history: an account of German Nazi enthusiasm in 1933, the Nuremberg welcome of Hitler at the National Socialist Party rally in 1936 (*Austerlitz* 222E, 321G), the "collective paroxysm on the part of the Viennese crowds" (*Austerlitz* 170E, 248G), and the German invasion of Czechoslovakia, 1939 (*Austerlitz* 171E, 250G), the inevitable Kindertransport (*Austerlitz* 173E, 253–54G), the edicts progressively laid out against the Czech Jews, one after another (*Austerlitz* 172–73E, 251–52G), and the deportation of Austerlitz's mother (*Austerlitz* 177E, 258ffG).

TEREZÍN

With his newly gained knowledge in hand, Austerlitz takes the train as did his mother before him, from Holešovice station to Terezín. The alphabetic archive has brought him back to his Vera and to his verity: has it convinced this wanderer, after all, that it is possible to go from point A to point B? For never, he tells us, has the feeling been stronger than on that evening with Vera in the Šporkova "as if I had no place in reality, as if I were not there at all" (*Austerlitz* 185E, 269G). As he travels to Terezín he cannot imagine "who or what I was." The tracks of the train seem to run "away into infinity on both sides" (*Austerlitz* 185E, 269–70G). And yet he feels "as if I had been traveling for weeks, going further and further east and further and further back in time" (*Austerlitz* 186E, 270–71G).

Terezín has two scenes in store for him, a junk shop whose doors remain closed to him, the ANTIKOS BAZAR, and then the Ghetto Museum—the intricate ambiguities of a window display and the simplicity of a museum exhibit. In a sense, one might take them as paradigmatic of the double experience of *Austerlitz*, displaying as they do a pattern of alternation that both disrupts and drives the flow of the narrative. The one he sees from the outside, the other from within; the first leaves him with questions, the second has pretensions of offering explanations.

The streets are deserted but for a ghostly figure of infirm old age and a madman babbling in broken German ("swallowed up by the earth"; *Austerlitz* 189E, 274–75G), in a town whose facades are dumb and whose windows are blind *Austerlitz* 189E, 275G). The photographs of its forbidding doors progressively assume the appearance of the gas chamber ovens (*Austerlitz* 190–93E, 276–79G). It is in these streets that Austerlitz comes upon the town square. Here he is overwhelmed by the "power of attraction" (*Anziehungskraft*; *Austerlitz* 195E, 282G) of the ANTIKOS BAZAR.[16] That is the easiest way to tell it, but it is not what Austerlitz and *Austerlitz* relate to the reader. For we arrive at this last site only by way of the narration of a dream. "Not long ago, on the threshold of awakening, I looked into the interior of one of these Terezín barracks. It was filled from floor to ceiling with layer upon layer of cobwebs woven by those ingenious creatures. I still remember how, in my half sleep, I tried to hold fast to . . . *the trembling dream image* and to discern what lay hidden in it, but it dissolved all the more and was overlaid by the memory, rising up in my consciousness at the same time, of the flashing *panes* of the display windows of the ANTIKOS BAZAR" (*Austerlitz* 190–94E, emphasis mine).[17]

As Austerlitz tells it, he stands on the threshold of waking, a half-conscious state in which, while occupying the more material threshold of a barracks building, he has "looked into the interior." The webs of spiders fill the space from floor to ceiling, layer upon layer, in a half-sleep vision (*Traumbild*) that fails to grant knowledge of what is hidden within. This is an image of which he cannot catch hold. For this dream of layering is overlaid (*überlagert*) in turn by something else that is not quite the store itself, nor simply its memory, but the memory of its glittering panes of glass (*die blinkenden Schaufensterscheiben*), the next to nothing that stands between Austerlitz and what is inside. This is no doubt what Evan spoke of, "says Austerlitz," when he observed: "nothing more than such a piece of silk separates us from the next world" (*Austerlitz* 54E, 84G), something like the "invisible border" (*Austerlitz* 41E, 64G) of which the narrator had earlier written. Ever caught up in "[der] Baugeschichte," both as the history of architecture and also as the story of the vain hope that we might fully enter, inhabit, much less plan and understand any construct, this is the dreamlike tale that Austerlitz will tell over and over. It is a tale of layering and shifting ground, of webs that do not catch hold, of nets of interrelation that tantalize with the ever receding horizon of system and from which we can never escape.[18] "Of course, I could see only what was set out for display in the windows. . . . But even these four still lifes obviously composed entirely at random, which appeared to have grown quite naturally into the black branch-work of the lime trees standing around the square and reflected in the glass of the windows, exerted such a power of attraction on me that it was a long time before I could tear myself away, and, my forehead pressed against the cold window . . ." (*Austerlitz* 194–95E).[19] Meaning, hidden secrets, an oracular utterance (*Austerlitz* 195E, 283G), these are the siren songs whispered in the chaos of the unfathomable interrelations (*unerforschliche[n] Zusammenhänge*; *Austerlitz* 285G)[20] of which Austerlitz too becomes part: "I was now able to perceive among them, weak and hardly recognizable, my own shadow image" (*Austerlitz* 197E, 285G), the phantom silhouette we the readers can (barely) find in the photo of "Austerlitz"-as-photographer, overlaid on a porcelain figure whose allegory we suddenly all too easily fathom: "the ivory-colored porcelain group of a hero on horseback turning to look back, as his steed rears up on its hindquarters, in order to raise up with his outstretched left arm an innocent girl already bereft of her last hope, and to save her from a without doubt cruel fate not revealed to the observer" (*Austerlitz* 197E).[21] Without doubt, the wishful saga of Jacques and Agáta.

And yet there are also a hundred other remnants of former lives on the other side of the glass. These and Austerlitz along with the branchwork (*Astwerk*) behind him, which the play of reflections leaves at once outside and within, not to mention that difficult nodal point, the camera he holds to his face, the instrument of documentation through which Austerlitz sees (as do we), from which perspective he reports, the invisible image maker and his reflected image: it is impossible to disentangle them all, to find their precise space, or even to find a proper train of thought that might lead to an unequivocal answer about them: "[I studied] the hundred different things . . . as if from one of them, *or* from their relationship to one another, an unequivocal answer might be deduced to the many impossible to think through questions that moved me" (*Austerlitz* 195E, emphasis mine).[22] Let us remember that phrase, hold it fast, if we can: "from one of them, *or* from their relationship to one another," for we are on to something here in the choice, if there is one, between the certain presence and specificity of the *one* and the *relation-to* the other.

And yet again, as a counterpart to the interwoven branchwork (*Ast-werk*) from one side, appears the branch stump (*Aststummel*) from the other, a broken fragment perhaps, but an escape from the reflected labyrinthine confusion: "the stuffed squirrel, already moth-eaten here and there, perched on the stump of a branch in a showcase the size of a shoebox, which had its beady button eye implacably fixed on me, and whose Czech name—*veverka*—I now recalled like the name of a long-lost friend" (*Austerlitz* 196E).[23] Thus might we not read here, perhaps also too easily once again, the serendipitous access to the mother tongue but also, embedded, the name of that friend for so long lost: the Vera in the somewhat stammered version of *veverka*? "I also asked Vera about the Czech word for a squirrel, and after a while, with a smile spreading slowly over her beautiful face, she answered that it was *veverka*" (*Austerlitz* 204E, 294G).

Still another, not entirely unambiguous answer branches off from Austerlitz's question, for Vera herself adds another, less direct explanation: the unsettling questions are not at an end. Reading aloud to the child from his favorite book about the change of seasons: "And Vera said, said Austerlitz, that every time we reached the page which described the snow falling through the branches of the trees, soon to shroud the entire forest floor, I would look up at her and ask: But if it's all white, how do the squirrels know where they've buried their hoard? . . . How indeed do the squirrels know, what do we know ourselves, how do we remember, and what is it we find in the end?" (*Austerlitz* 204E).[24] Less the happy return to the mother tongue, the recognition of *veverka* reminds, rather, of a possible dead end to knowledge, or, at best, that recognition immediately brings us to the knowledge discovered of an end and death. For Vera immediately follows it by the report of Agáta's second deportation, from Terezín—"to the East" (*Austerlitz* 204E, 295G).[25]

And that grim reality of the factual past, of course, is what the Ghetto Museum, the second vignette of Terezín, confirms. It is here, for the first time, that Austerlitz is presented with "some idea of the history of the persecution" (*Austerlitz* 198E, 286G). Every detail of the "origins and places of death of the victims," the clearest of documents: "I saw balance sheets, registers of the dead, lists of every imaginable kind, and endless rows of numbers and figures, which must have served to reassure the administrators that nothing ever escaped their notice" (*Austerlitz* 199E, 287–88G).²⁶ Yet, rather than offering a solid ground of certainty, this historical account in all its precision "far exceeded my comprehension": "I understood it all now, yet I did not understand it" (*Austerlitz* 199E, 287G).

Two scenes, then, in Terezín: In the haphazard jumble of the shopwindow: where no answers can arise, where no questions can be formulated, where the endless overlappings of individual pasts and of past and present, inside and out, photographer and photographed, Austerlitz and the ghostly but recognizable figure of W. G. Sebald posing as Austerlitz lie—all these things, apparently distant from one another, are patiently engraved and linked together in a web ("im geduldigen Gravieren und in der Vernetzung . . . weit auseinander liegender Dinge"; *Campo Santo* 200E, 244G).²⁷ Still there arises a clear allegory of redemption, a promise of something that might be caught there, of the recuperation of the mother tongue, a hint of Vera and her verity, perhaps even the alpha-betical order in the *B* follows *A* of *Antikos Bazar*. And yet again, in the brutal unrelenting certainty of the Ghetto Museum's order, and alongside the strangely gentle tones of reason's promise, lies a threat to understanding.

BETWEEN PRAGUE AND HOEK VAN HOLLAND

This back and forth is also the lesson of the journey that follows: the attempt to replicate the summer of 1939. Austerlitz had studied "the maps of the Greater German Reich" at the Ghetto Museum on which he traces the railway lines running through it (*Austerlitz* 198E, 286G). He returns then to Prague, himself to take up one of those lines from the main train station on the Wilsonova to Hoek van Holland. This is a train (and a train of narrative) that never quite reaches its destination but rather gets lost in Germany. It is a trip we mentioned earlier in "a nameless land without borders and entirely overgrown by dark forests" (*von finsteren Waldungen*; *Austerlitz* 224E, 324G), in which, nevertheless, the *Buchen* (beech trees), in good alphabetical order—as *B* might follow *A*—do indeed follow the *Eichen* (oaks)—if not quite the *Aychen* (*Austerlitz* 324G)[28]—and this is "the original" "of the images that had haunted [him] for so many years," Austerlitz tells us (*Austerlitz* 224E, 324G).

The renovated Wilsonova station itself "did not correspond in the least to the idea I had formed of it from Vera's narrative" (*Austerlitz* 217E, 314G). But as the train leaves Prague, it dawns on Austerlitz "with perfect certainty that I had seen the pattern of the glass and steel roof above the platforms before . . . and in the same half-light" (*Austerlitz* 219E, 316G). And as they cross the Moldau: "Then it really was as if time had stood still since the day when I first left Prague" (*Austerlitz* 219E, 318G,). What does it mean that time might stand still for Austerlitz, as he looks out of the corridor window of his train? This is no pane of the display window of Terezín, with all the complications brought on by its layered reflection: the pane of glass, here, does not stand between him and the object of his view. But if time seems at first to stand still, Austerlitz surely does not. He repeatedly shifts his ground on just how time functions.[29] He passes at first through scenes that bring the past back or him back to the past. But then, with the eye of the architectural historian, he notes that, passing through the valley of the Rhine, "it is difficult to say even of the castles standing high above the river . . . whether they are medieval or were built by the industrial barons of the nineteenth century" (*Austerlitz* 226E, 326G). What this train races through, its stations so to speak, are first the identity of the self's past with its present ("as if time had stood still"; *Austerlitz* 219E, 318G); then a neutral, matter-of-fact indeterminacy—of architectural historical periods in the objects outside the train; from this Austerlitz shifts rapidly to an entanglement of periods in his own experience: "At least, I no longer knew in what period of my life I was living as I journeyed down the Rhine valley" (*Austerlitz* 226E, 326G).

Time between Prague and Hoek van Holland does not stand still: it is maddeningly on the move. It has jumped from the still stand of present with past to the jumble of historical eras to the multiplicity of personal pasts. "Even today . . . when I think of my Rhine journeys, the second of them hardly less terrifying than the first, everything becomes confused in my head: my experiences of that time, what I have read, memories surfacing and then sinking out of sight again, consecutive images and distressing blank spots where nothing at all is left" (*Austerlitz* 226E).[30] What he has lived and what he has read, the Wales of his childhood memories alongside the images made centuries earlier by Victor Hugo and Joseph Mallord Turner, his memories and those of others. No barriers, none, between now and then, self and other, art and life. The journey to a particular point in the past branches out uncontrollably in dimensions of time-space impossible to take in at a glance. It is no coincidence, then, as we learn, that the narration of this journey takes place among the decaying gravestones of Tower Hamlets and on the border of St. Clement's Hospital, a no-man's-land between the place for the dead and their monuments and the place for the mad and their memories. At the outset of the trip is the experience of an absolute and almost reassuring certainty of repetition, a perfect coincidence of the past and the present. The narrative shifts over the next pages to the sense of rediscovery, a return to an original whose images had always haunted (*heimgesucht*). This gives way to an absolute certainty (*absolute Gewißheit*) of the way in which the past had made his childhood *unheimlich*—and then the horror of the second experience becomes as great as that of the journey it repeats. He loses all sense of his current temporal place so that in the present everything is jumbled about in his head until finally all these temporal loci become thoroughly entangled with the way others have portrayed the scenes. It makes sense that the story is interrupted by a shift into the present telling of the tale by Austerlitz as he and the narrator walk from Alderney Street to the cemetery of Tower Hamlets. A map of London tells us that they pass by St. Clements where mental breakdown has a home (*Austerlitz* 226–27E; 325–28G). Where Austerlitz heads on that train is no particular point of his past, but to breakdown: perpetual regression toward increasingly diverging, varied, and impenetrable ramifications ("immer mehr sich verzweigenden und auseinanderlaufenden Aufzeichnungen"; *Austerlitz* 371G). Like the branching footnotes he researched in the Bibliothèque Nationale on the rue de Richelieu, like the tracks of a railroad that run with great precision from A to B, and yet with an impulse not really understood (*Austerlitz* 33E, 52G), he gets lost in a fantastic nightmare of an unsystematic network of space and time.

And so haven't we captured it, understood what Sebald is about? Haven't we found an image at least of his mode of writing or several— too many—perhaps: as Sebald puts it in another context—"Snapshots he took with his equally sympathetic but ice-cold eye."[31] Might we develop and print these snapshots taken by the author's restless eye, fix in place this squirrely writer who, that restlessness notwithstanding, fixes us from the first, or so it seems, with a glassy button-eye relentlessly directed at us (*Austerlitz* 196E, 284G)? *Austerlitz*, one wants to say, is a "trembling dream image" (*erschauernde[s] Traumbild*; *Austerlitz* 194E, 281G) impossible to hold fast, with both completely arbitrary juxtapositions (like the still lifes that are "vollkommen *willkürlich* [zusammengesetzt]") as well as seemingly natural intergrowths (*naturhaften [Hineinwachsungen]*; *Austerlitz* 195E, 282G) that refuse entry to what lies hidden within (*Austerlitz* 195E, 281G); it is the flashing pane of a display window (*blinkende Schaufensterscheibe*; *Austerlitz* 194E, 281G) we try to gaze through, while it reflects both the gazer and creator without. And, laying out for us in cold facts and statistics, one by one, a reality we would perhaps rather not view, *Austerlitz* is also a museum of sorts,[32] a house of documents, reason, and order, setting in motion the train of thought of a perfect (if perfectly conventional) restitution that nevertheless exceeds by far our capacity to comprehend (*Austerlitz* 199E, 287G).

CAMPO SANTO—STUTTGART

And is *Austerlitz* not there in order to answer the query: *A quoi bon la littérature?* (What's the good of literature? *Campo Santo* 204E, 247G), to which Sebald, having posed the question in *Campo Santo*, responds: "Perhaps only so that we remember, and learn to understand that there are strange connections that cannot be grounded in a causal logic" ("An Attempt at Restitution," *Campo Santo* 204E, 247G). And, he continues, "There are many forms of writing; but only in the literary form is it a question, over and above the mere registering of facts and over and above scholarship, of an attempt at restitution" ("An Attempt at Restitution," *Campo Santo* 205E, 248G).

Austerlitz lays these unsteady, flickering images out, layer on layer, as a spider a web, in the uninhabited space of a dream, in a dream house of sorts, our *Zuhause*, which welcomes everything in but ourselves. If we follow this thread in another text, if we turn to another train ride, we might recognize the spider. In 2001, shortly after the publication of *Austerlitz*, Sebald writes of a visit to the artist Jan Peter Tripp in Stuttgart, when he, like the narrator of *Austerlitz*,[33] returns to Germany in the mid-seventies. "At the time Tripp gave me a present of one of his engravings, and on this engraving, on which the mentally ill judge Daniel Paul Schreber with a spider in his skull is to be seen—what can there be more terrible than the ideas always scurrying around in our minds?—on this engraving much of what I later wrote goes back, even in my method of procedure: in adhering to an exact historical perspective, in patiently engraving and linking together in a network apparently disparate things in the manner of a still life" ("An Attempt at Restitution," *Campo Santo* 200E).[34]

The interruption of the remark enclosed in dashes, the repetition of the phrasing, all this mimics the path of the scurrying spider. What Sebald later wrote is also in the manner of the spider in the skull, that creator of, that embodiment of the ceaselessly scurrying and recurring thoughts that traverse *Austerlitz* to our distraction. As we might say in German, Sebald *spinnt*; which has all the senses of weaving a web, spinning a tale, being a bit mad. When we faced the display window of Terezín, "an unequivocal answer" seemed deducible from one or another of the hundred things "*or* from their relationship to one another" (*Austerlitz* 195E, 283G, emphasis mine). The dilemma is that of choice. It distracts us between "adhering to an exact historical perspective," with its promise of conventional recuperation, and "linking together in a network [of] apparently disparate things" ("der Vernetzung . . . anscheinend weit auseinander liegender Dinge"), the interrelationship among the multiple, open to no simple procedure of representation. And yet, in *Campo Santo*, as we read, literature goes "over and above the mere registering of facts and over and above scholarship," beyond the recapitulation of the singular. Literature, insofar as it might offer a horizon of restitution, does so in relationships (*Zusammenhänge[n]*; "Ein Versuch der Restitution," *Campo Santo* 247G) that cannot be grounded in a logic of causality. We come to terms with this concept of literature as relationship, it seems, in a time that eludes the present: it takes place either insofar as "we remember" in the past or in the projected future of a "learn[ing] to understand" (*daß wir begreifen lernen*; *Campo Santo* 204E, 247G). The basis of this concept of literature is not as the success of but as the "attempt [*Versuch*] at restitution" (*Campo Santo* 205E, 248G): it is not grounded in the realm of knowledge.

PARIS—ELYSÉES

The alphabetic archive brings Jacques Austerlitz back to his past without detour, but it goes without saying how much in *Austerlitz* speaks the disturbance of that order and also the danger it brings, asking us, lulling us, to read over the vocabulary of interconnection (*Zusammenhang, Vernetzung*)[35]—the interconnection of terms one nevertheless trips over at every turn of this volume, which will ultimately lead to the more radical and unreadable version of those multiplying lines.

Thus it should be no surprise: Prague, Terezín, and the retraced trajectory of the Kindertransport return Austerlitz to his childhood but deliver him as well to yet another in a series of mental collapses. For, as miraculously as the Prague archive had done its work, "It was obviously of little use that I had discovered the sources of my distress and, looking back over all the past years, could now see myself with the utmost clarity as that child suddenly cast out of his familiar surroundings: reason was powerless against the sense of rejection and annihilation that was now pouring forth out of me" (*Austerlitz* 228E).[36]

The collapse on the return from Prague comes, of course, and is only one in a long history of fainting fits. Long before this he had experienced "the first of the several fainting fits [he] was to suffer, causing temporary but complete loss of memory" (*Auslöschung sämtlicher Gedächtnisspuren*; *Austerlitz* 268E, 381G).[37] A disturbing branching (*Verzweigtheit*) was involved with, if not quite the single root of, the first such crisis. It is 1959: on those long weekends when his friend, Marie de Verneuil, set off in another direction, which always left him in a fearful mood, the young student living in Paris took off by himself for the outskirts of the city. It is a train, of course, that brings him there. At Maisons-Alfort he comes upon the Veterinary Museum, with its revolting celebration of pathological deformity. The "trees of bronchial tubes, some of them three feet high, their petrified and rust-colored branches" (more literally translated, branchedness, *Verzweigtheit*; *Austerlitz* 266E, 378G) are preserved in turn by Sebald, who gives this image of grotesque branching the honor of a full-page photograph. Unlike the other photos with branchwork in Terezín, those too taken by Austerlitz, this one is marked, not with "[his] own shadow image" (*Schattenbild*; *Austerlitz* 197E, 285G) but with his trace as obliteration. It takes the form of the camera's flash of light on the pane of the "glass-fronted cases reaching almost to the ceiling" (*Austerlitz* 265E, 377G).

"Monstrosities of every imaginable and unimaginable kind" (*Austerlitz* 266E, 378G) fill the glass cases (*Glasschränke* and *Vitrinen*; *Austerlitz* 377–78G),[38] says Austerlitz. Their place of display behind the glass as well as one of its objects recall a more benign counterpart in the display window of the ANTIKOS BAZAR. For, long before encountering the porcelain horse and rider of Terezín (in 1993), that white knight allegory of redemption and of the possibility of turning back, Austerlitz had found another rider and another horse, this one charging forward rather than rearing backward, in a scene that speaks not of salvation but rather of decomposition and in other grotesque colors. "Far and away the most disgusting, however, so said Austerlitz, was the exhibit in a glass case at the back of the last cabinet of the museum, the life-sized figure of a horseman, most artfully flayed . . . by the anatomist and dissector Honoré Fragonard, . . . so that in the colors of congealed blood *every strand in the tensed muscles* of the rider and his horse, which was racing forward with a panic-stricken expression, came forth clearly along with the blue of the veins and the ochre yellow of the *sinews and ligaments*" (*Austerlitz* 266–68E, emphasis mine).[39] What Fragonard lays bare are the individual sinews, ligaments, and every strand in the muscles of horse and rider, setting out to view the striations of bodies we would far more comfortably view as contained and whole. And mustn't we think these in connection to that other place of "skulls and skeletons," muscles, nerves, and sinews, namely the poverty-stricken quarter on which, in the late nineteenth century, the northeast train stations of London were built? It is a place where Sebald had forced us once before to confront the monstrosity of bodily display: "Before work on the construction of the two northeast terminals began, these poverty-stricken quarters were forcibly cleared and vast quantities of soil, together with the bones buried in them, were dug up and removed, so that the railway lines, which on the engineers' plans looked like muscles and nerve strands in an anatomical atlas, could be brought to the outskirts of the City" (*Austerlitz* 132E).[40] This is preceded by a ghastly full-page photo of a skeleton with broken skulls and is followed by a full-page, unsettling, image of the railway lines—which we now cannot fail to regard as muscles and nerves (*Austerlitz* 131E, 193G, 133E, 195G). One can hardly read Sebald, one can hardly read *Austerlitz*, without being drawn to, distracted to another passage. The spider is spinning its terrible, forever scurrying thoughts (*Campo Santo* 200E, 243G) everywhere. The strands we are following from Fragonard's work place at Maisons Alfort to the subterranean burial grounds under the streets of London, strands of muscle and nerves and train lines, are rather arbitrary juxtapositions and thus a choice of one out of many paths we as readers might take, to keep us going, if not quite straightforward at least with a struggle to make sense, in scenes that portend a certain mental collapse. In Sebald collapse and interconnection (*Zusammenbruch* and *Zusammenhang*) are never far from, and always implicate, one another.

In 1959, at the site that precipitates his first collapse, the Veterinary Museum of Maisons Alfort, Austerlitz tells of Honoré Fragonard: "Fragonard . . . must . . . have been bent over death day and night, surrounded by the sweet smell of decay, and, apparently driven by the desire, in transforming its so readily corruptible substance into a *miracle of pure glass*, to secure for the frail body, by means of a process of *vitrification*, at least some participation in eternal life" (*Austerlitz* 268E, emphasis mine).[41] Fragonard's process, seems, however facetious the narrator may be here, an endeavor to secure an eternal life. Surrounded by the sweet smell of decay, does not Fragonard, this descendent of "the famous family of Provencal Parfumiers" (*Austerlitz* 268E, 380G), rather revel in the scent of corruption around him, forcing the viewer to come to terms with the decomposition of the one to the many while merely gesturing toward keeping the body intact?

And that gesture has much to do with vitrification and the miracle of glass here. At the ANTIKOS BAZAR the panes of the display windows present the still lifes within only as a quivering, flickering (*erschauernden, blinkenden*) nonlocus of sorts for the entanglements of viewing and reflection (*Austerlitz* 194–97E, 281–82G). Here the glass cases of the veterinary museum, with a sense of utter transparency, pitch one, if not blindly then thoughtlessly, into the space of their contents. But the glass of Fragonard is something else again: his process of vitrification , literally a transformation (*Umwandlung*) into glass, makes it the medium for a fixing in place that speaks of eternity. Still, it performs that glassy miracle by way of an all but unbearable violation of the body, striating what should remain one and whole, reminding us all too palpably of the frailty of the biological body—perhaps of the textual body as well.

Glass has a place in Sebald's world. He makes this clear when he writes of Bruce Chatwin. "The closed glass cabinet (*Glasvertiko*) with its enigmatic things became . . . the central metaphor both for the content and also for the form of Chatwin's work."[42] For Sebald, too, the glass display cases and windows become a central metaphor for what he has to say and how he says it—even though, as we have seen, just how glass functions may change from passage to passage. Nowhere is this clearer, if difficult to get a handle on, than in the following lines. The narrator continues shifting his stories of vitrification about. For, just when he ceases to speak of Fragonard's method of turning flesh into glass, he turns to describing the way in which Austerlitz tells his story. Glass appears, here too, although we are almost blind to it. It is Fragonard, then, who wishes: "in transforming its so readily corruptible substance into a *miracle of pure glass*, to secure for the frail body, by means of a process of *vitrification*, at least some participation in eternal life. In the weeks following my visit to the museum of veterinary science [thus Austerlitz {casting his glance to the boulevard outside} continued his story], it was impossible for me to remember anything of what I have just told" (*Austerlitz* 268E, emphasis, parentheses, and brackets mine).[43] Sebald draws a blank here—perhaps two. While speaking of the continuity of the story ("thus Austerlitz . . . continued his story"), the narrator forgets to mention the windowpane that interrupts the narrative, through which Austerlitz gazes ("casting his glance outside to the boulevard").[44] He also speaks of a total loss of memory. What we have read as narration, "what I have just told," was to him a total blank. The sentence is structured to include a double frame within. The narrator interrupts his report with "thus Austerlitz . . . continued his story" and ruptures that phrase in turn with a description of Austerlitz's gesture: "casting his glance outside to the boulevard." A double window, one might say, flung open in the continuation of Austerlitz's words, so deftly inserted we hardly notice. The first, "thus Austerlitz . . . continued his story," pulls us back from the content of Austerlitz' narrative to the form of its telling. The second is more difficult to locate. We must remember where we are. Austerlitz casts his glance "outside to the boulevard." Sixteen pages earlier the narrator gave names to that locus, names that, by way of their sounds, give one a sense of the glass and the blank to come: the interlocutors meet "in the Bistrobar Le Havane on the Boulevard Auguste Blanqui, not far from the Metro station La Glacière" (*Austerlitz* 255E, 363G). Thus as Austerlitz casts his glance outside it must pass through a glass window that is left unmentioned.[45]

And indeed what Austerlitz silently narrates with this gesture (as he both continues [*seine Geschichte fortsetzt*] and interrupts his story) is both a hint of and a threat to consciousness. This is akin to the various and unregulated, understated, ways we have seen glass function in the passages we have read. "In the weeks following my visit to the museum of veterinary science [thus Austerlitz {casting his glance to the boulevard outside} continued his story], it was impossible for me to remember anything of what I have just told you, for it was in the Métro on my way back from Maisons-Alfort that I had the first of the several recurring fainting fits I was to suffer, with a temporary erasure of all traces of memory" (*Austerlitz* 268E, parentheses and brackets mine).[46] The "erasure of all traces of memory" is the continual experience of reading *Austerlitz*. It echoes Austerlitz's sense of obliteration on his return from Prague. It leaves us uncertain if Sebald's narrator displays the past or splays it out and displaces it.

If the interconnections (*Zusammenhänge*) are perversely intricate, paradoxically the collapses (*Zusammenbrüche*) are more lucidly telling. They bring us at least to some common places, perhaps also commonplaces about this text. In 1959, in the train coming back from Maisons-Alfort, Austerlitz falls unconscious. "I did not return to my senses until I was in the Salpêtrière, to which I had been taken and where I was now lying . . . somewhere in that gigantic complex of buildings where the borders between institutions of healing and punishment have always been blurred, and which seems to have grown and spread of its own volition over the centuries until it now forms a universe of its own between the Jardin des Plantes and the Gare d'Austerlitz" (*Austerlitz* 269E).[47] And is this not also the place of Sebald's *Austerlitz,* somewhere between that other *Jardin des Plantes,* that appears in the opening pages (the narrative of Claude Simon about Gastone Novelli and his paintings of *A*s), as we must also remember, and the Gare d'Austerlitz, which, given a book so obsessed with both trains and its title character, inevitably becomes Austerlitz's final point of departure (*Austerlitz* 290ffE, 409ffG). And is *Austerlitz,* too, not a place in which the border between healing and punishment remains uncertain, in which any healing implicitly promised also recapitulates previous suffering.

Austerlitz continues his story: "In the semi-unconsciousness in which, for days, I found myself there, I saw myself wandering around a labyrinth of mile-long passages, vaults, galleries and grottoes [*Gängen, Gewölben, Galerien und Grotten*] in which the names of various Métro stations—Campo Formio, Crimée, Elysée, Iéna, Invalides, Oberkampf, Simplon, Solferino, Stalingrad—. . . ." (*Austerlitz* 269E, 382G). Here the letter makes a comeback in *Austerlitz.* Austerlitz stammers in *G*s of architectural spaces that alternate passageways (*Gänge, Galerien*) and the more dubious, open spaces of possible arrival (*Gewölbe* and *Grotten*), followed by an alphabetical arrangement of métro stations[48], almost all names of battles or with resonances of war.[49] Unlike the conspicuously absent name (*Gare d'*) Austerlitz (also the name of a significant battle), about which the boy of fifteen had asked "but what does it mean?" (*Austerlitz* 68E, 104G), the place of these metro stations seems a given.

As though wishing to struggle against the maze of the Paris metro map, a web that pervades the subconscious of every Parisian inhabitant, Austerlitz organizes the stations into an orderly alphabetic progression. The final stop is something akin to, but not quite the same

as, the Elysian Fields. Austerlitz continues his story: "Solferino, Stalingrad—and certain discolorations and flecks in the air seemed to
indicate that this was a place of exile for those who had fallen on the
field of honor, or lost their lives in some other violent way" (*Austerlitz* 269E, 382–83G). The heroes of Austerlitz's story find their place,
finally, among flecks in the air (*Flecken in der Luft*), the small and indefinable marks to which we return, which continually come back to
us (as black flecks and even snowflakes), and which we never escape,
not only in this the crisis of his student days but also at the close of
Austerlitz's final breakdown after his return from Prague.

As Austerlitz narrates it: having visited Prague, it nevertheless was
of little use to him that he had found the source of his distraught
state of mind (*Austerlitz* 228E, 330G). He, the historian of architecture,
becomes like the burnt out walls of a roofless and broken house.[50] "I
walked around in this place . . . up and down the corridors, staring for
hours through one of the dirty windows at the cemetery, where we are
standing now, and felt nothing inside my head but the four burnt-out
walls of my brain" (*Austerlitz* 230E, 332G). Repeatedly overwhelmed
by a horrific terror: "All of a sudden my tongue and palate would be
as dry as if I had been lying in the desert for days, more and more
I had to fight harder for breath . . . and everything I looked at was
veiled by a black hatching. I felt I had to scream but could bring no
sound across my lips." (*Austerlitz* 228–29E, 331G). Without the capacity
to cry out, much less speak, as though lost in the desert, Austerlitz
is surrounded by a black hatching (*Schraffur*), not unlike the flecks
(*Flecken*) in the air of his first collapse.

LONDON

Let me leave that thread hanging here to scurry first to a more than
obvious family likeness between the narrative voice and that of Austerlitz. For the narrator, too, has his breakdowns, also related to childhood, to memory, to the possibility of seeing straight. It is 1967. We
are told of the early encounter with Austerlitz who has concluded an
elaborate discussion of those fortresses built to defend Antwerp with
a description of Breendonk, "the last link in the chain" (*Austerlitz* 18E,

31G). The narrator ventures out there the following day, the first of a series of museums in *Austerlitz*. Like Austerlitz at the Ghetto Museum in Terezín, he is overwhelmed by the monstrosity of the experience.

> No one can explain exactly what happens within us when the doors behind which our childhood terrors lurk are flung open. But I do remember that there in the casemate at Breendonk a nauseating smell of soft soap rose to my nostrils, and that this smell, in some strange place in my head, was linked to the bizarre German word for scrubbing brush, *Wurzelbürste*, which was a favorite of my father and which I had always disliked, that *black striations* began to quiver before my eyes, and I had to rest my forehead against the wall, which was gritty, covered with *bluish spots* [*Flecken*], and seemed to me covered with cold beads of sweat.
>
> (*AUSTERLITZ* 25-26E, EMPHASIS MINE)[51]

Posed like Austerlitz, who, in the stairwell of his childhood house, "had to lean his head against the wall" (*Austerlitz* 151E, 223G), or like Austerlitz with his "forehead pressed against the cold window pane" (*Austerlitz* 195E, 282–83G) at the ANTIKOS BAZAR,[52] and like Austerlitz in his moments of crisis with black hatch marks before his eyes, the narrator prefigures Austerlitz and gives us again the strange language of their connection to one another (*Bezug zueinander*; *Austerlitz* 195E, 283G): hatching, striations, flecks: *Schraffur* (*Austerlitz* 35E, 55G), *Gestrichel* (*Austerlitz* 25E, 37G), *Flecken* (*Austerlitz* 25E, 41G). We remember and learn to understand that these are strange relationships that cannot be grounded in causal logic (*Campo Santo* 204E, 247G). This, after all, is literature.

And so it should be no surprise, given that their paths keep crossing in a manner impossible to understand (*Austerlitz* 27E, 44G), after a twenty-year hiatus when yet another completely chance encounter takes place between Austerlitz and his scribe (*Austerlitz* 41E, 64G), isolated snowflakes float by,[53] another recurring version of the flecks in the air. And, as with Austerlitz before him,[54] a black hatching returns to also define the perspective of the narrator (*Austerlitz* 35E, 55G). It is December of 1996. Taking up his long-neglected writings coincides with taking up once again the relationship to Austerlitz, which had been equally close and distant (*Austerlitz* 34E, 54G), and coincides as well with another crisis. "I was in some anxiety at the time because I had noticed, looking up an address in the telephone book, that the sight in my right eye had almost entirely disappeared overnight, so to speak. Even when I glanced up from the page open in front of me and turned my gaze on the framed photographs on the wall, all my right eye could see was a row of dark shapes curiously distorted above and below—the figures and landscapes familiar to me in every detail having resolved indiscriminately into a black and menacing cross-hatching [*Schraffur*]" (*Austerlitz* 34–35E).[55] What does it mean that the narrator, as in the story of Austerlitz he will soon come to know, has lost the familiar figures and landscapes that usually surround him? Lost them at least with one eye.[56] What does it mean that the perspective from which the tale of Austerlitz's childhood will be told is veiled by black hatch marks (*von einer schwarzen Schraffur*; *Austerlitz* 229E, 331G). How does this way of seeing define the perspective of *Austerlitz*, become the condition of possibility less of what it says (perhaps the left eye accounts for this) than of what it performs? Less a threat than that which enables a new form of sight. "I kept feeling as if I could see with undiminished clarity on the edge of my field of vision, and had only to look sideways in order to make what I took at first for a merely hysterical weakness in my eyesight disappear" (*Austerlitz* 35E, 55G).

What if a certain clarity can be maintained only on the edge of our field of sight—what if we must learn, as the narrator does in time, to make do with this new perspective of clarity at the limits and black hatching at dead center? What if hatching itself becomes a new way of viewing and writing, the network on the pupil left by a spider in the skull, perhaps? We have already begun to see that. What if Sebald's text comes to us like a suitor to a young woman on whose retina (*die Netzhaut*), as was the custom, "a few drops of liquid distilled from belladonna, a plant of the nightshade family, [were placed] . . . whereby her eyes shone . . . but she herself could perceive next to nothing" (*Austerlitz* 35E, 56G)? Can we accept this, in order all the better to read? These are the conditions under which he writes: the power of sight of the right eye opens out on a row of distorted forms, not unlike the rows of Novelli's *A*s, while the left eye remains temporarily as it was before, though continually threatened with a certain impairment of sight.

The narrator takes a train to London, to visit a Czech ophthalmologist with the name of Zdenek Gregor.[57] The visit accomplishes no

cure. It is, rather, the scene of describing and measuring the disturbance: "There was a considerable uncertainty, said Zdenek Gregor.
All that was really known was that it occurred almost exclusively in
middle-aged men who spent too much time reading and writing. After the consultation, in order more precisely to determine the defec-
tive area in the retina,[58] yet another . . . series of photographs of my
eyes or rather . . . of the back of the eye through the iris, the pupil and
the vitreous humor [*Glaskörper*] needed to be made" (*Austerlitz* 38E).[59]
Here, too, one sees through (something that reads like) glass.[60]

And indeed this middle-aged man, too much devoted to reading
and writing, has come to the (non)knowledge offered by Gregor by
first flitting his way through a strange concatenation (*eigenartige Ver-
kettung*; *Austerlitz* 34E, 54G) of thoughts. Taking the train to London, a
few isolated snowflakes were floating down. The falling of snowflakes
reminds him of a childhood fantasy in which his whole village might
be buried in snow; while in the waiting room he thinks of a poem he
leaves unidentified that brings him to thoughts of a city thus over-
fallen, a London that takes on all the character of the crisscrossing
and furrowing we have come to expect in this text:

> I imagined that out there in the gathering dusk I could see the dis-
> tricts of the city of London crisscrossed by innumerable streets
> and railway lines, crowding ever more closely as they marched east
> and north, one reef of buildings above the next and then the next,
> and so on . . . and that now on this huge outcropping of stone the
> snow would fall . . . until everything was buried and covered up . . .
> London a lichen mapped on mild clays and its rough circle without
> purpose . . . It was a circle of this kind with its edge going over into
> the approximate that Zdenek Gregor drew on a piece of paper as he
> attempted . . . to illustrate to me the extent of the gray zone in my
> right eye.
> (*AUSTERLITZ* 37E)[61]

The drawing of the eye, which no doubt the narrator's right eye cannot directly observe, follows from a poem that branches out from the
imaginings of a snow-laden London with their origin in a childhood
fantasy. And are not these unpredictable leaps and starts, the "gap for

clarity" of which Stephen Watts writes, the poet whose name is omitted in the lines we have read? For the full opening lines of the poem "Fragment," which Sebald does not identify, and of which he gives us, so to speak, only the edge, go like this:

> And so I long for snow to
> sweep across the low heights of London
> from the lonely railyards and trackhuts
> —London a lichen mapped on mild clays
> and its rough circle without purpose—
> because I remember the gap for clarity
> that comes before snow in the north . . .[62]

Having left the world of ophthalmology behind, the narrator waits at the Salon Bar of the Great Eastern Hotel in Liverpool Street for the next train home (*Austerlitz* 39E, 61G). And here on the periphery of his vision, at the edge of the crowd, he notices a solitary figure who can only be Austerlitz whom he has missed all these twenty years (*Austerlitz* 39E, 61–62G). Yet another of the marvelously coincidental meetings between Austerlitz and the narrator: "And when he now met me here in the bar of the Great Eastern Hotel, which he had never before entered in his life, it was, contrary to all statistical probability, according to an astonishing, positively imperative inner logic" (*Austerlitz* 44E, 68G). The logic of the story, however (were causal logic that which drives literature), is that only *because* the narrator has problems with his sight does his path cross that of Austerlitz. This is the inverse of Austerlitz finding Vera by way of the perfectly maintained archive.

Some eighty-five pages later, at three in the morning, as the narrator records it, he retreats to a room in the hotel and sits down at a poorly lit desk in order to write down as much as possible, in notes and disconnected sentences, of what Austerlitz had just told him (*Austerlitz* 97E, 146G). It is not that his sight is miraculously cured: only that, we are given to understand, writing with a "gap for clarity" as Watts puts it, from the perspective of the "rough circle without purpose" of his right eye, with clarity at the edge and hatch marks at the center, is simply the way in which *Austerlitz* must be conceived.[63]

THE DESERT

Nowhere do we get a clearer sense of this than when Austerlitz recalls an encounter with another text, long before Stephen Watts. Before we shifted to the edge of the story, and to that of the narrator, we had traced the way in which Austerlitz had been haunted by flecks in the air and black hatching. And Austerlitz had said of his most severe attack, in 1993, that he felt as though he had lain in the desert for days (*Austerlitz* 228–229E, 331G). The return to Prague and to his identity had brought this about. Still, there was another moment of wandering in the desert, a milder sense of where he really belonged, that reassuringly overtook him in earlier childhood, another image whose lines of connection are at once both tenuous and compelling and in which the hatch marks have an oddly different role to play.

Brought to Great Britain from Prague on the Kindertransport at the age of four and a half (*Austerlitz* 147E, 216G), his early years are a captivity of sorts in the arid home of a Calvinist preacher and his timid wife (*Austerlitz* 44–45E, 69G). He spends his childhood and the decades that follow lost in a wilderness, living the life of a nomad, without his mother tongue, housed, so to speak, in only the most provisional of architectural forms that punctuate (also visually) the story of his life.[64] But "after long years in the desert [he will] finally [find] the path to the promised land" (*Austerlitz* 169E, 248G) of a restored past.[65] The two-page illustration from the Welsh children's Bible (*Austerlitz* 56–57E, 86–87G) had always testified to this. In a sense this image anticipates his encounter with Vera, for in these pages he had already begun to understand his origins, to find his rightful place, long before setting out for the state archives in Prague.

> Further on in the story of Moses, said Austerlitz, I particularly liked the episode where the children of Israel cross a terrible wilderness. . . . I . . . immersed myself, forgetting all around me, in a full-page illustration showing the desert of Sinai looking just like the part of Wales where I grew up, with bare mountains crowding close together and a gray-hatched background, which I took sometimes for the sea and sometimes for the air above it. And indeed, said Aus-

terlitz on a later occasion when he showed me his Welsh children's
Bible, I knew that my proper place was among the tiny figures pop-
ulating the camp. I examined every square inch of the illustration,
which seemed to me uncannily familiar. I thought I could make out
a stone quarry in a somewhat lighter patch on the steep slope of the
mountain over to the right, and I seemed to see a railway track in
the regular curve of the lines below it. But my mind dwelt chiefly on
the fenced square in the middle and the tent-like building at the far
end, with a cloud of white smoke above it. Whatever may have been
going on inside me at the time, the children of Israel's camp in the
wilderness was closer to me than life in Bala, which I found more
incomprehensible every day, or at least, said Austerlitz, that is how
it strikes me now.
(*AUSTERLITZ* 55–58E)[66]

Long before the discovery of his obliterated name and his subsequent return to Prague, there is a possible escape from a life that,
with each passing day, becomes more and more incomprehensible.
Leave aside the very evident ironic details suggesting a quarry that
echoes the toil of the prisoners at Breendonk; leave aside the echo as
well of the layout of the concentration camps and the infamous cre-
matoriums with their smoke stacks. That escape from Bala is made
possible by the examination (*Durchforschung*) of the image before
him.[67] Still, if we, with Austerlitz, sense his belonging to the "Camp of
the Hebrews," it is not simply because of the biographical fact of the
Kindertransport. *Lager der Hebräer* speaks of the biblical liberation of
the Jews to whom God sent the pillar of clouds to show the way out of
slavery (*Austerlitz* 55E, 85G), but the camp of the Jews speaks as well—
no one can fail to hear the echo—of another "camp." Austerlitz's
sense of belonging is as ominous and ambiguous as it is reassuring.

What punctuates the biblical illustration are a number of soon-to-
be-familiar terms that flicker in and out of Austerlitz's description.
As we follow his lead and investigate every square inch of the three-
hundred-page text at hand, the reiterated traces, the ever recurrent
topoi that float in and out, return to haunt us, their fine lines drawn
and redrawn throughout the entire extended narrative (*Austerlitz* 14E,
24G): not only the tents but also the miniaturized figures, the train

tracks, the cloud of white smoke. And, above all, behind all, or rather constituting most everything, the hatch marks, the scratchings. For those marks that sometimes merely fill in the ground of a delineated line, also, just as often, create the figures we are sure we see. They do this not by outlining a figure (how could they?) but by the juxtaposition of different slants to the stroke. It is hatch marks, then (which in other passages threaten with an impending madness), that in the biblical scene create the semblance of heaven and earth, air and sea—and, yet again, we read, also make them interchangeable. Those scratchings give us the sense, though hardly with certainty, that we too might find the quarry or the regularly curved lines suggesting the tracks of a train. Thus the critical term here, even though it disappears into the background of Austerlitz's description, is, of course, *gestrichelt* (hatched), the unobtrusive kin of the flecks in the air at the Salpêtrière and the black hatching of his 1993 collapse. For *Austerlitz* is really a haunted text in which our mode of understanding, were understanding the appropriate concept, wavers between the simple recovery of the well outlined past, the very heart of the plot that Sebald offers up, and a mode of writing (with its requisite reading) that quivers before our eyes and forces us to read outside any certain perspective.

Hatch work can create the image, but, alternately, it challenges the sight and sanity of the viewer, just as the inconsistent hauntings of given images, their multiple appearances, promise us understanding while bewildering us with their nonsystematic difference. Thus the white tents in the Egyptian wilderness reappear on a postcard that Austerlitz sends the narrator signed with a (tent-shaped) "*A* for Austerlitz." "But at any rate, one day my mail included a picture postcard from the 1920's or 1930's showing a camp of white tents in the Egyptian desert, a picture taken during a campaign now remembered by no one, the message on the back saying merely *Saturday 19 March, Alderney Street*, a question mark and a capital *A* for Austerlitz" (*Austerlitz* 117E).[68] And they reappear once again from the bird's-eye view of a Nazi propaganda film that looks down at a party rally. As though to remind us that such wanderers in the desert often go astray, this is also the image that Maximilian, Austerlitz's father, uses for the Germans who come to see the Führer: "No, said Vera, Maximilian told us that a bird's-eye view showed a city of white tents extending to the horizon, from which as day broke the Germans emerged singly, in couples, and in small groups, forming a silent procession and pressing ever closer together as they all went in the same direction, following, so it seemed, some higher bidding, on their way to the Promised Land at last after long years in the wilderness" (*Austerlitz* 169E).[69]

Later it is the suppliant readers who find a place in the desert in a description of the visitors to the new Bibliothèque Nationale:[70] "these figures crouching close to the ground, some by themselves and some in small groups, have alighted here on their way through the Sahara or the Sinai peninsula in the last glow of the evening" (*Austerlitz* 278–80E, 396G).[71] What does it mean that Sebald can thus align the Hebrews wandering in the desert in the illustration from Austerlitz's childhood Bible with the Germans in Maximilian's description? How to compare the Hebrews in the Bible with Nazis in the Fatherland on their way to a rally with Hitler, Hess, and Himmler; and these in turn with suppliant readers at the present-day library monstrosity of Paris? What happens to our instincts of thematic reading or of repetition with regard to a text of fiction? How are we to find our moral compass with such unexpected, unpredictable, ungodly interconnections? And what does this have to say about Sebald's practice of ethics and textuality?

Faced with the disturbing ambiguity of intertwining strands, we, like Austerlitz, might wish to obey the not fully understood impulse that draws him to a fascination with organized totality, say "with the idea of a network, such as that of the entire railway system" (*Austerlitz* 33E, 52-53G). It gives a sense of control and of mapped comprehension.[72] Yet in similar figures we encounter the menacing branchings of the oversized trees of bronchial tubes of Maisons-Alfort or the railway lines in the engineer's plans for the Northeast terminals, similarly monstrous once we are told they resemble the sickening strands of muscles and nerves. We might assume that a cluster of recurring images wink at us from a textual heaven of sorts, that they might form a constellation in which recognition is made possible. Still, there is nothing strictly systematic about them. And, as Austerlitz puts it, it is precisely in its familiarity that the uncanny appearance of the image resides (*Austerlitz* 58E, 84G). Like the nomadic phrase "camp of the Hebrews," or like the image of the tent in its several variations whose portent and meaning will not hold still, the most familiar of Sebald's repeated images are signs that lead us on with rather uncertain guidance.

GREENWICH TIME

Perhaps we can nevertheless learn something from the inconsistency of such repeated gestures. Perhaps we can see something in the recurring encounter with hatch marks that both create the images, making reading possible, and menace our ability to understand. The challenge in reading Sebald's disturbingly labyrinthian prose is to orient oneself with respect to an ever branching, ever shifting subject matter. It is not possible for literature to work out complicated chaotic patterns in a systematic way ("Auf ungeheuer dünnem Eis" 187), Sebald once said. Can we as readers, at least, step back, then? Can we gain the critical distance that first makes possible what is "acceptable in literary scholarship" ("Auf ungeheuer dünnem Eis" 147)?

After a cautionary note on the illusions of alphabetical organization, the sections of this chapter are grounded in place names. Prague, Terezín, and the subsequent journey that Austerlitz undertakes from Prague to Hoek van Holland are designations that follow the path of Austerlitz. A side step then—to the Stuttgart of *Campo Santo* and the tale of Sebald's visit to Jan Peter Tripp. Back to Paris (by way of Maisons-Alfort) and Austerlitz's brush with madness; then on to London and the narrator's crisis with seeing things straight on. The actual thread is a shifting theoretical meditation on the complexities of Sebald's prose, but the stamp of geographical locations (which continues almost till the end of the chapter) seemed more likely to create a sense of stability and a mnemonic link to particular passages.

Along with place, also time, of course, is the inevitable guidepost of narrative progress: both are endlessly disturbed by Sebald's writings. In this monumental text the stories that Sebald's narrator passes on to us are interwoven with the stories of the changing places of their telling. Also the dates of the telling flow in and out of the dates of the events told.[73] While the menace to consciousness has been couched in spatial terms in the many passages we have been tracing until now (hatch marks, branchings, mazes, spiderwebs), the reader of *Auster-litz* frequently endures a similar sense of vertigo, caught in the force of a temporal whirlpool. Every moment of the past has the potential of opening out onto others of another time.

It is 1996 as Austerlitz engages us with the tale of his last visit to the home of his closest childhood friend (*Austerlitz* 109–12E, 161–64G). Both of Gerald's uncles have died within days of one another. The funeral procession moves in the direction of the cemetery of Cutiau. The dark figures, the trees, the light, the water, the massif: these are the elements of the double burial in Wales that Austerlitz describes. Our thoughts are rooted with him in 1957, when he tells us he discovered those same elements again a few weeks ago (1996) in watercolor sketches of Turner's *Funeral at Lausanne* the artist had made in 1841, toward the end of his life, out of his memory, as he tries to hold on to the fleeting visions of his past. Our thoughts have leapt back from 1957 to 1996 and then to Turner in 1841. But what really draws Austerlitz to the scene at Lausanne is not only his memories of the funeral at Cutiau but also those of his last walk with Gerald in 1966 near Lake Geneva. But, then again, in studying Turner, Austerlitz discovers that Turner, in turn, or out of turn, had himself in 1798 traveled through the same corner of Wales at precisely the age that Austerlitz had attended the funeral at Cutiau: 1996–1957–1996–1841–1966–1798–1957. The network of nominally different moments of time belies our conventional sense of progressive history, here in two pages, to be sure, but also relentlessly throughout Sebald's volume in a more or less overwhelming manner.

Moreover, alongside the frequent entanglements of specific historical frames, we are asked to take in a series of theorizations about time that cannot necessarily be reconciled with one another. This is particularly obvious in Austerlitz's long disquisition on time as he and the narrator walk through the Royal Greenwich Observatory. Home to Greenwich Mean Time, the prime meridian, and standard measures of length, the Royal Observatory stands as a monument to a belief in the reigning powers of time and space. With an irony the reader glimpses only in retrospect, the narrator first tells of their stroll to Greenwich: it takes place always in relation to a river and its flow. "As we walked down to the river through Whitechapel and Shoreditch he said nothing for quite a long time. . . . Only on the riverbank, where we stood for a while looking down at the gray-brown water rolling inland, did he say . . ." (*Austerlitz* 98E, 147G).[74] We take for granted the description of the river as the two men make their way together. The narrator writes of the natural landscape, and the reader, understandably, fails to take special note. We hardly notice that it is only on the bank that Austerlitz speaks. That moment of conversation takes place at the side of and to the side of the river as they glance down: what they have to say is as yet untouched by it. Here, with language mapped onto objective reality in a conventional and unproblematic way, it is like seeing with the left eye of the narrator.

Inside the observatory, however, it is another story. To be sure, here too we read another lengthy piece of description. It too regards a river and it too has much to do, not only with what one says but also with the way in which one speaks. This is Austerlitz's "disquisition on time," of which, the narrator writes, "much has clearly remained in my memory [*Erinnerung*]" (*Austerlitz* 100E, 149G). Austerlitz criticizes Newton's insistence that time is like a river. As he speaks, even beyond his particular fixation with Newton's metaphor, images of water and its flow overtake all Austerlitz wishes to say. If time is not like the linear, contained river, that Newton suggests, still Austerlitz will offer his own definition of time by in turn immersing himself in the image of water.

If Newton thought, said Austerlitz, pointing through the window and down to the curve of the water . . . glistening in the last of the daylight, if Newton really thought that time was a river like the Thames, then where is its source and into what sea does it finally flow? Every river, as we know, must have banks on both sides, so what, seen in those terms, what are the banks of time? What would be this river's qualities, qualities perhaps corresponding to those of water, which is fluid, rather heavy, and translucent? In what way do objects immersed in time differ from those left untouched by it? Why do we show the hours of light and darkness in the same circle? Why does time stand eternally still and motionless in one place, and rush headlong by in another? Could we not claim, said Austerlitz, that time itself has been non-concurrent over the centuries and the millennia?

(*AUSTERLITZ* 100E)[75]

Several things are taking place concurrently here: first a rejection of a metaphor which has time move in an even unidirectional flow, with an origin and a destination, defined by banks that enclose it along the way; then a rejection of time conceived as divisible into regulated units of measure. Austerlitz, who proudly announces that he has never owned an alarm clock, pocket watch, or wristwatch, much less a pendulum clock (*Austerlitz* 101E, 151G), calls time the most artificial of all our inventions: an arbitrary calculation based on the movement of the earth, and the calculation of an imaginary average measure of sunlight each day. Time, he says, might just as well be based on the growth of trees or the disintegration of limestone (*Austerlitz* 100E, 149–50G). Isn't much of the earth, then, ruled by that which cannot be so regulated? And is not human life thus ruled "by an unquantifiable dimension which disregards linear regularity [*Gleichmaß*], does not progress constantly forward but moves in eddies, is marked by congestion and irruption, recurs in ever-changing form, and evolves in no one knows what direction?" (*Austerlitz* 101E, 151G)

Austerlitz may reject Newton's metaphor of the river, but, in contrast to the narrator who had them standing calmly by the banks of the Thames and observing with detachment its gray-brown water rolling along, Austerlitz's language takes another turn. In describing and resisting Newton's river of contained, regulated, progressive time, Austerlitz's speech is inundated by its own fluid subject matter, with eddies and backups and the proposal that things might be "immersed in time" (*Austerlitz* 100E, 150G). Austerlitz rejects the linear, standardized units of measure, as though time were a uniform thing that language might describe, itself undisturbed, from the outside, as though time might escape a relation with subjective experience (say that of the sick or the dying) or escape a relation with language. If time is not like an evenly flowing river, Austerlitz still wonders about the specific characteristics of time that might correspond to or even converse with those of water. How does time find its linguistic counterpart in water? How does Austerlitz's language change its form to correspond with that which it speaks of? This is what Austerlitz surreptitiously asks. His answer is a sense of time that becomes immersed in the watery possibilities he lists.

This linguistic gesture is the countercurrent to the impositions of controlled, unchanging, regulated measure celebrated at the Royal Greenwich Observatory. And, given the opening scene in the Antwerp station, Austerlitz's resistance to regulated time is also a resistance to political violence and power.

> And Time, said Austerlitz, represented by the hands and dial of the clock, reigns supreme among all these emblems. The clock is placed about twenty meters above . . . the stairway . . . just where the image of the emperor was to be seen in the Pantheon in a line directly prolonged from the portal; as governor of a new omnipotence it was set even above the royal coat of arms and the motto *Eendracht maakt macht.* The movements of all travelers could be surveyed from the central position occupied by the clock in Antwerp Station, and conversely all travelers had to look up at the clock and were obliged to bring their activities into line with its demands.
> (*AUSTERLITZ* 12E)[76]

But these are hardly the only alternatives to mark time as we encounter it in *Austerlitz*: on the one hand the conventional, regulated time of the Greenwich Observatory along with the ominous clocks at the Antwerp Centraal Station and on the other the whirlpools, eddies, dammings, and overflows that actually more closely approximate human experience. Sebald's volume is populated with theories of time, explicitly expressed, or elegantly performed, not so much conflicting with one another as floating about and unpredictably surfacing in the back and forth of the text.

THE SCHELDE

Already at the very beginning of their relationship, there was another river, this time the Schelde, and another conversation that falls to the incomprehensibility of time. Austerlitz's thoughts flow among the temporary conclusions at which he seems to arrive.

Leaving his tale of the station behind, the narrator understands that it is Austerlitz's mode of speaking that above all calls out for attention. "From the first I was astonished by the way Austerlitz put his ideas together as he talked, forming perfectly balanced sentences out of his distractedness, so to speak, and the way in which, for him, the narrative imparting of his knowledge seemed to become a gradual approach to a kind of metaphysics of history, bringing that which was remembered back to life" (*Austerlitz* 12–13E).[77] It is by storytelling that Austerlitz, his scribe, and Sebald as well offer to approach a meditation on history and also story (*Geschichte*). But do Austerlitz's sentences bring the past back to life? If the name *Austerlitz* stands for anything, we will eventually learn, it is for the uncertainty that language, art, and even history might ever perfectly recapture the past. Thus while Austerlitz is trying to make sense of his newly acquired name (the more often the word was spoken, the more it seemed to become the young boy's name; *Austerlitz* 72E, 110G), his teacher Hilary proves to his students that no account of the past can begin to replicate lived life. He does this by describing at length the Battle of Austerlitz: "Hilary could talk for hours about the second of December 1805, but nonetheless it was his opinion that he had to cut everything much too short in his presentations, because, were one to really report what happened on such a day . . . it would take an endless length of time" (*Austerlitz* 71E, 108G).

The narrator's optimism about bringing the past to life is placed in ironic proximity to an elaborate scene by the Schelde River. What Austerlitz's narrative communication brings back there is not a lived moment but a canvas of the sixteenth-century painter Lucas van Valckenborch. It pictures ice skaters on the frozen river. "Pointing to the broad river sparkling in the morning sun, he spoke of a picture painted . . . towards the end of the sixteenth century . . . showing the frozen Schelde from the opposite bank. . . . And there on the river now before us some four hundred years later, said Austerlitz, the people of Antwerp are amusing themselves on the ice" (*Austerlitz* 13E).[78]

Something has happened to the flow of time: the icy moment depicted from the sixteenth century is made one with that of the two conversationalists standing on a summer's day in the late 1960s on the river bank: there on the frozen river the people *are amusing* themselves. And that moment is not simply one of happy coincidence, the coming together of the sixteenth-century past of the painter with that of the twentieth-century present, nor of the simple preservation of a moment by the painter's hand. "In the foreground, close to the right-hand edge of the picture, a lady has just fallen. She wears a canary-yellow dress. . . . When I look out there now, and think of that painting and its tiny figures, it seem to me as if the moment depicted by Lucas van Valckenborch had never come to an end, as if the canary-yellow lady had only just fallen over or swooned . . . as if the little accident [*Unglück*], no doubt unnoticed by most viewers, were always happening over and over again, would never cease, and nothing and no one could ever remedy it" (*Austerlitz* 13–14E).[79] It is a moment that has never come to an end, or is, at least, ever again repeated, still, also a moment that has just happened and has thus just slipped into the past and a moment that is the outcome of fall, accident, chance, unconsciousness, and pain. It does not simply make the remembered come alive again, as the narrator would have liked to have it (*Austerlitz* 12–13E, 22–23G.) The incident on canvas is that which usually escapes perception. Rather than bringing the past to life, it reminds of the frailty of the moment, a frailty endlessly repeated and a past that simply cannot be made whole again.

Time on the Schelde is accident, blankness, and loss, and also an ever repeated moment, but elsewhere the narrator will speak of his friend's entire life as a blind spot without duration: "for Austerlitz certain moments had no beginning or end, while on the other hand his whole life had sometimes seemed to him a blank point without duration" (*Austerlitz* 117E, 173G). And yet again, all moments present and past, Austerlitz will also seem to imply, have such endless capacity for duration that time as a concept might well rather give way to space.

> It seems to me then as if all the moments of our life occupy the same space, as if future events already existed and were only waiting for us to find our way to them at last, just as when we have accepted an invitation we duly arrive at a certain house at a given time. And might

it not be, continued Austerlitz, that we also have appointments to keep in the past, in what has gone before and is for the most part extinguished, and must go there in search of places and people who have some connection with us on the far side of time, so to speak? (*AUSTERLITZ* 257–58E)[80]

THE PLACE OF TIME

And yet again, so much of the temporal imagination of *Austerlitz* is structured, rather, not by interlocking spaces, much less a single shared space, but by the most simple of spatial relations: a layering of sequential eras of time such as one might find recorded in an archaeological dig. Thus beneath the site of Broadgate Station in London one finds the overcrowded burial grounds thick with human bones, piled over one another, whose disinterment Austerlitz chose to photograph (*Austerlitz* 131E, 193G). At the site of the other northeast terminal, Liverpool Station, were marshy meadowlands, once spread out and subsequently drained to make way for fish ponds, trees, and gardens. Here the priory of St. Mary of Bethlehem stood, as well as the infamous Bedlam hospital for the insane (*Austerlitz* 129E, 191G). The Great Eastern Hotel now has its place there—with the Liverpool Station just adjacent. Having narrated the striations of history at this spot, Austerlitz tells of his critical, almost mystical rediscovery, the return of the memory of his arrival in London at the age of four and a half, his wretched displacement by the Kindertransport, and the strange apparitions of the wrong people who had stood in for his parents all those years.

Thus also the new Bibliothèque Nationale is built on the same ground where, in 1959, the young student had been so moved by the melancholy Eastern music of the Bastiani family circus and their snow-white goose who seemed to understand its fate and that of the others (*Austerlitz* 272–75E, 387–90G). As Austerlitz looks out on the inner courtyard of the library, where its stone pines are caught by the winds, that circus enters his reverie; "In the daydreams in which I fell in the reading room, said Austerlitz, I sometimes felt as if I saw circus acrobats climbing the cables slanting up from the ground to the ever-green canopy, placing one foot in front of the other as they made their way upwards with the ends of their balancing poles quivering" (*Austerlitz* 281E, 397G).

That performance, we read a few pages later, as Austerlitz is told by Henri Lemoine, was in turn at the site of the Austerlitz-Tolbiac depot during the war (*Austerlitz* 288–89E, 407–8G). The Bibliothèque Natio-nale, unusable storehouse of knowledge, which Austerlitz so loathes, had been built on the storehouse of the stolen possessions of the murdered Jews of Paris.[81]

> Sometimes, said Lemoine, said Austerlitz, he seemed to feel up here the streaming of time around his temples and brow, but probably, he added, that is only a reflex of the awareness formed in my mind over the years of the various layers which down below have grown over one another on the ground of the city. Thus, on the waste land between the marshaling yard of the Gare d'Austerlitz and the Pont de Tolbiac where this library now rises, there stood until the end of the war an extensive warehousing complex to which the Germans brought all the loot they had taken from the homes of the Jews of Paris.
>
> (*AUSTERLITZ* 287–88E)[82]

It is perhaps this layering of the site, the almost obliteration of one era by the next,[83] at once brutal and melancholy, that contributes to the progressive dissolution of our capacity to remember and the col-lapse of the institution once vaunted as maintaining *toute la mémoire du monde* (the entire memory of the world).[84]

Maintaining perfect memory of the world, of course, is hardly Se-bald's thing. *Austerlitz* seems rather an extended and bewildering ex-ercise in how one might differently conceive the relations between periods. Different moments of individual, subjective time as well as the apparently more matter-of-fact dates of history, are intertwined with one another not unlike the branchings and webs of which we have read before. Still, the conventions of Newtonian time and Car-tesian space never lose their stability of reference altogether, just as the left eye of the narrator seems to hold its own. Thus, at the close of Austerlitz's long disquisition on time in Greenwich, the narrator has this to say. "It was around three-thirty in the afternoon and dusk was gathering as I left the Observatory with Austerlitz. We lingered for a while in the walled forecourt. Far away, we could hear the hollow grinding of the city, and the air was full of the drone of the great planes flying low and as it seemed to me incredibly slowly over Greenwich from the northeast, at intervals of scarcely more than a minute, and then disappearing again westwards towards Heathrow" (*Austerlitz* 101–2E).[85] This reassuring if ultimately absurd passage that reintroduces conventional clock time follows on a rejection of Newtonian time and the performed insistence that the language theorizing temporality must be immersed in the object of its description. The passage comes in the wake of envisioning time as a whirlpool rather than a unidirectional, regulated, measured flow, in the wake of leaving behind a concept of time coupled with the omnipotent brutalities of political dominion, judgment, and power.

Still time, we have read, might not be the brutal move toward the future as death, like the slicing off of "the next sixtieth of an hour" (*Austerlitz* 9E, 17G) in the movement of the minute hand at Antwerp Centraal Station. Time might rather consist of moments that "never come to an end" or that happen over and over (*Austerlitz* 14E, 24G). If certain moments seem to have no beginning and no end, an entire life, on the other hand, might also be a blind spot with no duration whatsoever (*Austerlitz* 117E, 173G). Yet again, we might conceive time such that all moments of any individual life occupy the same space (*Austerlitz* 257E, 367G) so that we might make our way to both past and future, if only we know how to find the path. But then time might also be spatialized as layers in which one era builds on top of and buries what came before, though this leaves us haunted, to be sure, by the ghosts of past suffering.

Sebald's prose both theorizes and performs all these possibilities, leaving the reader to be tossed about by its narrative eddies and whirlpools. Nevertheless, the narrator keeps an eye out for what might be remembered, for what should not be forgotten, for how time comes to us, and we to time, for how we speak the language of memory and history and how we misspeak it. There is nothing perfect here and nothing entire.

FIGURE 5.1 Time piece in three parts. Copyright © W. G. Sebald. Reprinted
by permission of the Wylie Agency, LLC *Austerlitz* 99).

Perhaps this is what the single photograph from the Royal Observatory is meant to convey. Something of a counterpoint to the museum at Maisons-Alfort with its monstrous, unimaginable anomalies
behind glass, the observatory is filled with "ingenious observational
instruments and measuring devices, quadrants and sextants, chro-
nometers and regulators, displayed in the glass cases [*Vitrinen*]" (*Austerlitz* 98E, 148G). Unlike the clocks in the Antwerp Centraal Station,
each with its single, omnipotent eye surveying, ruling, and judging
all in their domain, the single measuring device we encounter as image leaves us uncertain about what we have before us.

The two round pieces cite the pairs of eyes, some human, some an-
imal, in the opening pages of *Austerlitz*. Or they come to us like a pair
of glasses in which one lens lies strangely darkened, perhaps like the
right eye of the narrator. In the image, actually, three pieces are laid
out carefully for display. On the right we see what looks like the face of
a pocket watch, but with three unfamiliar, single dials, each occupied
by a single hand. In contrast to this white-faced instrument, on the
left lies a smaller piece. One wants to believe it the movement that,
if properly placed in the other's casing, might drive those hands of
measure. Their juxtaposition seems to promise that we might make

time work, even if we fail to understand how the various dials function and whether they are calibrated to that which we can comprehend. Between them sits a crank of sorts in the shape of a sideward *z*. Its function is elusive, the face of the timepiece, after all, already has the traditional knob with which to wind and set it. Might the *z*-shaped piece serve to connect the two? Why does it provocatively figure as something of an approximation sign (~) between the round pieces? On the face of it, they are neither the same nor of a piece, and yet, nevertheless, we sense the insistence on their relationship.

IVER GROVE

The puzzle image appears alone, unexplained, unrelated in any clear way to either Austerlitz or the narrator. But perhaps it finds its place less in relation to them or even to its kin in the observatory glass cases than to other images, both visual and linguistic, that soon appear as the narrative continues. Shortly after their visit to Greenwich, Austerlitz tells of his visits to the collapsing houses of the English countryside in his student days. Iver Grove is at once a house doomed like the others to dilapidation and yet a place in which time has been made to stand still. James Mallord Ashman brings his visitors to rooms that had been sealed off for years on end:

> And when these partitions . . . were taken down in the autumn of
> 1951 or 1952, and he entered the nursery again for the first time in ten
> years, it wouldn't have taken much, said Ashman, to overset his reason altogether. The mere sight of the train with the Great Western
> Railway carriages, and the Noah's Ark with the pairs of well-behaved
> animals saved from the Flood looking out of it, had made him feel
> as if the chasm of time were opening up before him . . . and before
> he knew what he was about he found himself standing in the yard
> behind the house, firing his rifle several times at the little clock
> tower on the coach house.
> (*AUSTERLITZ* 108E)[86]

What does it mean to take aim and kill time, here and elsewhere in *Austerlitz*, and each time in a different and still more bewildering

way? What does it mean that the details of Ashman's nursery rever-
berate with the scene of Austerlitz and the narrator some fifty pages
earlier and four decades later in 1996? The Great Western Railway of
the children's toy (*Austerlitz* 108E, 161G) echoes the Great Eastern Hotel (*Austerlitz* 41E, 65G), each with its respective Noah's Ark. How are
we to make connections in the whirlpools and echo chambers of objects and eras?

The room in Iver Grove that most radically defies the passage of
time is the refuge of Ashman's ancestor who had originally built
the structure. At the top of the house is an observatory, we read,
dedicated to selenography, the "delineation of the moon" (*Austerlitz*
104E, 156G). But while the moon was not to be seen, when veiled by
clouds—if not hatch marks—the selenographer occupied another
space that remained "exactly as it must have been one hundred and
fifty years before" (*Austerlitz* 105E, 157G). "It was as if time, which usually runs so irrevocably away, had stood still here, as if the years behind us were still to come, and I remember, said Austerlitz, that when

FIGURE 5.2 Billiard balls or celestial eclipse. Copyright © W. G. Sebald.
Reprinted by permission of the Wylie Agency, LLC (*Austerlitz* 106–7E).

we were standing in the billiards room of Iver Grove with Ashman, Hilary remarked on the curious confusion of emotions affecting even a historian in a room like this, sealed away so long from the flow of the hours and days and the succession of the generations" (*Austerlitz* 108E).[87] The still stand of time connects the university days of Austerlitz to the future of his encounter with the narrator.

Accompanying the tale that speaks of Iver Grove is another unlabeled, uncommented image. Is this the billiards table of Ashman's ancestor? Is it an eclipse of the moon? Is this an act of selenography in which the one orb might move to stand in place of the other, or billiard balls in place of celestial orbs? Billiards and an eclipse have this in common: one sphere is destined to knock the other out of our field of vision. But this image of two round objects had spoken to us already, of course, in the timepiece from Greenwich broken in two (or three) on which time stood still; also in the orbs of the eyes of the creatures caught in the Nocturama near the Antwerp Centraal Station; in the searching gazes of painter and philosopher that follow the opening pages; and in the ophthalmological descriptions of the narrator's eye problems.

BREENDONK—LITHUANIA

Can it be any wonder, then, that at the close of *Austerlitz* a similar figure takes its place? Austerlitz has set off from the Gare d'Austerlitz in search of his father. Austerlitz to Austerlitz. The narrator too doubles back. He returns to Breendonk in Belgium which he had visited shortly after their first meeting in the opening pages, though this time he cannot bring himself to cross the moat to the penal colony. All relations to the past are possible in *Austerlitz* except sustained, perfect repetition. Instead he takes the book his friend had given him, Dan Jacobson's *Heshel's Kingdom*.[88] Jacobson's book follows the traces of his grandfather, Heshel, a Lithuanian rabbi whose life was cut short in 1920 by a heart attack. "All that came down from Heshel to his grandson was a pocket calendar, his Russian identity papers, a worn spectacle case containing not only his glasses but a faded and already disintegrating piece of silk, and a studio photograph of

Heshel. . . . His one eye, or so at least it looks on the cover of the book, is shaded; in the other it is just possible to make out a white fleck, the light of life extinguished when Heshel . . . died of a heart attack" (*Austerlitz* 296–97E).[89] One eye in shadow, the other with a small fleck, this time white and as a sign of life. The double orbs of the spectacles, and then again the eyes of Heshel, one beflecked, are the last in a long line of such figures.[90]

The closing pages of *Austerlitz* borrow from chapter 15 of *Heshel's Kingdom* in an act of half-citation, the incorporation of the words of another so prevalent throughout Sebald's publications.[91] Those pages speak through the work of Jacobson and ultimately offer a sign of the life of W. G. Sebald found in the writings of yet another.

> In 1941 [the Lithuanian forts] fell into German hands, including the notorious Fort IX where Wehrmacht command posts were set up and where in the following three years more than thirty thousand people were killed. . . . Transports from the west kept coming to Kaunas until May 1944, when the war had long since been lost. The last messages from those locked in the dungeons of the fortress bear witness to this. One of them, writes Jacobson, scratched the words Nous sommes neuf cents Français in the cold limestone wall of the bunker. Others left only a date and place of origin with their names: Lob, Marcel, de St. Nazaire; Wechsler, Abram, de Limoges; Max Stern, Paris, 18.5.44.
> (*AUSTERLITZ* 298E)[92]

The writing returns us to the letters of the alphabet, something like those of Novelli, for these, too, are scratched in: it is no longer the repetition of a single letter that is always the same while never repeating itself, no longer the inarticulate scream, though the attempt is once again to record the same horror. In Kaunas the scratchings are clear and matter-of-fact, a statement of presence past, a precise if minimal record of history. Max Stern of Paris inscribes his name along with the date of that signature. Just how are we to understand the significance of the names and date?[93]

In the last pages it is no longer Austerlitz's personal story, but that of the narrator. He chooses Jacobson to speak for him in lines

so close to *Heshel's Kingdom* it is difficult to say whom we are reading. Yet the citation is not exact. Jacobson writes: "Also, among many
others, were 'Lob, Marcel, Mai 1944'; 'Wechsler, Abram, de Limoges –
Paris, 18.5.44'; 'Max Stern, Paris, 18.5.44.'"[94] May 1944 belongs to three
of the names: Sebald reserves that date for one alone. As *Austerlitz*
closes, only Max Stern inscribes his name with the date 18.5.44, which
is also the day on which Max Sebald was born.[95]

The identity of dates is and is not an accident. The author of *Austerlitz* calls on us to take note. The selective citation from Jacobson
is a strangely self-effacing and self-announcing culminating gesture.
Is it meant to suggest that the stars of Max Stern and Max Sebald are
crossed? Does it stand to remind us, as Sebald not unoften does, that
he was born only at the end of the nightmare, too late to have borne
witness with his own eyes? Still, *Heshel's Kingdom* returns us to much
we have seen to define the movement of *Austerlitz* throughout. We
might wish to call it Sebald's vision.

Sebald's alphabet takes us from *A* to *A* (in Novelli's paintings to begin with and in all the subsequent entanglements), but also from *A*
to *Z*, as in the name of his book and that of his protagonist. The alphabet fulfills its promise of communication, saves the name of Max
Stern, to be taken up in turn by Jacobson and then by Sebald. The
alphabet orders the state archives of Prague, brings Austerlitz back
to his Vera, his childhood back to Austerlitz, and his mother tongue
back to the victim of the Kindertransport. It also salvages the bitter
historical facts as found in the Ghetto Museum of Theresienstadt or
in the seemingly endless, pages-long, single sentence that gathers
together the horror of the ghetto's organization when Austerlitz recounts his reading of H. G. Adler (*Austerlitz* 232ffE, 335ffG).[96]

Both ethical and aesthetic satisfaction elude us here: We cannot
align order exclusively with evil and conventional modes of discourse
and disorder with the suffering of the victim as well as radical forms
of narrative.[97] Just as the archive both serves as a restitution of Austerlitz's past and stands as a sobering reminder of Nazi efficiency in
Theresienstadt (*Austerlitz* 283–85E, 401–3G), alphabetical order cannot definitively be called into service by either the one side or its os-
tensible challenger.[98] This is no less the case for the other forces of
organization we have been following, the delineation of both spatial

and temporal systems: clarity of sight and form in relation to flecks, branching, webs, and hatch marks—and Newtonian time in relation to the myriad jumbles of different moments.

Newtonian time, Austerlitz tells us, and right from his first conversations with the narrator in the Antwerp Centraal Station, stands as an ally to political, state power of the most ruthless kind. And yet the disturbance of and challenge to that linear, inexorable progress of the clock also marks Austerlitz's lifetime of suffering with its repeated mental collapses, but then again makes possible his hope of making contact with the past, of one point in time passing into the other. *Austerlitz* itself gives us the clear narrative of a series of progressive encounters between the narrator and Austerlitz from 1967 to 1997 as well as the dizzying experience of intertwined moments in their conversations reported therein. Something similar might be said of the visual representations of space. In a logical wish to distinguish power and its victims, one might, for example, pit the clear architectural plans of fortifications, say of Theresienstadt (*Austerlitz* 234–35E, 336–37G) or the "architectural style of the capitalistic era [with its] compulsive sense of order" (*Austerlitz* 33E, 52G) against the slow-motion version of the Theresienstadt ghetto film, sprinkled with its black flecks,[99] out of which Austerlitz, nevertheless, yearns to salvage an image of his mother.[100]

Still, the narrator's eye problem, to explain which his Czech doctor offers an unviewable, indistinct outline drawing (*Austerlitz* 37E, 59G), might show us, once again, how problematic such will to distinction is. He who writes the text, we read, experiences what seems a complete loss of sight in the right eye (*Austerlitz* 34–35E, 54–55G). He sees only a row of distorted forms, a threatening black hatching. This attack on his sight occurs just when he takes up his long-neglected writing (*Austerlitz* 34E, 54G). Are we to presume, therefore, that *Austerlitz* is entirely defined by distorted forms, wayward lines, hatch marks carved into or by the vision of the writer?

On the edge of his field of vision, after all, he apparently sees with a clarity that has not been deeply compromised (*Austerlitz* 35E, 55G). Moreover, if the right eye, on the one hand, has lost most of it capacity to see while maintaining, peripherally, a hope of clarity, the left eye, on the other hand, seems to maintain the possibility of sight.

What else could explain the detailed descriptions of the passing land-scapes outside the narrator's train window as he travels to the oph-thalmologist in London? Still in the left eye, too, he senses an im-pairment of vision. This dance from left to right, between center and periphery, between hatched blindness and clarity of form, this inexo-rable movement between, so goes the fiction, is what runs through the writing of *Austerlitz*.

Does *Austerlitz*, then, in its refusal to rigorously regulate its spatial and temporal forms, betray the certainty of an ethical commitment? How could that be in a life's work that, from beginning to end, calls attention to the tragic violence and destruction all around us? How are we to think this unsettling failure to fix in place—which is per-haps also, in another sense, a critical triumph? The narrator's pre-carious relation to recountability means that the reader is left with a troubling task: decision and reinterpretation, ever anew. This might be an ethics of another order with no self-certainty that we have seen clearly or gotten it right perhaps.

6

DÉJÀ VU OR . . .

"Like Day and Night—On the Pictures of Jan Peter Tripp"

NOT LONG after he had made his way to the other side, two years after he had passed over the border, as Sebald himself might have put it,[1] a volume entitled *Unerzählt* (*Unrecounted*) was published under the names of W. G. Sebald and Jan Peter Tripp. It is arranged with facing pages of Tripp's images of pairs of eyes and Sebald's laconic lines and implicitly contemplates the issues of perception, reality, and citation: this is a constellation at play, we saw, in the last lines of both *Austerlitz* and *The Emigrants* and which we pondered more pointedly in "Air War and Literature."[2]

There had also been another, earlier encounter of Sebald's writing and Tripp's images in *Logis in einem Landhaus* (*A Place in the Country*).[3] How shall we pose the question of that relation? At the close of the preliminary remarks to that volume, we read:

> And beforehand as a reader I therefore pay my tribute in what follows to the colleagues who went before in the form of several extended marginalia which otherwise make no particular claim. That at the end there is an essay about a painter—that is quite in order [*Ordnung*], not only because Jan Peter Tripp and I went to the same school in Oberstdorf for a rather long time and because Keller and Walser are equally meaningful to both of us, but also because I

learned from his pictures that one has to look into the depths, that
art does not get on without handwork and that one has to take many
difficulties into account in enumerating things.
(*LOGIS IN EINEM LANDHAUS* 7G)[4]

The tribute to previous colleagues takes the form of "marginalia."[5]
What would it mean to write marginalia, to write on the margins of
another's work, just outside its frame? Is it the same as what the narrator of *Austerlitz* speaks of as vision at the edge of the field of sight
(*Austerlitz*, 35E, 51G)? Would this account as well for Sebald's essay on
the painter? Or does Sebald's attempt here to read Tripp's work, particularly at the close of that essay, go off in a different direction? What
does it mean to look into the depths? Moreover, the essay on Tripp
has its own order and is bound up with the difficulties of listing, enumeration, accounting for things.

As I account for this accounting I want, if at all possible, to set
out on the right foot. And so I begin with a citation, and with a citation within that citation, from the works of Jan Peter Tripp that I take
from "Like Day and Night: On the Pictures of Jan Peter Tripp" ("Wie
Tag und Nacht—Über die Bilder Jan Peter Tripps").[6] I wish to speak of
what remains untold in the story of two paintings and to do so by way
of Sebald's essay, which in its closing pages purports to do just that
and yet still leaves a thing or two unrecounted.

"Remembrance is fundamentally nothing but a citation" ("As Day
and Night" 90E, 184G),[7] Sebald tells us. Echoing Umberto Eco, he
goes on to write: "And the citation incorporated in a text (or image)
by montage compels us . . . to probe [literally: to the looking through
of] our knowledge of other texts and pictures and our knowledge of
the world. This, in turn, takes time. By spending it, we enter into narrated time and into the time of culture" ("As Day and Night" 90–91E).[8]
Already we are out of time, or compelled at least to spend it, by enter-
ing into another time, "narrated time" and "the time of culture," in
which our own "knowledge" (*Kenntnisse*) is put to the test. What does
it mean to step into the frames of time recounted or the time of culture? What can we know of other texts and other images? What can
we know of time that has been narrated, given over, thus, to storytelling? What can we know of the world?

Sebald proposes to "show" the necessity of all this by citing, that is, by the incorporation by montage (*Einmontierung*) of Jan Peter Tripp's *La Déclaration de guerre* into his text. Despite its apparent lack of ambiguity, something is immediately amiss.[9] There is indeed a war raging, as the title of the painting insists, though perhaps not openly declared, and certainly not explained (*erklärt*),[10] in the juxtaposition of the two patterns. "Let us finally try to show that in the picture 'La déclaration de guerre' measuring 370 by 220 centimeters and in which an elegant pair of ladies' shoes is to be seen on a tiled floor. The pale blue-natural white ornament of the tiles, the gray lines of the joints, the lozenge-net from a leaden glass window cast by sunlight onto the picture's middle section, in which the black shoes stand between two shadow areas, all this makes a geometric pattern of a complexity not to be described in words" ("As Day and Night" 91E).[11]

A challenge is made to the pattern of the ornamental tile on which the shoes stand, a challenge made by the rhomboid net, a second pattern, cast as shadow by the sunlight passing through the leaden glass window we are compelled to imagine at the right ("As Day and Night" 91E, 184–85G).[12] The right shoe is aligned with the grid of the shadow;

FIGURE 6.1 Jan Peter Tripp, *Déclaration de guerre.*
Copyright © Jan Peter Tripp. Reprinted by permission
of the artist (in "As Day and Night" 91E, 185G.).

the left shoe with that of the grouted tile joints. A war is played out as well between the visual complexity all this produces and the descriptive word that is bound to fail: a complexity that is not to be described in language. If there is some sort of *declaration of war*, it jumps to the eye, then, as a question of form and it announces as well the limits of representation. This takes place with respect to an object that, nevertheless, apparently claims to communicate as a "mediating object of [the] representation" (*Darstellung*; "As Day and Night" 92E, 186G).

Still, suddenly thereafter, we enter a realm in which description proves to be no challenge whatsoever. "A picture puzzle arises out of this pattern illustrating the degree of difficulty of the different relationships, connections and interweavings and the mysterious pair of black shoes—a *picture puzzle* which the *observer* who does not know the *prehistory* will hardly be able to solve. To which woman do the shoes belong? Where did she go? Did the shoes pass over into the possession of another person?" ("As Day and Night" 91E, my emphasis).[13]

The narrator shifts the stakes abruptly from the clashing formal relations between texts and images into a realm we might call "narrated time," a "time of culture," or even "knowledge of the world" ("As Day and Night" 90-91E, 184G). The essay turns from the war of patterns within the image to finding a woman without. It passes as well from the incommensurability of image and text to assuming that the enigma of the picture might be solvable. It poses the frame-jumping question 'To whom did the shoes belong?' and will venture to show us what has happened to her. This will take place by way of Tripp's second painting. The two shoes of the *Déclaration* do not declare and do not explain. They do not give away their secret ("As Day and Night" 91E, 185G), at least not before they are mounted into a subsequent work of the artist. What Sebald himself creates is a picture puzzle (*Bilderrätsel*).

What sort of solution will that second citation make possible? Can it bring about the shift from image to language that we expect in a rebus? The pages solving the puzzle begin with the description of what we observe and end with us as the object of observation. This solution stands, admittedly, in place of the formal conundrum in which words were seen as incapable of either describing or explaining the *Déclaration*. We find tales of people and dogs, of time and space, of

FIGURE 6.2 Jan Peter Tripp, *Déjà vu oder der Zwischenfall* (*Déjà vu or the Incident*). Copyright © Jan Peter Tripp. Reprinted by permission of the artist (in "As Day and Night," 92E, 186G).

paintings and their painters, and the artist as creator, observer, and witness; stories of fidelity and secrets revealed, of knowledge and perspicacity, of domestication and wildness, and, above all, of the inexplicable losses and gains implicit in citation's relation to realism.

> Two years later, to be sure, the painter shifts his puzzle-image at least a bit further into the public sphere. In a work of a significantly smaller format (100 x 145 cm) the larger painting reappears, not only as a quotation but as a mediating object of representation. Filling the upper two-thirds of the canvas, it now evidently hangs in its place; and in front of it, in front of "La Déclaration de guerre," turning away from the viewer, sideways on a white-upholstered mahogany chair, sits a flamingly red-haired woman. She is elegantly dressed, but somehow is someone tired by evening of the day's burdens. She has taken off one of her shoes—and they are the same that she contemplates on the large picture.
> ("AS DAY AND NIGHT" 92E)[14]

Just as the smaller painting, has, in the act of citation, shrunk the scale of the much larger one reproduced therein, the name of the larger will also soon be shortened and domesticated into the German *Kriegserklärung*. The woman in white contemplates the image of the two shoes. Turned away from us, the observers, she sits in for us as well, domesticating not only the foreignness of its title but also of its representation. For she appears as an answer to the questions it first posed (To which woman do the shoes belong? Where did she go?), and she poses in turn, in a compelling manner, the third and most puzzling of the narrator's queries: "Did the shoes pass over into the possession of another person?" ("As Day and Night" 91E, 185G). For only here, as we observe the second painting, just as we seem to account for the initial pair in *La Déclaration de guerre*, just as we seem to have found the woman to whom the shoes belonged, one of her pair goes missing.

Thus we must recognize "that one has to take many difficulties into account in enumerating things" (*Logis* 7G) and that art is no simple doubling of this world into an aesthetic realm: it cannot be accounted for by the "obliteration of the visible world in interminable series of reproductions" ("As Day and Night" 84E, 178G). In this regard, art distinguishes itself from photography, as Sebald chooses to understand it. "The photographic image turns reality into tautology. . . . Roland Barthes saw in the by now omnipresent man with a camera an agent of death, and in photographs something like the residue of a life perpetually perishing" ("As Day and Night" 84E).[15] In photography, life dies into and becomes the image. But, Sebald insists, art is in need of "the transcendence of that which according to an incontrovertible sentence is the case" ("As Day and Night" 84E, 178G). Thus Tripp's second painting only half-heartedly suggests that the shoes in the work of art result from reality being ferried over into a nether world by an agent of death. Were that inexorably the case, how to explain the anomaly that, while both shoes appear in *La Déclaration de guerre*, the left shoe remains on the woman's foot?[16]

What citation generates, just as the narrator had forewarned, requires turning to yet other texts and other images, to the time of culture and narrated time. For what Sebald now invents to explain the puzzle is a series of stories about what happened over time, to the woman and to the dog, speaking of them, so caught up in their realism is he, as if they had lives independent of Tripp's creation. Thus it is evening and the woman, "wearied from the burdens of the day" ("As Day and Night" 92E, 186G), has removed one of her shoes, which is now no longer to be seen—shoes that are (but are also not) the *same* as those in the puzzling *La Déclaration de guerre*. She ponders an inexplicable loss (*unerklärlichen Verlust;* "As Day and Night" 93E, 188G).

As surely as we regard her from outside the frame of art, she too, from within, regards the painting hanging before her. "Originally, so I was told, she held this shoe taken off in her left hand, then it lay on the floor on the right, next to the chair, and finally it had wholly vanished" ("As Day and Night" 92E).[17] How are we to understand this slide from left to right and ultimately to nowhere? If the elegant woman held the shoe to one side, was it she who, taking on a life of her own, then shifted it and laid it on the floor to the right? What to make, moreover, of the utter lack of agency in its ultimate disappearance: "and finally it had totally vanished" ("As Day and Night" 92E, 186G). Or are we to understand, pairing this passage with the one to come, that what the narrator has heard told, what has taken form in "narrated time," is, rather, three versions of the painting, the first with the shoe in her left hand, then with it laid on the floor at her right, and finally out of sight? For not only the shoe but the dog as well has done some moving around. "The woman with the one shoe, alone with herself and the enigmatic declaration of war, alone except for the faithful dog at her side, who, to be sure, is not interested in the painted shoes, but looks straight ahead out of the picture and into our eyes . . ." ("As Day and Night" 92E).[18] The woman and dog are a couple, but are, then again, like night and day: she aligned with the right shoe, the dog with the left in *Déclaration de guerre;* the one with her back to us seems caught up in the painting, the other, indifferent to that which is painted, casts his eyes outside the frame and confronts us head on. The woman makes us the observer of the observer. With the dog we become the observed. Still, since "an X-ray would show that earlier on he had once stood at the center of the picture" ("As Day and Night" 92E, 186G), it might tell us, then, as well, that the dog, who gives such evidence of a conscious, intentional gaze, is himself merely paint and was once painted over.

And yet, we go on to read, between finding his original place in the middle (as the materiality of the artist's medium) and shifting his stand to the left (where he appears as mimetic representation), he takes on a mysteriously kinetic and embodied presence (as though *real*): a fanciful story redelivers the dog to narrated time and the time of culture: "*Meanwhile* he has been *underway* and has brought in a sort of wooden sandal, from the fifteenth century or more specifically from the wedding picture hanging in the London National Gallery which Jan van Eyck painted in 1434" ("As Day and Night" 92–93E, emphasis mine).[19]

More is left hanging than the pictures: of marriage and war, of union and conflict. The dog makes something of a trip between the paintings of the two Jans. And doesn't this explain the title of the painting, which Sebald has chosen to obliterate: *Déjà vu oder der Zwischenfall?* What we contemplate is the citation of *La déclaration de guerre* (this is the déjà vu) *or* the announcement of a small and almost unnoticed incident (*Zwischenfall*), perhaps the breaking out of a conflict of another kind, as the dog moves between (*zwischen*) one version of the painting and the next: "Meanwhile he has been underway." ("Inzwischen ist er unterwegs gewesen"; "As Day and Night" 92–93E, 186–87G). What marked the middle of Tripp's picture (the dog) now finds its place at the left. The narrator tells of what happened in between (*inzwischen*)—between middle and left, between the twentieth and fifteenth centuries, *or* between continental Europe and London. In this story the canine, which was formally conceived in minute strokes of color, takes form as in the machinations of a trick film and comes, like one of its living, furry counterparts, to occupy and pass through time and space. It brings back a sandal, we read, either by returning to the concrete, three-dimensional world of a historically earlier time or by jumping the space of the Channel to the formal, two-dimensional realm of van Eyck's painting in the London National Gallery. At the same time, it figures as a creature for whom space and time are no object. The dog runs "with ease over the abysses of time, because for him there is no difference between the fifteenth and the twentieth centuries" ("As Day and Night" 94E, 188G).

While the woman in white, something of a bride without a bridegroom after all, "ponders the history of her shoes and an inexplicable loss, [she] never guesses that the disclosure of her secret lies behind her—in the shape of an analogous object from a world long past" ("As Day and Night" 93–94E, 187–88G). The dog, having left its place in the middle of the canvas, and, having turned its back on the enigmatic image and image puzzle (*Rätselbild* and *Bilderrätsel*; "As Day and Night" 91–92E, 185G) cited therein, has in the meantime become the "bearer of a secret" ("As Day and Night" 94E, 188G). But is the revelation of the secret, even to us, a certainty? Is the "inexplicable loss" ("As Day and Night" 93E, 188G) of her shoe explained? Do we discover thereby whether or not her shoe has gone over into the possession of another ("in den Besitz eines anderen"; "As Day and Night" 91E, 185G)? Doesn't the dog remain, rather, as the text reads, simply the bearer of the secret rather than the agent of its revelation? Isn't it this that contemplating the painting of van Eyck (and reading the narrator's ostentatiously faulty description of it) tells us?

[The dog] brought in a sort of wooden sandal, from the fifteenth century or more specifically from the wedding picture hanging in the London National Gallery which Jan van Eyck painted in 1434 for Giovanni Arnolfini and the Giovanna Cenami affianced to him in a morganatic marriage "of the left hand," as a token of his witness. *Johannes de Eyck hic fuit*, one is told, on the frame of the round mirror in which the scene, reduced to miniature format, can once more be seen, from behind. In the foreground, near the left lower edge of the picture, lies that wooden sandal, this curious piece of evidence, beside a little dog that probably entered the composition as a symbol of marital fidelity.

("AS DAY AND NIGHT" 93E)[20]

Spending some time with the painting, one sees that here it is not a question of a complexity that cannot be described in words ("As Day and Night" 91E, 185G). It is, on the contrary, a work that both calls for and performs the act of description. The convex mirror that inevitably draws the eye (while functioning as one) reduces the scene to a miniature format, as Sebald tells us. In this it plays the same role as Tripp's second painting, considerably reducing the larger, initial image and introducing the figure of the observer. In Van Eyck's painting,

FIGURE 6.3 Jan van Eyck, *Portrait of Giovanni* (?) *Arnolfini and His Wife*. Copyright © the National Gallery, London.

although Sebald neglects to remind us of it, the mirror not only lets us see the initial scene again, this time from behind, it also adds what is presumably the image of van Eyck as a sign of his having been witness to the event (*zum Zeichen seiner Zeugenschaft*) and adds as well, alongside the painter, another observer at his side. Whereas Sebald speaks of one sandal, in van Eyck's painting there are, of course, two. Whereas van Eyck has signed *Johannes de Eyck fuit hic*, Sebald inverts the word order to *hic fuit*—putting in question precisely the hereness of the "was" in a statement that is said to fix it in place: *Johannes de Eyck was here*. Sebald tells us that the declaration is to be found "on the frame of the round mirror" when it is, in fact, outside that frame, prominently and elegantly displayed on the wall.[21]

If the photographic image turns reality into tautology, this is not the case as the narrator describes van Eyck's painting. Let us just say in passing, in place of a more thorough reading of Sebald's gloss, which shifts things around so obviously, that the more subtle lesson to be learned here is less that of the narrator's divergences and differences from the wedding picture as the object of his description than the nature of the union that van Eyck actually celebrates. One wonders how it could be anything but intentional that what we witness van Eyck witnessing (or creating) is "a morganatic marriage 'of the left hand'" ("As Day and Night" 93E, 187G). This was a marriage with the provision that the passing on of the husband's property or title was, from the beginning, out of the question. It is a relation in which all inheritance, even that of a wooden sandal, simply could not take place. The ritual sign of this declared impossibility was the offering of the left hand instead of the right: it is echoed in Tripp's second painting by the substitution of the left, not quite "analogous," sandal from van Eyck for the missing right leather shoe. Were the weary lady to slip on its replacement, she would hobble unevenly at best. It disturbs the desire to create a couple, to form a pair.

What the dog carries over both challenges and testifies to the prohibition against such activities, against delivering it "into the possession of another." The sandal's anomalous appearance definitively explains the van Eyck as the source of Tripp's citation. The figure of the dog in Tripp's painting is a witty stand-in for the conventional rhetoric of art history, which would explain the appearance of Arnolfini's left sandal as a citation or allusion to the fifteenth-century master-piece and as a testament to Tripp's stunning skills of mimicry.[22] But the story of the dog in Sebald's essay "Like Day and Night" is, after all, not an answer to the questions apparently posed by the real-life setting of the painting, or, rather, by Sebald's fabula—not an answer, for example, to the query "Did the shoes pass into the possession of another person?" Nor does it explain the "inexplicable loss" that, we read, the red-haired woman ponders. The "secret" of that loss is no-where revealed.

Still, the dog is the locus of knowledge: he "knows a great deal more precisely than we do" ("As Day and Night" 94E, 188G). What he knows, like his movement, is marked as an abyss between left and right and is evidenced in a strange double gaze.[23] Sebald's last im-age, a cropped citation of the second, smaller painting, places the dog once again in the middle of the frame. "Attentively his left (do-mesticated) eye is fixed on us; the right (wild) one has a trace less light, strikes us as averted and alien. And yet it is precisely by this overshadowed eye that we feel ourselves seen through" ("As Day and Night" 94E).[24]

In the essay we find a previous history of this state of affairs, which, while not solving the riddle of the dog, might help us to frame that cropped image of it from another perspective. Under the aegis of what might be left behind, it is again a question of an inheritance of sorts and of painting and the observer in relation, this time, to the *nature morte*. Citing Maurice Merleau-Ponty, Sebald writes:

> The *nature morte*, for Tripp . . . is the paradigm of the estate we leave behind. In it we encounter what Maurice Merleau-Ponty . . . called the *regard préhumain*, for in such paintings the roles of the observer and the observed objects are reversed. Looking, the painter relin-quishes our all too facile knowing; fixedly/unrelatedly,[25] things look across to us. "Action et passion si peu discernables . . . qu'on ne sait plus qui voit et qui est vu, qui peint et qui est peint." ("Action and passion so little separable . . . that one no longer knows who is look-ing and who is being looked at, who is painting and who is being painted.")
> ("AS DAY AND NIGHT" 80E)[26]

FIGURE 6.4 Detail of Jan Peter Tripp painting *Déjà vu oder der Zwischenfall* (*Déjà vu or the Incident*). Copyright © Jan Peter Tripp. Reprinted by permission of the artist ("As Day and Night" 94E).

Our *knowing* is ill-considered, frivolous, and must be relinquished (unlike that of the dog). Perhaps this is because, as observers (and isn't this what the dog sees through?), we foolishly presume to know what Tripp (and art) are about. Sebald, too. For is not much of the essay "Like Day and Night" a series of ever shifting takes on Tripp's work, perspectives that are implicitly cited, if not precisely kept in view, and ironically undone by the closing passage?

In thinking of Tripp, this is what Sebald tells us all along: we cannot avoid the question of realism and of fidelity to reality: *Wirklichkeitstreue.* "What seems to me worth considering in it is only the assumption . . . according to which the inherent quality of a picture by Tripp, just in view of what one might believe to be its purely objective and affirmative nature, probably cannot be attributed to that identity with reality which all its viewers admire without fail—or to its photographic reproduction—but to the far less apparent points of divergence and difference" ("As Day and Night" 84E).[27] If the narrator dismisses such fidelity to reality in Tripp's art as completely off the mark, for most of the essay, nevertheless, it remains his point of departure. Thus art may call for ambiguity and polyvalence and for the transcendence of that which seems to be the case, but Tripp's art is repeatedly viewed less as a radical departure from than as modification of the faithful replicating material of the photograph: with additions, interventions, divergences, and differences ("As Day and Night" 84–85E, 179G). His claims notwithstanding, the narrator fundamentally maintains the assumption of this art's almost fidelity to, and even identity with, reality ("As Day and Night" 80E, 174G and 84E, 178G) with which Tripp's work inevitably lures every observer: for what Sebald writes, at least early in the essay, is that just a small shift needs to take place: "Something is shifted to another place" ("As Day and Night" 84E, 179G).

Still, toward the end of the essay there is a shifting sense of shifting (*rücken*) that gets quite out of hand. The *Déclaration de guerre,* we read, closes itself off in a private realm, but, when cited in a second work, "the painter *shifts* (*rückt*) his puzzle-image at least a bit further into the public sphere" ("As Day and Night" 92E, 185G, emphasis mine). This shift in the name of openness and revelation is immediately followed by the shift of the shoe in the hand of the woman in white, the shift of the dog from the middle to the left, the shift of the dog in and out of the frame, and the shift of van Eyck's sandal into Tripp's picture—shifts that cannot simply be grounded in fidelity to reality. The outlandish tale Sebald finally creates responds to his essay's initial naïveté. So does the title of Tripp's second painting, which Sebald keeps secret: *Déjà vu oder der Zwischenfall* (*Déjà vu or the Incident*). The title gives us a choice—or perhaps rather insists on our seeing double. The second painting presents art as *Déjà vu*. The painting of the two shoes, *Déclaration de guerre*, which we see imaged in this second work, previously had a place in a more immediate realm. *Déjà vu or the Incident,* because it contains a replica of the first painting, announces its fidelity to a reality outside its canvas (the *Déclaration de guerre*) that is passed from this world over the threshold to that of art. It is the passage to death (*nature morte*) of which we have already read—passing over the border on the way to the other side ("As Day and Night" 86E, 180G).

Moreover, one can think of the shoe on the woman's foot (or the missing shoe, for that matter) as one of the original pair in the *Déclaration de guerre:* they are the same as those she contemplates on the large picture ("As Day and Night" 92E, 186G). In this sense, once again, not only what we see but also what she sees in the *Déclaration de guerre* is *Déjà vu.* The painting is a matter of fidelity to reality, as a replica of objects of the world, the painting, the woman's shoe(s).

"*Déjà vu* oder *der Zwischenfall*" (*Déjà vu* or *the Incident*): what the canvas and Sebald's storytelling also make of this incident (*Zwischenfall*) is the *inzwischen,* the intervening time, the time that falls between, of the outrageously elaborated adventure of the dog underway through time and space. In this little story of a little trip Sebald thereby claims to present as explanation for the woman's loss that which is both beside the point and impossible.

Mimetic language had already met its match when confronted with the *Déclaration de guerre* as an image of such complexity, we were told, that it cannot be described in words. Shifting that image into Tripp's second painting seemed a move toward bringing it into a more public sphere. The scene of the woman contemplating the *Déclaration de guerre* pretends to speak of, or even partially explain, the relation between what is inside and what is outside of art. It hints at but fails to fully account for a conventional economy of art. The narration of the essay, however, then takes an entirely different tack with regard to *Déjà vu or the Incident* in the totally far-fetched story of the dog, which violates all norms of time and space. The story conjures reality (but then who is to say that the dog really *is?*) out of the material and materiality of art rather than the other way around. This purely paint-of-a-dog, shifting in and out of the frame of the picture, moves miraculously and indifferently through the no longer meaningful parameters of time and space, or so the narrator was informed ("As Day and Night" 92–93E, 186–87G). And, through no act of imitation, he does what no real dog could do: he brings van Eyck's sandal into Tripp's frame, carrying it both like a secret and a real thing. This is at once a testimony to (Tripp's) exemplary mimetic, artistic accomplishment and/or a writerly tale of a painter forced to give up his own "all too facile knowing" ("As Day and Night" 80E, 174G).

And yet, the paintings are cited to begin with in order to explain that "Remembrance is fundamentally nothing but a citation" ("As Day and Night" 90E, 184G): and that citation sends us scurrying out of our present context into storied time and the time of culture. It is a test of all that we know: texts, images, the world. Sebald's tale both mirrors life and creates it: it is both déjà vu and that which comes to invent the no-man's-land of an incident (*Zwischenfall*) that falls in between. It tells us that, between the dog's obliterated, painted-over place in the middle of the canvas and his final place at the left as representation, the illusory creature created in colors entered into lived (three-dimensional) space or back in time or, more outrageously, into another work of art to rob it of an object/image. Thus all the frames that mark off art from reality are both perfectly intact and utterly blasted. This is no less true for the imaginary plane that (as with all paintings) separates *Déjà vu* from the locus of its observer. What might it mean that across that divide the alien eye of that same dog seems to see right through us? This is a tale we reserve for the "Endnote" to follow.

7

A CRITICAL EYE

The Interviews

That is precisely the secret of fiction, that one never knows
where the line of demarcation runs.
("AUF UNGEHEUER DÜNNEM EIS" 181)

EVERYTHING LIES all jumbled up in the abysses of history Sebald had written in "Air War and Literature" ("Air War" 74E, 79–80G). Perhaps it is he, then, who authorizes the academic misstep in the jumble of chapters. I situate the reading of "As Day and Night," first published in 1993, only after the readings of his other texts, which otherwise follow one another in good chronological order.[1] Still, I wanted to close with Sebald's essay on Tripp, not necessarily as a culminating point of progress, but because, in more ways than one, it is here that Sebald puts critique on the line or that the lines of its different conceptualizations intersect. One might call this the crux of Sebald's vision, if one were foolish enough to reduce it to a single term.

Sebald often reminded his many interlocutors, and they him,[2] that he had begun not by writing literature but rather literary criticism.[3] He remained, ultimately, wildly skeptical about the academic enterprise.[4] And yet Sebald never really relinquished a certain respect for the critical eye. By respect, I do not suggest unquestioned admiration, only that he accorded critique, in its various forms, over and over, a place, a role to play, a position that must be forever called to account. Thus when Ralph Schock says, in response to Sebald's reading of "Dr. K. takes the waters at Riva" (chapter 3 of *Vertigo*), "You are a professor of German literature in Norwich." ("Auf ungeheuer dünnem Eis" 96), Sebald replies: "Well, this text which I just read marks— that is one of the first prose texts that I did—, it already marks, as you say, to a certain extent the crossing over from the description of literature to literature itself" ("Auf ungeheuer dünnem Eis" 97). One might say the same for "Like the snow on the Alps" which shifts back and forth between describing the works of Matthaeus Grünewald and spinning a literary text about their creator.

Yet even before he embarked on his literary path in the mid eighties, Sebald will insist, he was already on the path from science or scholarship (*Wissenschaft*) to fiction. "Yes, it was about the middle of the 80's. And one needs to mention first that already as a literary scholar actually I was working in an unorthodox manner and I always went to the limits of what was possible or acceptable in literary scholarship. This rather essayistic procedure moved then, I believe, more or less naturally in the direction of the more fictive" ("Auf ungeheuer dünnem Eis" 147) To be sure, he explains, while frequently calling into play the same image, his current work, it too, requires research; but this research is hardly academic. It never goes straight forward, its path can never be retraced, and it places him in the role of a dog.[5]

> When I do research for my books, I don't do it according to academic methods. One follows rather a diffused instinct; the trajectory of the research can then no longer be replicated because it looks like the way a dog runs across a field to follow a scent. That is a rather primitive form of research, always with the nose or muzzle on the ground.
> ("AUF UNGEHEUER DÜNNEM EIS" 118)

In this way one always finds very peculiar things which one would never have reckoned on, things which you can never find in a rational way, that is when you do research as you learned to do it at the university, always straight ahead, right, left, right angles, and so on. One has to search in a diffuse way. It should be a matter of discovering

precisely in the manner that a dog seeks, back and forth, coming out
and going back down, sometimes slowly, sometimes fast.
("AUF UNGEHEUER DÜNNEM EIS" 214)

If Sebald's manner of research isn't precisely rational, if it is a bit all
over the place, we, his readers, know at least what he collects: photos,
documents, citations. Their function, however, Sebald readily admits,
is ambiguous. Photographs, he says, are the "true documents," they
make it possible to hold onto things. "It's necessary to hold onto these
things somehow or other. Of course you can do that by writing, but the
written is no true document. The photograph is the true document
par excellence. People let themselves be convinced by a photograph"
("Auf ungeheuer dünnem Eis" 168). And yet holding onto things and
convincing the reader is not quite or not all that Sebald is after.[6] For
what interests him more than a document that seems incontrovert-
ibly "true" is the suggestion of the faint, the dim, the indistinct. "I
don't want to mount pictures of high photographic quality into the
texts, rather they are simply documents of found material, something
secondary. It is actually very nice when this lack of clarity enters into
the photos" ("Auf ungeheuer dünnem Eis" 169) Photographs are therefore at once "the true document par excellence" that convinces the
onlooker, and yet they are also there to unnerve the reader: they rightfully introduce irritation and insecurity.[7] "Thus many of these documents are in fact documents. . . . On the other hand there is the one
or the other of the photographs, one or other of the documents that is
put in with another end in view, where, really . . . that is the falsification theme, which is to say: it is also a matter of making the reader
uncertain. The reader should indeed think about: what is true in these
stories, no?" ("Auf ungeheuer dünnem Eis" 99).

The photographs have therefore a double function, as Sebald will
go on to reiterate in another interview.[8] They make the improbable
seem authentic, but at the same time they introduce the possibility
of the counterfeit. "And this is a very complicated, self-contradictory
process which finally leads either consciously in the head of the
reader or subliminally to a feeling of continuous irritation—which, I
hope, somewhat corresponds to the feeling I myself have" ("Auf ungeheuer dünnem Eis" 141).

For all that, what the photos inhabit and illuminate cannot simply be declared "fiction." Sebald insistently refuses to call his works novels. Prose book, prose text, prose literature ("Auf ungeheuer dünnem Eis" 97, 236): just not novel.[9] Speaking of *Austerlitz,* he says that it is "in my eyes not a novel. It is a prose book of an indeterminate kind" ("Auf ungeheuer dünnem Eis" 199). Indeterminacy is indeed his trademark. When Volker Hage suggests to Sebald in 2000 that in the case of Kluge one never knows what is fiction, what citation, and what invented citation, Sebald replies: "I consider that very productive. I'm often asked whether the lives I tell of are authentic or not. That is precisely the secret of fiction, that one never knows exactly where the line of demarcation runs" ("Auf ungeheuer dünnem Eis" 181).[10]

That unlocatable line runs not only between fiction and citation, but also between fiction and fact. What Sebald strives for is the smooth transition back and forth between the two such that the reader is never certain where she is. "When you drive a car with automatic transmission you only have this strange rolling feeling when it goes from one level to the next. And that is what I try to simulate there—that one comes, through a kind of *lissé de main,* from *fact* into *fiction* and back again, that one never knows precisely where one is actually. I've always admired that in Alexander Kluge" ("Auf ungeheuer dünnem Eis" 117). Reading Sebald, then, would be giving oneself over to a no-man's-land where the borders between literary scholarship (describing a text),[11] fact, document, citation, and fiction are ever shifting. One experiences the object read somewhat like Simplicius experiencing Baldanders (chapter 3). Or one might (also with Sebald) say the fictive, the documentary, and the cited come together over and over at seams or join together like the rows of teeth on opposing sides of a zipper. "There you've put your finger on one of the seams or borders, one of the seams in the text where the fictive more or less puts itself together with the documentary or that which is cited like a zipper" ("Auf ungeheuer dünnem Eis" 56)

This has some kinship with the slide one experiences in "Air War and Literature," from the demand for a language fully adequate to its object to a scene of observation in which even the most basic promise of learning from what one sees is probably out of the question. Some kinship as well with the drift back and forth in "Like the snow on the Alps" between the biographical events of Grünewald's life and a language that enacts the disintegration of his name.[12] Some kinship, yet again, with the pseudoscholarly descriptions of Tripp's work, zippered together as they are with fictions about the figures portrayed therein.

Or should we say, as Sebald does, given that it's a matter of designating reality, that the reality of reality (*Wirklichkeit der Wirklichkeit*) is an old problem that hasn't been resolved and that is rather a matter of point of view? "It depends on the point of view from which one looks at something, in what light, in what atmosphere. Each time different perspectives, different panoramas come into being. And it is actually a question of explaining in writing, finally, that reality can actually only be thought up. That it doesn't exist as a concrete object out there but exists rather only in the relation that we create with it as individuals" ("Auf ungeheuer dünnem Eis" 141–42).

That, ultimately, reality can only be thought up or contrived, that there is no concrete object present to hand, except perhaps in relation to an individual observer, what has this to do with Sebald's enterprise? What aspirations does the writer hold for that particular observer, the narrator in a Sebald text, even while recently having insisted on the necessity of inventive thinking (*Ersinnen*) in relation to so-called reality (*Wirklichkeit*)? In a 1997 conversation with Andrea Köhler, he has this to say: "The narrator in my texts refuses to give any *interpretation*. He doesn't avail himself of the possibilities of the *explanation* of the catastrophe, he indicates that people earlier thought about it in this or that manner. With regard to himself, I believe I can say that he has no answer to this form of radical contingency. He stands perplexed confronted with it, can only describe how it looked, how it came to that" ("Auf ungeheuer dünnem Eis" 160, emphasis mine).

Interpretation and explanation are out of the picture.[13] Except perhaps, Sebald will go on to say, the explanation that invokes *natural history* (*Naturgeschichte*). The shift from the history of civilization to natural history could have been seen very clearly, say, in the bombings of Hamburg ("Auf ungeheuer dünnem Eis" 161). And what characterizes natural history, what distinguishes it from every other form of history, is that it refuses any attempt "to establish sense" (*Sinn zu stiften;* "Auf ungeheuer dünnem Eis" 161). "But the natural historical course is by definition something that is fully neutral, into which no sense of any kind can be projected, at least not from the viewpoint of today" ("Auf ungeheuer dünnem Eis" 161). Köhler, subtle interpreter of texts that she is, brings the sequence together: Sebald's refusal to have his narrator interpret, to offer up explanations, on the one hand, and the senselessness of natural history. She asks him if he himself doesn't aspire to the neutrality of natural history (at least, it is understood, in the context of "Air War and History"). "Yes that would be approximately my ambition. The attempt to describe things in the most neutral way possible—though not detached. One cannot tell about them from the perspective of complete indifference. But I believe the greatest possible neutrality is the only possible stance with respect to these things" ("Auf ungeheuer dünnem Eis" 162.

In passages that move us from literary criticism (as the description of literature) to literature; from the photograph as a true document to its role of falsification, uncertainty, and the capacity to irritate; from Sebald's dogged, if always unguided and irrational "research" that can never be duplicated to the repeated call to the reader to think about "what is true about these stories" ("Auf ungeheuer dünnem Eis" 99) we arrive at last at a confession. What reads in *Campo Santo* as threat, the apocalyptic tipping into a natural history devoid of human autonomy, it turns out, was all along, from a certain perspective, a model for Sebald to emulate. He attempts to achieve in his own writings, or at least in the voice of his narrator, utter neutrality in the face of radical contingency. None of what he excoriates in his diatribe against the conventional practice of literary criticism ("Kafka Goes to the Movies" 195–96) is to be found in the words of his narrator—no interpretation, no explanation: just his own perplexity. Such a narrator, then, like the reader, is also adrift.

History itself was that way from the beginning. "We know in the meantime that history doesn't proceed in its course in the way that the historians of the nineteenth century have told us, that is according to some logic or other dictated by important people, or according to any logic whatsoever. It's a question of completely different phenomena, of something like a drifting, of scatterings, of natural-historical patterns, of chaotic things which coincide sometime or other and then run off in different directions again. I believe that it would be important for literature and also for history writing to work out these complicated chaotic patterns. That is not possible in a systematic way" ("Auf ungeheuer dünnem Eis" 187).

Such a coherent argument has its ironies, fashioned as it is from a patchwork of citations—from the bricolage of Sebald's conversations, as though the interview alone might escape those shifting lines of demarcation among fact, fiction, document, and citation.[14] A return to Sebald writing of Tripp could set us straight or at least remind us just where we are: that reality, which has no place as a concrete object, is invented each time anew from a different perspective. "Like Day and Night" performs. It frolics about, though not frivolously, among different modes of discourse—criticism, theory, fiction; among different takes on the object of its observation—as works of art, the materiality of those works, their formal qualities, or the doings of living individuals portrayed in them. It jumps about as well between opposing accounts of its own position—as observer and observed. This seemingly modest piece of prose performs, moreover, much that takes place in the other chapters of this book.[15] So let us rehearse, as a closing gesture, some of its complicated, chaotic patterns. It is, Sebald has reminded us, not possible to do this in a systematic way.

"Like Day and Night" poses at first as a critical commentary on the work of Jan Peter Tripp: with its description of individual works,[16] the ritual invocation of well-recognized theoretical voices (Ernst Gombrich, Merleau-Ponty, Eco), and the historical account of the development of the artist's oeuvre. Still the reader senses all along that something else is at play. The essay puts forth some of the most outrageous fictional moments in Sebald's work and some of the most interesting metacritical thought-as-practice. In the final pages Sebald writes of two paintings, the large format *Déclaration de guerre* and the smaller format *Déjà vu oder der Zwischenfall* that cites and incorporates its predecessor (see chapter 6). We see, to begin with, an image of the first. The narrator describes it—two shoes and several patterns at odds with one another: the ornamental lines and those that divide the individual tiles of the floor, which is to say the decorative and the functional (still both presumably a direct representation of what is present to hand), and the lines of shadow cast on those tiles by the unseen frames in a leaden glass window as the indirect trace of what is absent. The narrator announces the incommensurability between words and the formal complexity of what is pictured in this conflict. Thus the observer who wishes to record what she sees is bound to fail; the possessor of the critical eye cannot represent the object of its vision.

It is here a shift occurs. The narrator leaves behind the challenge of formal complexity and puts forth instead a puzzle that might well have solutions.[17] That shift is made possible as he gives up description and becomes instead a storyteller, displacing the endlessly complex formal aspects of art—its relationships, connections, and interweavings—for a story line of human events.[18] The narrator asks who had possessed the shoes we see in *Déclaration de guerre,* where she went, and whether the shoes later belonged to someone else. This is a realm of another order, a quest for content and implicit reality of sorts, invented, of course, by Sebald.

It is only by mounting *Déclaration de guerre* into a second painting, only by citing it in *Déjà vu or the Incident,* setting it up as previously seen, that such answers can be offered. Sebald, following Tripp, then, has jumped the frame of the earlier painting, reducing it, citing it, and making it the object of a different observation. Suddenly, the formerly unreadable *Declaration* can now be pondered not as a formal jumble of lines and patterns but as a circumscribable object read for the plot. That plot, however, is also something of a frame jumper since it crosses the borders of what is open to view in the second painting as well. Sebald's narrator begins to fabulate. The woman is tired at the end of the day, and he seems to know of her what is not portrayed: that she held the missing shoe first in one hand, then laid it on the floor, until it went missing (into *Déclaration de guerre,* we might presume). Or is he, we might also understand, speaking of three moments in the production of the painting, so that the woman, as we now see her, who had seemed for a brief moment to come to life in the story's telling, is, rather, the result of the artist's whims? The resolution of the enigmas invented for the first canvas is fleeting indeed, since it depends on the momentary, fictive embodiment of the woman in *Déjà vu or the Incident.*

Still Sebald's narrator takes another turn. The dog at the edge of the canvas, we are reminded, is merely a matter of formal composition, for once, in an earlier version, he stood at the middle of the canvas, but now he has landed a bit to the left. In the meantime, however, no sooner reduced to the materiality, its arbitrary application, of paint, the story has him running across time and space, a real dog, one is tempted to say, to fetch a souvenir from a fifteenth-century painting: the narrator's verbal animation of the dog explains the presence in Tripp's work of a wooden sandal from Van Eyck's masterpiece. And this dog who vacillates between the purely formal figure in the painting and the embodied, living being in a raucous art history, makes us the object of his glance. The dog in *Déjà vu* is not simply observed by us, he confronts us head on.[19] And thereby, no less than the woman in white and the dog, the narrator/critic/observer/reader also has a multiple role to play. The dog stares directly out of the canvas with his left eye, affirming our position, no doubt. With the dog's domesticated eye directed at us,[20] we become the object of the painting's gaze and feel thereby, perhaps, assured of our reality and existence and that of Sebald and his narrator as well.

But his right eye is far less reassuring.[21] What might it mean that we are seen through? It is the critic and observer who are in question in Tripp, and especially in Sebald. Are we then unreal, at best irrelevant, or could we be the object of moral judgment? Is this a commentary on our too facile knowing ("As Day and Night" 80E), our overly simple concept of knowledge bound to powers we associate with critique and observation? Are we, in our search for revelation, inevitably seen through. With the gaze of his wild right eye that sees right through us, we are made to feel that the revelation of our secrets (like those of the woman) will, if anywhere, inevitably take place behind our backs and will never be open to view. Let us remember, in this pointedly serious moment (a declaration of war, perhaps) that the figure who judges us was, but a few lines earlier, the whim of a painter who had obliterated the dog's first location on the canvas.

Forgetting all that, let us review. Already as a literary scholar, Sebald had said, he was working in an unorthodox manner and moving in the direction of fiction. Here too, in the essay on Tripp, what sets out as art criticism moves back and forth, in and out of the scene directly before him and culminates in unusually pointed fiction. First assuming the role of the scholar, devoted to describing the work at hand, Sebald then crosses over to literature itself ("Auf ungeheuer

dünnem Eis" 97). Along the way, we have the obligatory facts, the documents, as citation, in this case the montage into his text of Tripp's
two paintings, their dimensions, their dates. A faithful enumeration
of *what* is to be seen confirms his point of view as writer and ours in
turn as reader. Still, from the very beginning with the citation from
Eco, this is a test: a test with respect to our knowledge, not only of the
images cited but also of other texts and pictures and our more gener-
alized knowledge of the world ("As Day and Night" 90–91E, 184G).

Let us go back. We have been in this position before. It is where,
at the most critical moments, Sebald tends to place us. In *Rings of
Saturn* we stand before Rembrandt's *Anatomy Lesson of Dr. Nicolaas
Tulp*, precisely where those who were present at the dissection stood,
Rembrandt as well, and we believe we see what they saw (*Rings of Saturn* 13E, 23G). What we learn is that the much praised verisimilitude
of Rembrandt's picture proves, on closer examination, to be more
apparent than real, that Rembrandt (like Sebald) judged the various
viewers of the scene and did so in a performance that turns his otherwise true-to-life painting into a crass false construction (*Rings of Saturn* 16E, 27G).

At the close of *The Emigrants* we are placed in this same position
along with the narrator, Sebald too then, before a photograph of
three weavers at the ghetto in Łódź. It is the very spot where Genewein, the accountant, who fancied himself a renderer of reality, an
innovative documentarian, stood with his camera (*The Emigrants*
237E, 355G). The observer, as at the end of the essay on Tripp,[22] must
endure the gaze of the image looking back. The observer is called to
judgment.

It is a call to judgment of the observer we read in "Air War and Literature" as well. It condemns those whose writings avoided a concrete documentary approach ("Air War" 58E, 65G), who did not present the real circumstances ("Air War" ixE, 7G) by way of a steady gaze
at reality ("Air War" 51E, 57G), who did not make us see ("Air War" 57E,
64G). But that condemnation gives way to another scene of observation in which Kluge, the pseudodocumentarian who mixes fiction,
citation, and invented citation, looks down on the bombed-out city
of Halberstadt. It is here, we are to understand, as Sebald put it in
another context, that "natural history and the history of the human

species" iridescently become one another ("Auf ungeheuer dünnem Eis" 260).

Perhaps it is *Austerlitz* that performs the most complex vicissi-tudes of the critical position. We saw this when we traced, however unsystematically, the appearance of glass in that work. Glass, after all, is that which so often in Sebald separates the eye of the viewer and the object of the glance. This was certainly the case already in *Rings of Saturn* where the narrator's hospital window is set up as the metaphor for recapturing and retelling the journey through Suffolk that constitutes the book. When Austerlitz visits Terezín he gazes at remnants of former lives through the display windows of the An-tikos Bazaar. His search for the past is accompanied by a reflection of branch work from the trees behind him as well as his own faint reflec-tion. At the Veterinary Museum of Maisons-Alfort we are pitched into a description of the contents of the cabinets (as at the Royal Observa-tory), forgetting what stands between us. But one of the descriptions, it too of branch work (this time within the cabinet), is a counterpart to the scene of Antikos Bazaar. Where we once saw on the glass the reflection of Austerlitz (looking just like Sebald) now we encounter the flash of the camera used to take the photograph. It obliterates the observer. And there are still other incarnations of glass that make us rather forget the division between viewer and viewed,[23] like the miracles of pure glass brought about by Honoré Fragonard in which glass embodies its object through a process of vitrification. All that is framed, yet again, by the telling of the telling of the tale in which Aus-terlitz casts his eyes through the window of a café that looks out on Boulevard Blanqui near the Métro Glacière, a narration about a blank in memory and in which glass is reflected upon in linguistic play. Thus the varied appearances of glass practice different conceptual-izations of sight: direct, mirrored, self-reflective, blinding, playful.

In "Like Day and Night" the position from which narrative erupts leaps about. The scholarly observer offers a description of the *Décla-ration de guerre*, only to give up then with respect to its visual com-plexity. An act of montage makes possible the literary voice that spins the tale of the woman in white. She is left sitting and contemplating as the text turns to the liberating antics of the dog while the narra-tor also cavorts, celebrating his own capacity for a fiction no longer beholden to the visual object, a fiction that has, it seems, no bounds. A few years later Sebald spoke of the slide from academic writing to literature as follows: "This preoccupation with making something out of nothing, which is, after all, what writing is about, took me at that point. And what I liked about it was that if you just changed, as it were, the nature of your writing from academic monographs to something indefinable, then you had complete liberty."[24] The narrator of "Like Day and Night" cavorts, but then his considerable powers of invention give way under a judgmental gaze, though the terms of its accusation remain elusive. Sebald's texts come to us in unsystematic permutations of many voices: critic, scholar, fiction writer, recorder of citations. They are all there throughout his works. Each demands a different conceptualization of authority and truth and asks us in turn to modulate our positions, to accept the implicit permutations of reader, commentator, observer, and observed. "Each time different perspectives, different panoramas come into being" ("Auf ungeheuer dünnem Eis" 141–42). Each jump in the voice of the narrator dislocates the position of the reader as well. The space between text and observer is a porous border and "one never knows precisely where one is actually" ("Auf ungeheuer dünnem Eis" 117). That goes without saying. This take on things tells us something about Sebald's capacity for moral judgment: it has always been a puzzle, given that he declares the oblique indirection in his writings necessary, given that his ambition is to maintain neutrality, given his narrator's purposeful refusal of interpretation. The capacity for moral judgment as Sebald practices it has no set frame.[25] Nor is it bound to fixed truth or reality. What is essential in the works of those he most admires, Rembrandt, for example, or Tripp, is precisely a crucial deviation. His enduring question remains: Shouldn't the reader "think about: what in these stories is true, no?" ("Auf ungeheuer dünnem Eis" 99).

NOTES

PREFACE

1. As I was nearing the end of this study, Henry Sussman called it my book on Sebald's vision. I have taken that phrase as a gift, bearing as it does all the uncertainty of what this work might claim to be about.

2. These are the obvious readings of the German phrase: *nach der Natur* which can suggest either that which follows Nature temporally or also, as in the phrases draw or paint from nature (*nach der Natur zeichnen)*, an art that imitates its natural object. Many of Sebald's readers take us through these and other ambiguities of the title. Dorothea von Mücke ("History and the Work of Art in Sebald's *After Nature*") and Claudia Öhlschläger ("Der Saturnring oder Etwas vom Eisenbau") would be just two highly articulate examples. Eva Hoffman ("Curiosity and Catastrophe") gives a particularly beautiful formulation of this:

> But on another level, the poem is an exploration of the relationship between art and reality—and, not incidentally, an implicit gloss on various connotations of the book's title phrase. Grünewald's art, with its tormented imagery of death, extreme anguish and physical decomposition, is made "after nature," Sebald implies, in that it faithfully imitates the conditions the medieval master saw in his world—the "pathological spectacle" of crippled bodies, gangrenous diseases and the brutality of the Peasants' War. But the iconography of Grünewald's paintings and sculptures was also imbued with a more eschatological, apocalyptic conception of a post-natural world, a vision fed by portents and premonitions of "the ending of time."

3. Andrea Köhler's eloquent statement on vision as Sebald's most critical theme reads as follows: "Probably there is hardly a theme in his work as central to it as eyes are. . . . [The] dimming of vision and the penetration of darkness are the key metaphors in all his books for his most intimate concern: the work of remembrance, the work of witness, in the torrential flux of time" (Köhler, "Penetrating the Dark," 95–96).

4. *Sebald's Vision* takes up his work cognizant of a number of questions and poses them, neither by way of a historical, political, and sociological contextualization of his works nor by aligning Sebald's writings with the theoretical thinkers of the twentieth century. These approaches have been enormously successful in producing other understandings of the work. I am thinking in particular of J. J. Long's *W. G. Sebald: Image, Archive, Modernity*. An admirable piece of scholarly writing and broad historical and cultural thinking, it is concerned with Sebald's work in relation to a long view of the concept of modernity, or, in his own words, "the seismic social, economic, political and cultural transformations" in Europe (ibid., 1). Eric Santner's exceptionally intelligent and original book, *On Creaturely Life: Rilke/Benjamin/Sebald*, is conceived as a continuation of his volume on Franz Rosenzweig, from which the concept of neighbor love is central for the new work. Under the rubric of the *creaturely*, Santner magisterially puts Sebald's work in contact with that of previous writers and thinkers, not only Benjamin and Rilke but also Freud, Schmitt, Kafka, Scholem, Celan, Lacan, Heidegger, Agamben, Foucault, and others. Rather than looking elsewhere, the attempt here is to concentrate on the particularities of Sebald's poetry and prose, with occasional detours into the writings of authors explicitly embedded within his work.

5. One should think as well of those striking instances where the open, seeing eye is challenged by the different or even troubled sight of its counterpart: the image of Frank Auerbach, which only appeared in the German edition of *The Emigrants (Die Ausgewanderten* 240G), showing the black lines of a face with one eye closed and the other open, but unclearly so; the dog at the end of Sebald's essay on Tripp, one eye averted and in shadow, the other, we read, attentively fixed on us ("As Day and Night" 94E and "Wie Tag und Nacht," 188G); Saint Dionysius of Grünewald's painting whose open glance toward Saint George is strangely contradicted by the severed head with closed eyes he holds in his hands (*After Nature* 7E, 8G); the extended reminder in *Austerlitz* that the sight of the narrator is divided between a clear-sighted eye and another threatened at its core by black hatching.

6. This is only one strand of the argument. Sebald certainly doesn't let things rest with such assertions.

7. At about the same time he was writing the Tripp essay, Sebald says of his own writing that "every fiction, if it doesn't wish to be insipid, must pass

over on the edge into the fantastic and mysterious. It is from that it lives ultimately. Thus realism to which I am very attached on the one hand is not sufficient; one always has to transgress it at certain points" ("jede Fiktion [muß], wenn sie nicht platt sein will, irgendwo so am Rande in die Phantastik und ins Mysteriöse übergehen. . . . Davon lebt sie letzten Endes. Also Realismus, dem ich ja sehr verhaftet bin, einerseits, reicht nicht aus, man muß ihn immer an bestimmten Punkten übertreten.). "Auf ungeheuer dünnem Eis," 98. A related passage on realism from a conversation with Sven Boedecker (1993) would also be of interest here (ibid., 107).

8. Silverblatt, "A Poem of an Invisible Subject (Interview)," 80. And, in conversation with Jean-Pierre Ronda: "For me, it's that one can write about this horrific German history of the twentieth century or the first half of the twentieth century only from a certain distance, approaching the subject obliquely, tangentially, referring to it here and there" ("Auf ungeheuer dünnem Eis" 216).

9. "And of course what one also knows from a distance and what one didn't know, at least what I didn't know when I was there growing up, was the horrors that were associated with these places and that one really only afterwards, so to speak, learned to grasp from historical study" ("Auf ungeheuer dünnem Eis" 226).

10. We might also think in terms of someone who has visions, something akin to what happens in the last section of the final poem of *After Nature* in which the narrator speaks to God of the visionlike dream he has had.

11. "Now I know, as with a crane's eye / one surveys his far-flung realm" (*After Nature* 115 E, 98G).

12. Sebald used the name Aurach for the character in the German edition, but switched to Ferber in the English out of respect for the protests of the living artist on whom the character was based (Frank Auerbach). *Aurach* came too close to home.

13. Silverblatt, "A Poem of an Invisible Subject (Interview)," 80.

14. In "Curiosity and Catastrophe" Hoffman writes: "The language of 'After Nature,' as conveyed in Michael Hamburger's flawlessly clear translation, is almost classically lucid: No verbal games here, no self-conscious ironies." It is indeed neither simply a game nor a flatly self-conscious irony that drives the richness of the German original in particular, critical, moments of the poem: still, one finds a complexity in Sebald's use of Grünewald's name that should not be ignored. (Sebald was obsessed both with his own name and that of others throughout his works.)

15. I make the leap from glossing chapter 3 to chapter 5 here (returning to chapter 4 in the subsequent pages) simply to maintain the clearer logic of the theoretical argument. Any reader of Sebald, however, knows how distracting such gestures can be.

1. "LIKE THE SNOW ON THE ALPS"

1. Dante, *The Divine Comedy of Dante Alighieri, Inferno*, II, 139–42, translation modified.

2. This alternative to Michael Hamburger's translation ("all turns as white as / the snow on the Alps") might better enable us to see what Sebald is about.

3. In an essay on *Nach der Natur*, thoroughly admirable for its careful readings and its meditation on crucial theoretical issues, Dorothea von Mücke has this to say of the opening lines: "The first sentence doesn't just say what can be *seen* but rather what *happens* if one closes the altar's left shutter and encloses the carved figures in their housing. The opening sentence invites the reader of the poem to imagine herself in front of the altar of the parish church of Lindenhardt. . . . Yet, while the poem draws attention to the concrete material object or vehicle of the work of art, in the same sentence it also draws attention to the imaginary aspect of the representational work of art" (von Mücke, "History and the Work of Art" 9). Thus we are reminded, here as elsewhere in this essay, of the role of the reader. It is the last lines of "Like the snow on the Alps," as we shall see, that call the reader to an even more radical role.

   Way beyond this reading of the opening lines, von Mücke's essay offers an extensive analysis of the complex register of "Like the snow on the Alps," taking up repeatedly the ways in which Sebald casts aside the received views of art history with respect to the biographical Grünewald "and engages with the painter and his oeuvre in order to pursue questions about the relationship between artist and work of art and about the relationship between the work of art and history" (von Mücke, "History and the Work of Art" 8).

4. A more literal, if clumsier translation would read: "him, on the left panel, St. George approaches." Andrea Köhler ("Penetrating the Dark" 95) reminds us that Georg is one of Sebald's given names, as does Dorothea von Mücke. It is also the name of the subject of the second poem in *After Nature*, "Und blieb ich am äussersten Meer" ("And if I remained by the outermost sea"), Georg Wilhelm Steller. It is the understood name of the last section as well, devoted as it is to a double of W. G(eorg). Sebald.

5. *Wer die Flügel des Altars*
   der Pfarrkirche von Lindenhardt
   zumacht und die geschnitzten Figuren
   in ihrem Gehäuse verschließt,
   dem kommt auf der linken
   Tafel der hl. Georg entgegen.
   (NACH DER NATUR 7G)

6. *Zuvorderst steht er am Bildrand*
   eine Handbreit über der Welt

und wird gleich über die Schwelle
des Rahmens treten. Georgius Miles.
(NACH DER NATUR 7G)

7.   *in der Mitte des rechten Flügels*
des Lindenhardter Altars in Besorgnis
den Blick auf den Jüngling auf der anderen
Seite gerichtet jener ältere Mann, dem ich selber
vor Jahren einmal an einem Januarmorgen
auf dem Bamberger Bahnhof begegnet bin.
Es ist der heilige Dionysius,
das abgeschlagene Haupt unterm Arm.
(NACH DER NATUR 8G)

8. This is not an unusual claim for Sebald. In *Vertigo* (*Schwindel. Gefühle.*) the
narrator encounters, among others, Dante in the Gonzagagasse (35E, 41G),
King Ludwig II of Bavaria in Venice (*Vertigo* 53E, 61G), and also twins with
an uncanny resemblance to pictures of Kafka as an adolescent (*Vertigo*
88E, 101G).

9.   *Immer dieselbe*
Sanftmut, dieselbe Bürde der Trübsal,
dieselbe Unregelmäßigkeit der Augen, verhängt
und vesunken seitwärts ins Einsame hin.
. . .
Es seien dies merkwürdig verstellte
Fälle von Ähnlichkeit, schrieb Fraenger,
dessen Bücher die Faschisten verbrannten.
Ja, es scheine, als hätten im Kunstwerk
die Männer einander verehrt wie Brüder,
einander dort oft ein Denkmal gesetzt,
wo ihre Wege sich kreuzten.
(NACH DER NATUR 7-8)

See, for example, the image of Sebald's eyes in *Unrecounted* (*Unerzählt*)
(76E, 70G). One might add to these resemblances the figure of Sebald who,
like Grünewald, emerges again and again as witness and commiserator.

The face of the unknown
Grünewald emerges again and again
in his work as a witness
to the snow miracle, a hermit
in the desert, a commiserator
in the Munich Mocking of Christ.
(AFTER NATURE 5)

> *Das Antlitz des unbekannten*
> *Grünewald taucht stets wieder auf*
> *in seinem Werk als das eines Zeugen*
> *des Schneewunders, eines Einsiedlers*
> *in der Wüste, eines Mitleidigen*
> *in der Münchner Verspottung.*
> (*NACH DER NATUR* 7)

10. See, for example, the image of the dog in Jan Peter Tripp's "*Déjà vu or the Incident*," described in Sebald's "Like Day and Night: On the Pictures of Jan Peter Tripp ("Wie Tag und Nacht—Über die Bilder Jan Peter Tripps"), and discussed in chapters 6 and 7, who also jumps a centuries-long gap in historical time as well as moving in and out of the frame of the painting on which he is depicted.

11. > *Zuunterst in der linken Ecke kauert*
    > *der von syphilitischen Schwären*
    > *überzogene Leib eines Insassen*
    > *des Isenheimer Spitals. Darüber*
    > *erhebt sich eine doppelköpfige*
    > *Und mehrarmig verzwitterte Kreatur,*
    > *im Begriff, dem Heiligen mit einem*
    > *Kieferknochen den Garaus zu machen . . .*
    > *Rechterhand ein stelzenbeiniges Vogeltier,*
    > *das mit menschlichen Armen*
    > *einen Prügel erhoben hält. Hinter*
    > *und neben diesem, gegen die Mitte des Bildes . . .*
    > (*NACH DER NATUR* 23)

12. *After Nature* is the only major piece among Sebald's literary works that has no images within the text. The first edition included six bookend photographs of bleak landscapes.

13. Perhaps this explains the website that places the images of Matthaeus Grünewald side by side with Sebald's "Like the snow on the Alps": http://www.wgsebald.de/gruenewald.html. Thus, also, understandably, von Mücke chooses to support her reading of Sebald with images of Grünewald's paintings.

14. > *Der panische Halsknick,*
    > *überall an den in Grünewalds Werk*
    > *vorkommenden Subjekten zu sehen,*
    > *der die Kehle freigibt und das Gesicht*
    > *hineinwendet oft in ein blendendes Licht,*
    > *ist der äußerste Ausdruck der Körper dafür,*
    > *daß die Natur kein Gleichgewicht kennt,*

sondern blind ein wüstes
Experiment macht ums andre
und wie ein unsinniger Bastler schon
ausschlachtet, was ihr grad erst gelang.
(NACH DER NATUR 24)

15. *Wahrscheinlich hat Grünewald*
die katastrophale Umnachtung,
die letzte Spur des aus dem Jenseits
einfallenden Lichts nach der Natur
gemalt und erinnert, denn im Jahr 1502,

. . .

glitt zum 1. Oktober der Mondschatten
über den Osten Europas von Südpolen
über die Lausitz, Böhmen und Mecklenburg,
und Grünewald, der wiederholt mit dem Aschaffenburger
Hofastrologen Johann Indagine in Verbindung stand,
wird diesem von vielen mit großer Furcht
erwarteten Jahrhundertereignis der Sonnenverfinsterung
entgegengereist und Zeuge geworden sein
des heimlichen Wegsiechens der Welt,
in welchem ein geisterhaft Abendwerden
mitten im Tag wie eine Ohnmacht sich ausgoß
und im Gewölbe des Himmels,
über den Nebelbänken und den Wänden
der Wolken, über einem kalten und schweren
Blau ein feuriges Roth aufging und Farben
umherschweiften glanzvoll, wie nie
sie ein Auge gesehen und die der Maler
fortan nicht mehr aus dem Gedächtnis bringt.
(NACH DER NATUR 26–27)

16. *Mitte des Mai, Grünewald*
war mit seinem Gesprenge
in Frankfurt zurück, war
das Korn weiß zur Ernte,
zog die geschärfte Sichel
durch das Leben eines Heers von fünftausend
in der sonderbaren Schlacht von Frankenhausen

. . .

Als Grünewald am 18. Mai
diese Nachricht erreichte,
ging er nicht mehr außer Haus.
Er hörte aber das Augenausstechen,

das lang noch vorging
zwischen dem Bodensee
und dem Thüringer Wald.
Wochenweis trug er damals
eine dunkle Binde
vor dem Gesicht.
(*NACH DER NATUR* 31)

17. Sebald talks of his preoccupation with his birthday in an interview with Joseph Cuomo (Cuomo, "A Conversation with W. G. Sebald" 97).
18. Sebald also speaks in an interview of the play on the initials of his own name: "reference to an eighteenth-century German botanist and zoologist called Georg Wilhelm Steller, who happens to have the same initials that I have" (Cuomo, "A Conversation with W. G. Sebald" 99).

19. *Die Bewandtnis mit der Signatur M. N.*
   über dem Rahmen des Fensters sei die,
   daß sich der in den Archiven entdeckte,
   durch eigene Arbeit sonst aber nicht nachweisliche Maler
   Mathis Nithart hinter dem Namen Grünewald verberge.
   Darum die Initialen M. G. und N. Auf dem Schnee-
   Altar in Aschaffenburg. . . .

   . . .

   Und in der Tat geht die Figur des Mathis Nithart
   in den Dokumenten der Zeit in einem Maß
   in die Grünewalds über, daß man meint,
   der eine habe wirklich das Leben
   und zuletzt gar den Tod
   des anderen ausgemacht.
   (*NACH DER NATUR* 16–17)

20. *Zu Grünewalds Zeit . . .*

   . . .

   Nachts, am Sonntag um vier schon,
   werden sie eingeschlossen, und
   gehen dürfen sie nirgends,
   wo ein grüner Baum wächst,
   weder auf dem Scheidewall
   noch im Roß, noch auf dem Römerberg
   oder in der Allee. In diesem Ghetto
   war das Judden Enchin zuhause gewesen,
   eh sie, wenige Monate vor der Feier
   der Hochzeit mit Mathys Grune,
   dem Maler, auf den Namen
   der heiligen Anna getauft wurde.
   (*NACH DER NATUR* 13)

21.   *Daß aber er die ihm ein Jahr später*
      angetraute Anna zum Wechsel
      des Glaubens bewegt hat, dafür
      findet sich nirgends ein Anhalt.
      Vielmehr scheint es, sie selber
      habe sich den zu jener Zeit
      von besonderer Entschlußkraft
      oder Hoffnungslosigkeit zeugenden
      Schritt dadurch erleichtert,
      daß sie dem Maler mehrfach
      in die Augen sah, vielleicht zuerst
      sich auch bloß in seinen grünfarbenen
      Namen verliebte . . .
      (*NACH DER NATUR* 14)

22.   The loss of the green of the trees was already there in section 5: "while behind us already the green / trees are leaving their leaves" ("während hinter uns schon die grünen / Bäume ihre Blätter verlassen"; *After Nature* 27E, 24G).

23.   "Odenwald" is omitted from the English translation, but repeats that syllable *Wald*—a green-colored name (it means woods or forest). Among the many reverberations in the three poems, Odenwald will also appear in the last section of the final poem (*After Nature* 113E, 97G).

24.   *und stets zwischen dem Blick*
      des Auges und dem Anhub des Pinsels
      legt Grünewald jetzt eine weite
      Reise zurück, unterbricht auch viel öfter,
      als er sonst gewohnt, den Fortgang der Kunst,
      um sein Kind in die Lehre zu nehmen
      in der Werkstatt und draußen im grünen Gelände.
      Was er selbst dabei lernte, ist nirgends berichtet,
      nur daß das Kind im Alter von vierzehn Jahren
      aus unbekannter Ursach auf einmal
      gestorben ist und daß der Maler es
      nicht um viel überlebte.
      (*NACH DER NATUR* 32–33)

25.   *Späh scharf voran,*
      dort siehst du im Grauen des Abends
      die fernen Windmühlen sich drehn.
      Der Wald weicht zurück, wahrlich,
      in solcher Weite, daß man nicht kennt,
      wo er einmal gelegen . . .
      (*NACH DER NATUR* 33)

26. In the opening eight lines of section 6, we once again encounter a scene in which the eye is challenged and the green of the landscape is devoured.

> a landscape reaching so far into the depth
> that our eye is insufficient to see its limits.
> A patch of brown scorched earth
> whose contour like the head of a whale
> or an open-mouthed leviathan
> devours the pale green meadow plains . . .
> (AFTER NATURE 29)

> eine so weit in die Tiefe hineingehende Landschaft,
> daß unser Auge nicht ausreicht, sie zu ergründen.
> Ein Stück brauner verbrannter Erde,
> deren Umriß wie der Kopf eines Walfisches
> oder Leviathans mit offenem Maul
> die fahlgrünen Wiesenplane . . .
> . . . verschlingt . . .
> (NACH DER NATUR 26)

In the final section of the poem, however, by the time the forest recedes, the green has already been left behind.

27. James Martin has written intelligently on the polar landscapes of Sebald and notes the allusion to Dante here (Martin, "Campi deserti," 145).

28. *In view of this it seems to me*
> *that the ice age, the glaringly white*
> *towering of the summits in*
> *the upper realm of the Temptation*
> *is the construction of a metaphysic . . .*
> (AFTER NATURE 31E)

> *In Anbetracht dessen dünkt mich*
> *die Eiszeit, das hellweiße*
> *Turmgebäude der Gipfel im oberen*
> *Bereich der Versuchung,*
> *die Konstruktion einer Metaphysik . . .*
> (NACH DER NATUR 28G)

29. *und das Eishaus*
> *geht auf, und der Reif zeichnet ins Feld*
> *ein farbloses Bild der Erde.*
> *So wird, wenn der Sehnerv*
> *zerreißt, im stillen Luftraum*
> *es weiß wie der Schnee*
> *auf den Alpen.*
> (NACH DER NATUR 33)

30. We find this mode of creating images in Aurach/Ferber's manner of painting in *The Emigrants/Die Ausgewanderten*, and later in that of Novelli in *Austerlitz*.

31. Wachtel, "Ghost Hunter" 53.

32. In a 1992 interview with Piet de Moor, Sebald describes the evolution of his first prose literary work, *Vertigo*. The passage begins with Sebald's reminder that his first role as writer was as a literary critic. What enables the writing of the prose book and, presumably, that shift away from an academic writing that merely describes the work and author concerned, is the recognition of a series of coincidences, of dates, of place, first between the lives of Stendhal and Kafka, but then between those lives and his own. Thus the work moves from a writing about others to a search for himself.

> I am no writer in the actual sense of the word. . . . For many years I was active only academically: to be sure I always kept notebooks in which I made very chaotic entries. . . . I knew Kafka's work well, not Stendhal's and yet a curious coincidence touched me immediately: Stendhal was born in 1783, Kafka in 1883; Stendhal stayed in northern Italy in 1813, Kafka in 1913. After that I wrote two literary-biographical essays on the two authors whom I wanted to bring face to face with one another. While I was still writing, it suddenly occurred to me that in 1980 I too had traveled through northern Italy.
>
> ("AUF UNGEHEUER DÜNNEM EIS" 71)

33. From the opening line it speaks of Windsheim in Franken, making geographical connection with that place, which also appears in the two other sections of the poem. It is in the Windsheim woods ("Windsheimer Wälder," *After Nature* 34E, 30G) that Grünewald spoke to his brother artists of the tearing of the coat and the end of time. It is also in Windsheim that Sebald's mother realizes that she is pregnant with Sebald (*After Nature* 86E, 74G), and in the same place that Steller was born. Sebald himself comments on something of this coincidence in an interview, as well as on the shared initials with Steller. He tells this in the context of a book he just happened to read:

> reference to an eighteenth-century German botanist and zoologist called Georg Wilhelm Steller, who happens to have the same initials that I have [audience laughter], and happened to have been born in a place which my mother visited when she was pregnant in 1943, when she was going from Bamberg . . . down to the Alps . . . She couldn't go through Nuremberg, which is the normal route, because Nuremberg had just been attacked that night and was all in flames. So she had to go around it. And she stayed in Windsheim, as that place is called, where a friend of hers had a house.
>
> (CUOMO, "A CONVERSATION WITH W. G. SEBALD," 99)

34. The pastures, of course, bring back the green resignedly lost at the end of "Like the snow on the Alps."

35. The gray evening of the first poem, also returns as well: "there you see in the greying of the nightfall / the distant windmills turn" ("dort siehst du im Grauen des Abends / die fernen Windmühlen sich drehn") (*After Nature* 37E, 33G).

36. As well as the "the glaringly white / das hellweiße" in the scene from the Temptation cited in note 29.

37. *und weiter noch in der Ferne*
    das im schwindenden Licht sich
    auftürmende Schnee- und Eisgebirge
    des fremden, unerforschten und
    afrikanischen Kontinents.
    (*NACH DER NATUR* 99)

38. Speaking with Eleanor Wachtel about *The Emigrants,* Sebald had said: "You just try and set up certain reverberations in a text and the whole acquires significance that it might not otherwise have" (Wachtel, "Ghost Hunter" 54).

39. It was the ekphrastic language in the first poem that made visualizing the object of the text's narrative a daunting challenge.

40. The first part of Sebald's next book, *The Emigrants* (*Die Ausgewanderten*) also closes with snow, ice, and the Alps. At the end of the story of Dr. Henry Selwyn, his dear friend, Johannes Naegeli, rises up from the glacier on which, seventy-two years earlier, he had lost his life. The third chapter also ends with snow—and, this time, not blindness but dumbness, not a call for us to look closely, but rather an invocation, one of so many in Sebald, of the bird's-eye view: "My great-uncle also noted that late the previous afternoon it had begun to snow and that, looking out of the hotel window at the city, white in the falling dusk, it made him think of times long gone. Memory, he added in a postscript, often strikes me as a kind of dumbness. It makes one's head heavy and giddy, as if one were not looking back down the receding perspectives of time but rather down on the earth from a great height, from one of those towers whose tops are lost to view in the clouds" (*The Emigrants* 145E, 214–15G).

41. Cuomo, "A Conversation with W. G. Sebald" 96–97.

42. Ibid., 108.

2. WHAT DOES IT MEAN TO COUNT?

1. To be sure, in the second of the chapters Sebald has Paul Bereyter engage in similar activities: "It was only in the last decade of his life . . . that re-

constructing those events became important to him. . . . [He] spent many days in archives, making endless notes" (*The Emigrants* 54E, 80G). And the narrator also seems to take his cue from photographic documents: "Mme Landau put before me a large album which contained photographs documenting not only the period in question but indeed, a few gaps aside, almost the whole of Paul Bereyter's life, with notes penned in his own hand" (*The Emigrants* 45E, 68G).

2. Chapter 7 takes up these issues again by way of Sebald's interviews.

3. Mark McCulloh understands this (McCulloh, *Understanding W. G. Sebald*, 55). A review by Nicole Krauss in the *Partisan Review* ("Arabesques of Journeys"), however, a publication that surely has no interest in selling books (which may undercut my cynicism in reading the Fischer Verlag blurb) makes a similar claim, speaking of "the stories of four twentieth-century Germans of Jewish descent who left their country." But Henry Selwyn was not German and Ambros Adelwarth was not Jewish.

4. We read of "the fact that . . . old Bereyter was what was termed a half Jew, and Paul, in consequence, only three quarters an Aryan" (*The Emigrants* 50E, 74G).

5. Sebald changed the name from Aurach to Ferber in the English translation. Aurach is the name used in the course of this book.

6. Thomas Stachel wisely suggests another, possible, translation here: "Do not destroy the remnant/the last thing, (which is) memory."

7. "Allmählich kam ich auf meinen sonntäglichen Exkursionen über die Innenstadt hinaus in die unmittelbar angrenzenden Bezirke, beispielsweise in das . . . vormalige Judenviertel. Bis in die Zwischenkriegszeit hinein ein Zentrum der großen jüdischen Gemeinde von Manchester, war dieses Quartier von seinen in die Vororte übersiedelnden Bewohnern aufgegeben und seither von der Stadtverwaltung dem Erdboden gleichgemacht worden" (*Die Ausgewanderten* 231–32G).

8. Or are the inhabitants of Sebald's tale, Jews and non-Jews alike, already lost to us? Of Manchester, in general, he writes: "One might have supposed that the city had long since been deserted, and was left now as a necropolis or mausoleum" (*The Emigrants* 151E, 223G).

9. In a conversation with Burkhard Baltzer (1993) Sebald had this to say: "Yes. I believe that literature to a not small extent consists in holding conversations with the departed and setting off for the dark side of life." Sebald, "Auf ungeheuer dünnem Eis," 81.

10. "Einmal ums andere, vorwärts und rückwärts durchblätterte ich dieses Album an jenem Nachmittag und habe es seither immer wieder von neuem durchblättert, weil es mir beim Betrachten der darin enthaltenen Bilder tatsächlich schien und nach wie vor scheint, als kehrten die Toten zurück *oder* als stünden wir im Begriff, einzugehen zu ihnen" (*Die Ausgewanderten* 68–69G, emphasis mine).

190 2. WHAT DOES IT MEAN TO COUNT?

11. And these, in turn, perhaps have something to do with the advice of Paul Bereyter's doctor that "peaceful spells spent simply looking at the moving leaves would protect and improve his eyesight" (*The Emigrants* 58E, 85G).

12. "Wie meistens die Toten, wenn sie in unseren Träumen auftauchen, waren sie stumm und schienen ein wenig betrübt und niedergeschlagen. . . . Näherte ich mich ihnen, so lösten sie sich vor meinen Augen auf und hinterließen nichts als den leeren Platz, den sie soeben noch eingenommen hatten" (*Die Ausgewanderten* 180–81G).

13. One might compare in this regard the scene in *Vertigo* in which the narrator goes into the past with another gesture. He touches the centuries-old uniform on an old tailor's dummy only to watch it turn to dust: "But when I stepped closer, not entirely trusting my eyes, and touched one of the uniform sleeves that hung down empty, to my utter horror it crumbled into dust." Sebald, *Vertigo* and *Schwindel. Gefühle.*, 227E, 248G.

14. "als dort ein Mann mittleren Alters auftauchte, der ein weißes Netz an einem Stecken vor sich hertrug und ab und zu seltsame Sprünge vollführte. Der Adelwarth-Onkel blickte starr voraus, registrierte aber nichtsdestoweniger meine Verwunderung und sagte: It's the butterfly man, you know. He comes round here quite often. Ich glaubte einen Ton der Belustigung aus diesen Worten herauszuhören, und hielt sie daher für ein Zeichen der ... Besserung" (*Die Ausgewanderten* 151G).

15. The sections that close *After Nature* (*Nach der Natur*) and *Vertigo* (*Schwindel. Gefühle.*) also engage obvious figures of the author.

16. "I came across a sign on which TO THE STUDIOS had been painted in crude brush-strokes. It pointed in to a cobbled yard" (*The Emigrants* 160E, 236G).

17. "Wenn er versuche, sich in die fragliche Zeit zurückzuversetzen, so sehe er sich erst in seinem Studio wieder bei der mit geringen Unterbrechungen über nahezu ein Jahr sich hinziehenden schweren Arbeit an dem gesichtslosen Porträt *Man with a Butterfly Net*, das er für eines seiner verfehltesten Werke halte, weil es, seines Erachtens, keinen auch annähernd nur zureichenden Begriff gebe von der Seltsamkeit der Erscheinung, auf die es sich beziehe" (*Die Ausgewanderten* 259–60G).

18. Just as the return of Naegeli's body is on the way to Lake Geneva.

19. In the closing chapter, when the narrator arrives at the hotel Arosa, Mrs. Irlam asks: "And where have you sprung from?" (*The Emigrants* 152E, 224G), making him and perhaps Sebald himself something of a Butterfly Man.

20. "Die Arbeit an dem Bild des Schmetterlingsfängers habe ihn ärger hergenommen als jede andere Arbeit zuvor, denn als er es nach Verfertigung zahlloser Vorstudien angegangen sei, habe er es nicht nur wieder und wieder übermalt, sondern er habe es, wenn die Leinwand der Beanspruchung durch das dauernde Herunterkratzen und Neuauftragen der Farbe nicht mehr standhielt, mehrmals völlig zerstört und verbrannt" (*Die Ausgewanderten* 260G).

21. And yet this is not total obliteration for we are left haunted by the sense, if not of an individual, then of a long line of ancestors: "an onlooker might well feel that it had evolved from a long lineage of grey, ancestral faces, rendered unto ash but still there, as ghostly presences, on the harried paper" (*The Emigrants* 162E, 239–40G).

22. During the winter of 1990/91, in the little free time I had (in other words, mostly at the so-called weekend and at night), I was working on the story of Max Ferber given above. It was an extremely arduous task. Often I could not get on for hours or days at a time, and not infrequently I unravelled what I had done, continuously tormented by scruples that were taking tighter hold and steadily paralyzing me. These scruples concerned not only the subject of my narrative, which I felt I could not do justice to, no matter what approach I tried, but also the entire questionable business of writing. I had covered hundreds of pages with my scribble, in pencil and ballpoint. By far the greater part had been crossed out, discarded, or obliterated to the point of unreadability by additions. Even what I ultimately salvaged as a "final" version seemed to me a thing of shreds and patches, utterly botched.

     (*THE EMIGRANTS* 230–31E, 344–45G)

Moreover, already in 1989, before he finds Aurach's paintings in the Tate, the narrator says: "but I never succeeded in picturing him properly. His face had become a mere shadow" (*The Emigrants* 177E, 264G). Ambros Adelwarth is no less an artist of this sort. A photograph of his diary shows his letters layered over one another (*The Emigrants* 132E, 194–95G). In the German edition the image of Adelwarth's "Agenda" overlays the double pages of Sebald's book in a gesture of coincidence. See both *Die Ausgewanderten* 194–95G and 200–1G.

23. Da er die Farben in großen Mengen aufträgt und sie im Fortgang der Arbeit immer wieder von der Leinwand herunterkratzt, ist der Bodenbelag bedeckt von einer im Zentrum mehrere Zoll dicken, nach außen allmählich flacher werdenden, mit Kohlestaub untermischten, weitgehend bereits verhärteten und verkrusteten Masse, die stellenweise einem Lavaausfluß gleicht und von der Aurach behauptet, daß sie das wahre Ergebnis darstelle seiner fortwährenden Bemühung und den offenkundigsten Beweis für sein Scheitern. Es sei für ihn stets von der größten Bedeutung gewesen . . . daß nichts an seinem Arbeitsplatz sich verändere . . . und daß nichts hinzukomme als der Unrat, der anfalle bei der Verfertigung der Bilder, und der Staub, der sich unablässig herniedersenke und der ihm, wie er langsam begreifen lerne, so ziemlich das Liebste sei auf der Welt.

     (*DIE AUSGEWANDERTEN* 237–38G)

24. This returns us as well to the scene in *Vertigo* cited in note 14, reminiscent as well of Aurach's enterprise.

25. The narrator, too, speaks of "fragmentary recollections" (*The Emigrants* 42E, 63G) as does Luisa Lanzberg (*The Emigrants* 208E, 312G). This follows a scene in which the passage of time is carefully marked out. Here as in *Austerlitz*, conventional and inevitable measures of narrative time are juxtaposed with reminders of their artificiality. See, for example, the temporal guideposts that follow Austerlitz's long disquisition on arbitrary concepts of time (*Austerlitz*, 100–2E, 149–52G).

26. The play on *Staub* (dust) and *Bestäubung* is mine, but in the chapter on Ambros Adelwarth, at the site of those whose thoughts go wild, one can almost imagine hearing it. The narrator visits the now decaying mental institution in which his uncle had passed away, tortured to death in the name of science by an electric shock assault that passed for therapy. Here Dr. Abramsky lives on in regret, no longer practicing institutional violence. He keeps bees and acknowledges his own madness (*The Emigrants* 110E, 161G), and in his role as apiarist his thoughts cannot be far from pollination/*Bestäubung*. The impending collapse of Samaria Sanatorium will take place with the help of the "mouse folk," the "woodworm and deathwatch beetles" (*The Emigrants* 112E, 165G). "And that is precisely what does happen in my dream, before my very eyes, infinitely slowly, and a great yellowish cloud billows out and disperses, and where the sanatorium once stood there is merely a heap of powder-fine wood dust, like pollen" (*The Emigrants* 113E,166G). That *Bestäubung* might coincide with a certain liberation, despite its obvious destructive thrust, is something with which one must come to terms.

27. The names of characters transgress not only the chapter divisions but also the individuality of Sebald's works. (In this Sebald's practice is not unlike that of Werner Herzog, who, in elaborate acts of cross-film citation, carries over his actors and sometimes his characters from film to film.) Thus a Bereyter appears in *Vertigo*, and does so, tellingly, in the context of one person standing as a cipher for many others. "La Ghita, who reappears a number of times on the periphery of Beyle's later work, is a mysterious, not to say ghostly figure. There is reason to suspect that Beyle used her name as a cipher for various lovers such as Adèle Rebuffel, Angéline *Bereyter,* and not least for Métilde Dembowski, and that Mme Gherardi, whose life would easily furnish a whole novel . . . in reality never really existed, despite all the documentary evidence" (*Vertigo*, 21–22E, 26G, emphasis mine).

28. The scene haunts each of the volume's stories. Paul Bereyter and Lucy Landau have also been in the mountains and have seen the landscape of Lake Geneva. It passes by less perceptibly elsewhere as well: as when Adelwarth works in a hotel in Montreux, near the Grammont (*The Emigrants* 77–78E, 113G), and returns to Lake Geneva in 1911 with Cosmo (*The Emigrants* 91E,

132G), as when Aurach returns to Manchester after the war and looks down on the city with a bird's-eye view (*The Emigrants* 168E, 249–50G), which is not unlike a scene we are about to encounter in Herzog's film *Kaspar Hauser*. Moreover, Nabokov, already an important figure in the opening chapter, spent the last seventeen years of his life in Montreux.

29. A twinned image makes its appearance even before the opening lines of the first story. We see the photograph of a great tree spreading its branches among the tombstones of a cemetery. A remarkably similar tree appears in the final chapter, the reproduction of Courbet's *The Oak of Vercingetorix,* which the narrator speaks of as "the point of departure for [Aurach's] study of destruction" (*The Emigrants* 180E, 268-69G). This tree, so very similar to the first, lacks, however, the grave markers. Twinned images, once again, like the two glacier scenes in which the version marked by death precedes the double that restores the departed (in a newspaper photograph) or eradicates the remembrance of their loss (in a painting).

30. Als der Zug, langsamer werdend, über die Aarebrücke nach Bern hinein- rollte, ging mein Blick über die Stadt hinweg auf die Kette der Berge des Oberlands. . . . Eine Dreiviertelstunde später, ich war gerade im Begriff, eine in Zürich gekaufte Lausanner Zeitung . . . beiseitezulegen, um die jedesmal von neuem staunenswerte Eröffnung der Genfer Seelandschaft nicht zu versäumen, fielen meine Augen auf einen Bericht, aus dem hervorging, daß die Überreste der Leiche des seit dem Sommer 1914 als vermißt geltenden Berner Bergführers Johannes Naegeli nach 72 Jahren vom Oberaargletscher wieder zutage gebracht worden waren. –So also kehren sie wieder, die Toten.

(*DIE AUSGEWANDERTEN* 36G)

31. Other guides, notably blind, traverse these tales: the blind guide who shows Ambros and Cosmo er-Riha (*The Emigrants* 142E, 210G) and the blind Berber leader in Kaspar Hauser's final story, though the latter is never ex- plicitly mentioned by Sebald's narrator.

32. It may be coincidental, but not irrelevant, that the word for screen here, *Leinwand*, is that used in the story of Aurach for canvas.

33. This is not quite possible, since Nabokov was there not in spring of 1971 but in August of 1971, as the actual appearance of the photo in the Swiss press shows.

34. Hersch was the original name of Henry Selwyn before he changed it to Henry (*The Emigrants* 20E, 33G).

35. "Der im Süden die Ebene überragende, über zweitausend Meter hohe Berg Spathi wirkte wie eine Luftspiegelung hinter der Flut des Lichts. . . . Auch vor diesem Bild saßen wir lange und schweigend, so lang sogar, daß zu- letzt das Glas in dem Rähmchen zersprang und ein dunkler Riß über die Leinwand lief. Der so lange, bis zum Zerspringen festgehaltene Anblick der

Hochebene von Lasithi hat sich mir damals tief eingeprägt, und dennoch hatte ich ihn geraume Zeit hindurch vergessen gehabt" (*Die Ausgewanderten* 28–29G).

36. "Wiederbelebt ist [der Anblick] worden erst ein paar Jahre darauf, als ich in einem Londoner Kino das Traumgespräch sah, das Kaspar Hauser mit seinem Lehrer Daumer . . . führt und wo Kaspar, zur Freude seines Mentors, zum erstenmal unterscheidet zwischen Traum und Wirklichkeit, indem er seine Erzählung einleitet mit den Worten: Ja, es hat mich geträumt. Mich hat vom Kaukasus geträumt" (*Die Ausgewanderten* 29G).

37. "Es hat mich geträumt" is at best outmoded and certainly strange to the ear. Literally translated, it could read: *it dreamed me*, though, no doubt, *I dreamed* is more of what Kaspar has in mind. "Es träumte mir" is a phrasing that appears elsewhere in *The* Emigrants (for example *Die Ausgewanderten* 179G, 261G). For Freud even this phrasing gives a sense of alienation. "Our scientific consideration of dreams starts off from the assumption that they are products of our own mental activity. Nevertheless the finished dream strikes us as something alien to us. We are so little obliged to acknowledge our responsibility for it that [in German] we are just as ready to say '*mir hat geträumt*' ['I had a dream,' literally 'a dream came to me'] as '*ich habe geträumt*' ['I dreamt']. What is the origin of this feeling that dreams are extraneous to our minds?" (Freud, *The Interpretation of Dreams*, 77). Kaspar dreams a scene he could not possibly have known in reality ("in Wirklichkeit") and returns the narrator to a Crete he has also never known.

38. "Kaspar Hauser" opens with a scene of writing in which a young man with no identity learns without understanding to write his name. This is its point of origin. An unnamed figure forces the inmate to write his name (for he writes by himself as little as he later dreams for himself): "Write, Wrr-ite. Note this: write!" These are the first distinct words uttered in the film entitled *Kaspar Hauser*, about whom we are reminded repeatedly: "The riddle of his origins remains unsolved to this day."

39. Flickering images run throughout *Austerlitz* as well, often the sign of ghostly presences.

40. This is the same alternative, almost, as that we read of before: "as if the dead were coming back, or as if we were on the point of passing away into them" (*The Emigrants* 46E, 69G, emphasis mine).

Das *Wadi Halfa* war durchstrahlt von einem flimmernden . . . Neonlicht . . . [ich] sehe . . . Aurach, wenn ich zurückdenke an unsere Begegnungen in Trafford Park, ein jedes Mal sitzen, stets auf demselben Platz, vor einem von unbekannter Hand gemalten Fresko, das eine Karawane zeigte, die aus der fernsten Tiefe des Bildes heraus und über ein Wellengebirge von Dünen hinweg direkt auf den Betrachter zu sich bewegte. Infolge der Ungeschicktheit des Malers und der schwierigen Perspektive, die er gewählt hatte, wirkten die menschlichen Figuren sowohl als die

Lasttiere in ihren Umrissen leicht verzerrt, so daß es . . . tatsächlich war, als erblicke man eine in der Helligkeit und Hitze zitternde Fata Morgana. Und insbesondere an Tagen , an denen Aurach mit Kohle gearbeitet und der pudrig feine Staub seine Haut mit einem metallischen Glanz imprägniert hatte, schien es mir, als sei er soeben aus dem Wüstenbild herausgetreten oder als gehöre er in es hinein.

(*DIE AUSGEWANDERTEN* 243G, EMPHASIS MINE)

41. This is a reappearance of the desert caravans of which Cosmo and Ambros speak (*The Emigrants* 97E and 141E, 141G and 209G) and the caravan of Kaspar Hauser's tale.

42. Im übrigen, so fuhr er . . . fort, erinnere ihn die Verdunkelung seiner Haut an eine Zeitungsnotiz, die ihm unlängst untergekommen sei, über die bei Berufsfotografen nicht unüblichen Symptome der Silbervergiftung. Im Archiv der Britischen Medizinischen Gesellschaft werde beispielsweise, so habe in der Notiz gestanden, die Beschreibung eines extremen Falls einer solchen Vergiftung aufbewahrt, derzufolge es in den dreißiger Jahren in Manchester einen Fotolaboranten gegeben haben soll, dessen Körper im Verlauf seiner langjährigen Berufspraxis derart viel Silber assimiliert hatte, daß er zu einer Art fotografischer Platte geworden war, was sich, wie Aurach mir vollen Ernstes auseinandersetzte, daran zeigte, daß das Gesicht und die Hände . . . bei starkem Lichteinfall blau anliefen, sich also sozusagen entwickelten.

(*DIE AUSGEWANDERTEN* 244G)

43. *Litz as heddle*—a part of the warp on the web frame.

44. Sebald's description refers to an exhibition at the Jüdisches Museum Frankfurt am Main (the Jewish Museum in Frankfurt) to which I extend my gratitude for permission to use the images they provided. These were also gathered in the catalogue: *"Unser einziger Weg ist Arbeit."* The photograph of Genewein is on p. 76, that of the weavers on p. 119.

45. The Austrian-born Walter Genewein eagerly joined the NSDAP early in 1933 and worked in the Łódź ghetto from 1940 until its closure in 1944. In 1943, when ordering five hundred slide frames, he described his project as archival documentation. Still, he clearly regarded his photographs not only as a service to the German cause but also as an aesthetic accomplishment that placed him in the avant-garde of color photography. His correspondence with IG Farben Berlin, with its insistent complaints about the disappointing quality of the color of their film, attests to his artistic aspirations (Jewish Museum in Frankfurt, *"Unser einziger Weg ist Arbeit"* 54).

In 1947 he was brought before the Austrian Volksgericht for his role at Litzmannstadt. In addition to being starved, worked to death, and deported for annihilation, with Genewein's help the Jewish population was continuously charged for the services and provisions they received and in other ways systematically robbed of the little they had in goods and funds (Jewish Museum in Frankfurt, *"Unser einziger Weg ist Arbeit"* 22–23, 45) Genewein denied that the ghetto was a concentration camp, denied ever having shown the photographs, denied profiteering from his position in the ghetto administration (*"Unser einziger Weg ist Arbeit"* 54). The 1998 film *Photographer* directed by Dariusz Jablonski documents Genewein's slides and his trial statements along with the counternarration of a ghetto survivor, Arnold Mostowicz.

46. "Hinter einem lotrechten Webrahmen sitzen drei junge, vielleicht zwanzigjährige Frauen. . . . Wer die jungen Frauen sind, das weiß ich nicht. Wegen des Gegenlichts, das einfällt durch das Fenster im Hintergrund, kann ich ihre Augen genau nicht erkennen, aber ich spüre, daß sie alle drei herschauen zu mir, denn ich stehe ja an der Stelle, an der Genewein, der Rechnungsführer, mit seinem Fotoapparat gestanden hat" (*Die Ausgewanderten* 355G).

    The difficult light through the window, the obscurity, bring us back to Aurach's studio where contact with the past is equally problematic: "where Ferber had set up his easel in the grey light that entered through a high north-facing window layered with the dust of decades" (*The Emigrants* 161E, 237G).

47. The German racial laws concerning *Mischlinge,* if nothing else, would have taught him that.

48. Like Sebald's, the narrator's mother was Rosa (*The Emigrants* 76E, 110G), one of several echoes of the name in the text. Aurach's mother, whose diary occupies so many of the last pages, was Luisa.

49. The English translation anglicizes the name to Luisa, but the parallel world of Poland's Łódź Ghetto is important to maintain in its difference. If the Nazis germanified Łódź, the text pays them back in kind, transforming the German names Rosa and Luisa, to the Polish Roza, Lusia, and Lea. And lest we get caught up in the specificity of national identity, the narrative shifts to the mythic dimensions of the three Parcae.

50. "Die mittlere der drei jungen Frauen hat hellblondes Haar und gleicht irgendwie einer Braut. Die Weberin zu ihrer Linken hält den Kopf ein wenig seitwärts geneigt, während die auf der rechten Seite so unverwandt und unerbittlich mich ansieht, daß ich es nicht lange auszuhalten vermag. Ich überlege, wie die drei wohl geheißen haben—Roza, Lusia, und Lea oder Nona, Decuma und Morta, die Töchter der Nacht, mit Spindel und Faden und Schere" (*Die Ausgewanderten* 355G)

51. One need only think of Ambros Adelwarth who, in an institution removed from the eye of the public, willingly gives himself up to the cruel pseudo-experiments of a maniacal Eastern European doctor and his "annihilation method" (*The Emigrants* 114E, 168G).

52. There is a geographical version of this in which the structure of one thing becomes that of another—in which, suddenly, one terrain, Constantino-

ple, becomes associated with the terrain of Allgäu, of Switzerland, and of the *Judenviertel*, the place where Jews are quartered (*The Emigrants* 130–31E, 192–93G).

53. The practice of cross-pollination was also the practice of *Vertigo*. Sebald had this to say in an interview with Andreas Isenschmid in 1990 about the interrelation of the stories in that text. "Yes, on the surface very heterogeneous, as we said at the beginning, four actually different, disparate, discrepant stories. Interrelation runs across the locations that come up over and over again, runs through the dates that cross one another, runs across the emotional identifications and the recurrent, repeating themes" ("Auf ungeheuer dünnem Eis" 68).

3. FRAMES AND EXCURSIONS

1. Claude Lévi-Strauss makes a similar gesture in the opening pages of *Tristes Tropiques*, a text Sebald will go on to cite.

2. "An English Pilgrimage"/*Eine Englische Wallfahrt:* the subtitle was dropped in the English translation.

3. We have seen this passage between life and death in *The Emigrants* (*Die Ausgewanderten*) and we shall see it again in *Austerlitz* as well.

4. That is, this fragment "I am the beginning and the end and am valid in all places" (*Rings of Saturn* 23E, 35G) is a clue to decode the otherwise meaningless passage that follows. In Grimmelshausen's work the speaker, Baldanders, as we shall also see, boasts he can teach Simplicius how to make silent things speak.

5. *The Rings of Saturn: An English Pilgrimage* resists both a satisfying sense of the circular path suggested by its title and the sense of purposeful direction invoked in its subtitle. In a book divided into parts (*Teile*) rather than chapters, the dust particles (Staub*teil*chen) of the epigraph that circle the planet Saturn might have something in common with its chapters as "traces of destruction" (*Rings of Saturn* 3E, 11G). This is all the more disconcerting since, a few pages into the narrative, dust menaces the novelist (or at least Flaubert) with an onslaught of irresistible stultification (*Rings of Saturn* 7–8E, 17G) where "all that which has been written by him up to now consists in a series of stringing together the most inexcusable . . . errors and lies" (*Rings of Saturn* 7E, 16–17G).

   If the title speaks of circularity, doesn't the subtitle promise the purpose and destination of a pilgrimage? At the feet of which saint, one might wish to ask, does the narrator set out to worship? In a text in which St. Sebolt alone is extensively invoked among the saints, any sense of direction is also bound to be something of a joke.

6. "I set off to walk through the county of Suffolk, in the hope of escaping the emptiness that expands in me whenever I have completed a major work" (*Rings of Saturn* 3E, 11G).

7. "At all events memory preoccupied me in the period that followed, not only of the wonderful sense of freedom but also of the paralyzing horror" (*Rings of Saturn* 3E, 11G). This reverses the seductive rhythm of Proust's *mémoire involontaire* that pretends to vacillate between lived life and a return to it through written acts of remembrance. Walter Benjamin knew better, and Sebald, who moves here from writing as an emptying of experience to the gathering of new experience, now and then makes uncomfortably evident that in his work too the temporal relationship between experience and notation can often be unsettling. See Benjamin, "On the Image of Proust"; and Jacobs, "Walter Benjamin: Image of Proust," especially 50–53.

8. "[Ich] stand dann gegen die Glasscheibe gelehnt und mußte *unwillkürlich* an die Szene denken, in der der arme Gregor, mit zitternden Beinchen an die Sessellehne sich klammernd, aus seinem Kabinett hinausblickt in undeutlicher Erinnerung, wie es heißt, an das Befreiende, das früher einmal für ihn darin gelegen war, aus dem Fenster zu schauen. Und genau wie Gregor mit seinen trübe gewordenen Augen die stille Charlottenstraße . . . nicht mehr erkannte . . . *so schien auch mir*. . . ." (*Die Ringe des Saturn* 13G, emphasis mine).

9. The narrator, like Gregor, is a traveler. We are reminded repeatedly in Kafka's tale that Gregor is a traveler: "Samsa was a traveler." "'Oh God,' he thought, 'what a demanding profession I've chosen! Day in day out travelling'" (Kafka, *Sämtliche Erzählungen*, 56).

10. Victim, then, of a metamorphosis, rather like the *Bombyx mori* of part 10, the narrator's self-definition comes through his resemblance to and transformation into a fictional character, in a story by Kafka that tells once again of such a transformation.

11. Parkinson studied the works of Charles Ferdinand Ramuz, who, like Sebald, wrote under the sign of apocalyptic forebodings. One might consider Ramuz's *Présence de la mort,* in this regard. Parkinson's name, despite his long and difficult journeys on foot, haunts with a sense of the impaired gait of an all too tragic disease. Sebald himself, though perhaps not in this instance, plays on the coincidences of names. Writing of the attempt to harness the phosphorescence given off by dead herring: "Around 1870, when projects for the total illumination of our cities were everywhere afoot, two English scientists with the apt names of Herrington and Lightbown investigated the unusual phenomenon" (*Rings of Saturn* 58–59E, 76G). This is followed, unnoted, by the bizarre story of Major George Wyndham Le Strange who rewarded his housekeeper for thirty years of "Silent Dinners" (*Rings of Saturn* 63E, 81G). Rather than traveling the countryside, as Parkinson did, Dakyns seems to live on another planet, holding almost perfectly still in

a landscape generated without intention. Obsessed with Flaubert and his fear "that he would never again be able to bring even a half-line to paper" (*Rings of Saturn* 7E, 16G), she lives buried in "lecture notes, letters, and pieces of writing" (*Rings of Saturn* 8E, 17G). A "paper flood," a "paper landscape with mountains and valleys" that had moved to the edges of the writing table (*Rings of Saturn* 8E, 17G) "like a glacier when it meets the sea," continuing onto the floor and onto other tables, with the new accumulations representing "so to speak the later epochs in the development of the paper universe of Janine" (*Rings of Saturn* 8E, 18G). It is a world of paper, covered with text, about a writer who feared the blank page.

12. This is not quite the "colloquy with the dead" by way of which, Sebald writes, Edward FitzGerald, the translator of Omar Khayyām, tried to bring us news of them (*Rings of Saturn* 200E, 238G).

13. But Frederick Farrar, the narrator's recently deceased neighbor (*Rings of Saturn* 46E, 62–63G), St. Sebolt (*Rings of Saturn* 86E, 106G), Joseph Conrad (*Rings of Saturn* 104E, 126G), Conrad's Marlow (*Rings of Saturn* 120E, 146G), and Edward FitzGerald (*Rings of Saturn* 204E, 242G), among others, take over the narrative voice often before we know it in that colloquy with the dead (*Rings of Saturn* 200E, 238G) only to then cede their role again to Sebald's narrator and double.

14. Aren't these the unspoken reverberations of the next image, the skull of Thomas Browne, resting its brain cavity on the works of the author, its jaws wired in place? See Dickey, "The Fate of His Bones," where we are told that the photo was the frontispiece to the 1904 edition of Thomas Browne's work.

15. Even a glance at the table of contents gives one a sense of this.

16. That is to say, that Sebald's prose suggests the uncertainty of his narrator's certainty. Still it is likely that Sebald consulted a rather imposing volume on Rembrandt's painting that gave him reason to draw these conclusions: William S. Heckscher's *Rembrandt's ANATOMY OF DR. NICOLAAS TULP, an Iconological Study*. There one reads, for example: "It is possible that Dr. Tulp's anatomy of 1632 attracted Descartes, who, after all, was himself an avid amateur anatomist. Perhaps also a young Englishman was present, one who at that time was enrolled as a medical student at Leiden University: Thomas, later Sir Thomas, Browne" (Heckscher, *Rembrandt's ANATOMY OF DR. NICOLAAS TULP*, 26).

17. One might also ask what Sebald shows us. The image of Rembrandt's painting shown here is from the Mauritshuis. The image in *Rings of Saturn*, however, is spread over two pages (*Rings of Saturn* 14–15E, 24–25G), which brings about a distortion: the loss in the fold, for example, of part of the face of the most central figure, holding a written document and just to the left of Dr. Tulp. One can get a sense of such distortion by looking at another of Sebald's two-page images (figure 5.2).

18. "Und doch ist es fraglich, ob diesen Leib je in Wahrheit einer gesehen hat,
denn die damals gerade aufkommende Kunst der Anatomisierung diente
nicht zuletzt der Unsichtbarmachung des schuldhaften Körpers. Bezeich-
nenderweise sind ja die Blicke der Kollegen des Doktors Tulp nicht auf
diesen Körper als solchen gerichtet, sondern sie gehen, freilich haarscharf,
an ihm vorbei auf den aufgeklappten anatomischen Atlas" (*Die Ringe des
Saturn* 23G).

19.   Die Blicke der Kollegen des Doktors Tulp [sind] nicht auf diesen Körper als solchen gerichtet, sondern sie gehen, freilich haarscharf, an ihm
vorbei auf den aufgeklappten anatomischen Atlas, in dem die entsetz-
liche Körperlichkeit reduziert ist auf ein Diagramm, auf ein Schema
des Menschen, wie es dem passionierten, an jenem Januarmorgen im
Waagebouw angeblich gleichfalls anwesenden Amateuranatomen René
Descartes vorschwebte. Bekanntlich lehrte Descartes in einem der
Hauptkapitel der Geschichte der Unterwerfung, daß man absehen muß
von dem unbegreiflichen Fleisch und hin auf die in uns bereits ange-
legte Maschine, auf das, was man vollkommen verstehen, restlos für die
Arbeit nutzbar machen und, bei allfälliger Störung, entweder wieder in-
stand setzen oder wegwerfen kann.

(DIE RINGE DES SATURN 23–26G)

20. "Der seltsamen Ausgrenzung des doch offen zur Schau gestellten Körpers
entspricht es auch, daß die vielgerühmte Wirklichkeitsnähe des Rem-
brandtschen Bildes sich bei genauerem Zusehen als eine nur scheinbare
erweist" (*Die Ringe des Saturn*, 26G).

21.   Und mit dieser Hand hat es eine eigenartige Bewandtnis. Nicht nur ist
sie, verglichen mit der dem Beschauer näheren, geradezu grotesk dis-
proportioniert, sie ist auch anatomisch gänzlich verkehrt. Die offenge-
legten Sehnen, die, nach der Stellung des Daumens, die der Handfläche
der Linken sein sollten, sind die des Rückens der Rechten. Es handelt
sich also um eine rein schulmäßige, offenbar ohne weiteres dem anatomischen Atlas entnommene Aufsetzung, durch die das sonst, wenn man
so sagen kann, nach dem Leben gemalte Bild genau in seinem Bedeutungszentrum, dort, wo die Einschnitte schon gemacht sind, umkippt in
die krasseste Fehlkonstruktion.

(DIE RINGE DES SATURN 27G)

22. See Richard T. Gray's very careful reading of Rembrandt's procedure which
enables him to draw parallels between Rembrandt and Sebald's narrator.
Gray, "From Grids to Vanishing Points," 512–13.

23. Although one could say, with a certain perversity, that Rembrandt copies
the atlas at Kindt's feet with great verisimilitude, its errors included.

24. Sebald could well have had this in mind, given the description of a similar situation in a painting in *After Nature*. Describing a panel of Grünewald's Lindenhardt altar, Sebald writes:

> *Each of these,*
> *The blessed Blasius, Achaz and Eustace;*
> *Panthaleon, Aegidius, Cyriax, Christopher and*
> *Erasmus and the truly beautiful*
> *St. Vitus with the cockerel,*
> *each look in different*
> *directions without our knowing*
> *why.*
> (*AFTER NATURE* 7, *NACH DER NATUR* 8–9)

25. Sebald does something similar both at the close of his essay on Jan Peter Tripp and also, most notably, several times in the chapter *"All'estero"* in *Vertigo / Schwindel. Gefühle.*

26. In an important and convincing contribution, Gray follows the grid systematically through *The Rings of Saturn*. He demonstrates Sebald's use of the grid as a critique of Enlightenment rationality. Over and against the grid as a "sterile, rigid, rational order," Gray points out suggestions of an "alternative form of cognition and representation," more "subtle if complex forms of order" ("From Grids to Vanishing Points," 508). *The Rings of Saturn*, Gray tells us, represents an experiment in a form of writing that escapes the confines of the grid (ibid., 523).

27. Vielleicht war es der weiße Dunst, von dem er in einer späteren Notiz über den am 27. November 1674, über weiten Teilen Englands und Hollands liegenden Nebel behauptet, daß er aufsteige aus her Höhle eines frisch geöffneten Körpers, während er, so Browne im selben Zug, zu unseren Lebzeiten unser Gehirn umwölke, wenn wir schlafen und träumen. Ich entsinne mich deutlich, wie mein eigenes Bewußtsein von solchen Dunstschleiern verhangen gewesen ist, als ich, nach der in den späten Abendstunden an mir vorgenommenen Operation, wieder auf meinem Zimmer im achten Stockwerk des Krankenhauses lag.
(*DIE RINGE DES SATURN* 27–28G)

28. For Flaubert, Janine Dakyns has told the narrator, "clouds of dust" are related to a string of the most unforgivable errors and lies, the consequences of which were immeasurable (*Rings of Saturn* 7E, 16–17G). They are related also, perhaps, to "the relentless spread of stultification which [Flaubert] had observed everywhere, and which he believed had already invaded his own head" (*Rings of Saturn* 7E, 17G).

29. [Ich] sah . . . wie, anscheinend aus eigener Kraft ein Kondensstreifen
     quer durch das von meinem Fenster umrahmte Stück Himmel zog. Ich
     habe diese weiße Spur damals für ein gutes Zeichen gehalten, fürchte
     aber jetzt in der Rückschau, daß sie der Anfang gewesen ist eines Ris-
     ses, der seither durch mein Leben geht. Die Maschine an der Spitze der
     Flugbahn war so unsichtbar wie die Passagiere in ihrem Inneren. Die Un-
     sichtbarkeit und Unfaßbarkeit dessen, was uns bewegt, das ist auch für
     Thomas Browne, der unsere Welt nur als das Schattenbild einer anderen
     ansah, ein letzten Endes unauslotbares Rätsel gewesen.

     (*DIE RINGE DES SATURN* 29G)

30. To see the body of Aris Kindt "in truth" (though the phrase is missing from
     the English translation, *Rings of Saturn* 13E, 23G), to escape the "rigid Car-
     tesian gaze" (*Rings of Saturn* 17E, 27G), Rembrandt must be said to see both
     the body and the shadows: "He alone sees that greenish annihilated body,
     and he alone sees the shadow in the half-open mouth and over the dead
     man's eyes" (*Rings of Saturn* 17E, 27G).

31. Later, we find, just as the quincunx is everywhere to be encountered in the
     physical world, the thread of silk can turn up at any moment in *The Rings
     of Saturn*.

32.   It amazes me that even then, before the Industrial Age, a great number
        of people, at least in some places, spent their lives with their wretched
        bodies strapped to looms made of wooden frames and rails, hung with
        weights, and reminiscent of instruments of torture or cages. It was a pe-
        culiar symbiosis which, perhaps because of its relatively primitive char-
        acter, makes more apparent than any later form of factory work that we
        are able to maintain ourselves on this earth only by being harnessed to
        the machines we have invented. That weavers in particular, together with
        scholars and writers with whom they had much in common, tended to
        suffer from melancholy . . . is understandable.

        (*RINGS OF SATURN* 282–83E)

     Dann nimmt es mich wunder, in welch großer Zahl, zumindest an man-
     chen Orten, die Menschen bereits in der Zeit vor der Industrialisierung
     mit ihren armen Körpern fast ein Leben lang eingeschirrt gewesen sind
     in die aus hölzernen Rahmen und Leisten zusammengesetzten, mit
     Gewichten behangenen und an Foltergestelle oder Käfige erinnernden
     Webstühle in einer eigenartigen Symbiose, die vielleicht gerade auf-
     grund ihrer vergleichsweisen Primitivität besser als jede spätere Ausfor-
     mung unserer Industrie verdeutlicht, daß wir uns nur eingespannt in die
     von uns erfundenen Maschinen auf der Erde zu erhalten vermögen. Daß
     darum besonders die Weber und die mit ihnen in manchem vergleichba-

ren Gelehrten und sonstigen Schreiber . . . zur Melancholie . . . neigten, das versteht sich.

(*DIE RINGE DES SATURN* 334–35G)

33. Paul North's superb book, *The Problem of Distraction,* deals with a double register of distraction in a far more complex and profound way than is here the case. His second concept of distraction has "been released from its subordination to attention, to perception, to the subject" (North, *The Problem of Distraction,* 6), which is not really the case in our readings.

34. J. J. Long writes: "The universal resemblance that Browne discovers in *The Garden of Cyrus* is sustained by an extended metaphorical complex uniting the quincunx, the chiasmus and the net as the *tertium comparationis* that facilitates the perception of similitude across an incredible diversity of natural phenomena and cultural products" (Long, *W. G. Sebald,* 34).

35. Browne, "THE GARDEN OF CYRUS."

36. The description may also suggest that as one builds decussation on decussation, in their progression, the cross that appears as interior to an imagined lozenge also builds the outer sides of new rhomboid forms.

37. His name is populated, overpopulated, with the letter *A,* which become so important in Austerlitz and itself resembles the inverted *V.*

38. Gray writes of taxonomy as the counterpart to the grid: "a rational scheme for systematizing knowledge according to categories" (Gray, "From Grids to Vanishing Points," 499 and 513).

39. In other passages one reads "spruce" (Browne, "THE GARDEN OF CYRUS." 188), "rooted," "flourishing branch" (ibid., 190).

40. Elsewhere in *The Rings of Saturn* Sebald writes of Lévi-Strauss's *Tristes Tropiques.* There, in the facial designs of the Caduveo women of Brazil, something similar takes place. There is an unsettling dissolution of what seems like patterns of symmetry and balance and the marking out of spaces that include and contain in what Lévi-Strauss refers to as a conjuring trick. See Jacobs, *Telling Time,* 48–53.

41. In a long and remarkable piece that accounts for passages in so many of Sebald's works and brings together the readings of a plenitude of scholars, Matthew Hart and Tania Lown-Hecht take us through a series of "close readings of . . . Sebaldian topoi" that "are both spatial and thematic" (Hart and Lown-Hecht, "The Extraterritorial Poetics of W. G. Sebald," 217). What is strikingly astute throughout this study is the refusal of a static sense of the concept. What the authors understand is that in Sebald's writings it is not just this but also that. "The attempt to reterritorialize language from within is both irresistible and inadequate" (ibid., 219). They understand that "the irony of Sebald's style is that . . . points of view often overlap" (225). Reading Browne on the quincunx, one encounters an entirely ab-

stract version of what Hart and Lown-Hecht have called Sebald's extraterritoriality, a play between inclusion and exclusion. One might go on to suggest that Sebald's play of breaking frames, both here and in *The Emigrants*, excising pieces of canvas, both here in *The Rings of Saturn* and also in the essay on Jan Peter Tripp (see chapters 6 and 7), could also be theorized as more abstract versions of the extraterritorial.

42. Browne, and Sebald in turn, pull the silk over our eyes. The description of the quincunx does not correspond with the frontispiece from Browne's *The Garden of Cyrus*. Nowhere in this illustration is a five-pointed quincuncial form to be found "which is composed by using the corners of a regular quadrilateral and the point at which its diagonals intersect" (*Rings of Saturn* 20E, 31G). Either the middle (fifth) point of each diamond shape is missing or, if we take the basic module in this image to be a quadruple set of diamonds, the point in the center is formed by intersecting lines that depart, not from the corners of the equilateral rhombus, but from the mid-points of their sides. If the quincunx indeed partakes of a system with perfect conformity to natural law (*Rings of Saturn* 21E, 33G), the description of its law by Sebald's narrator, following Browne (*Garden of Cyrus* 194–95), seems to falter.

Jeremiah S. Finch, on the other hand, offers a very clear definition of the quincunx: "The term derives from *quinque-unciae*, or five-twelfths of a unit of weight or measure, and was used by the Romans to denote an arrangement of five trees in the form of a rectangle, four occupying the corners, one the center, like the cinque-point on a die, so that a massing of quincunxes produces long rows of trees with the effect of latticework" (Finch, "Sir Thomas Browne and the Quincunx," 274). Finch goes on to note that "the central idea of *The Garden of Cyrus*" is borrowed from the writings of others (ibid., 276) as is the diagram that serves as the frontispiece (282), along with the scholarly history in the first chapter (277).

Other readers of Sebald have noticed discrepancies between image and descriptive text in *Die Ringe des Saturn*. Claudia Öhlschläger writes of the failed "1:1 relation between text and image" when the narrator describes the herring (Öhlschläger, "Der Saturnring oder Etwas vom Eisenbau," 199). Anja Lemke goes on to remark that the fish actually portrayed is a predator of the herring (ibid., 257). See also Holger Steinmann, who points out several errors in source attribution in the Thomas Browne citations. He also discovers that the image of what should be the diary of Roger Casement appears to be rather in the handwriting of Joseph Conrad (Steinmann, "Zitatruinen unterm Hundsstern," 155). Ruth Franklin writes that for every photograph that seems to authenticate the text "there is another that firmly denies any easy correspondence" (Franklin, "Rings of Smoke," 124).

43. In this regard we should turn to the scene in *The Emigrants* (17E, 28–29G) in which the glass over a photographic slide cracks or to Jan Peter Tripp's picture of the cracked glass over the etched portrait of a man in "As Day and Night" (82E, 176G).

44. "so beschließt er mit einer schönen Wendung seine Schrift—das Sternbild der Hyaden, die Quincunx des Himmels senkt sich bereits hinter den Horizont *and so it is time to close the five ports of knowledge   We are unwilling to spin out our thoughts into the phantasms of sleep, making cables of cobwebs and wildernesses of handsome groves*" (*Die Ringe des Saturn* 32G).

45. It is a question, particularly, of the eyes, of course, which make it possible to observe the quincunx.

    In an exceptional reading of Browne's relation to Sebald in *Rings of Saturn,* Anne Fuchs reminds us that sense perception is explicitly privileged in Browne's *The Garden of Cyrus* (Fuchs, "Die Schmerzensspuren der Geschichte," 99–107). Still her reading rightly insists that this empiricism of Browne is also bound up with a speculative principle. Fuchs's reading of the Browne-Sebald connection includes a careful theorization of intertextuality and an ethics of remembering and is exemplary in its linguistic sensibility alongside scholarly erudition.

46. Before turning to Grimmelshausen, the narrator also speaks briefly of Borges.

47. Theisen, "A Natural History of Destruction," 566–67.

48. In Grimmelshausen's words: "da ich doch alle Zeit und Täge deines Lebens bin bey dir gewesen." Grimmelshausen, *Der Abentheurliche Simplicissimus Teutsch,* 506.

49. This begs us to think back on the narrator's dubious musings of where the spectators, Browne, and we might have stood before the "Anatomy Lesson of Dr. Nicolaas Tulp" (*Rings of Saturn* 13E, 23G, 17E, 27G).

50. "Ob ich nichts mehr von dessen Fundament sehen kundte, wurde aber nichts dergleichen gewahr, sonder, dieweil ich einen Hebel fande, den etwan ein Holzbaur ligen lassen, nahme ich denselben und stunde an dise Bildnuß, sie umbzukehren, umbzusehen, wie sie auff der andern Seiten eine Beschaffenheit hette; ich hatte aber derselben den Hebel kaum unterm Halß gesteckt, und zulupffen angefangen, da fieng sie selbst an sich zuregen und zusagen: lasse mich mit frieden ich bin Baltanders" (Grimmelshausen, *Der Abentheurliche Simplicissimus Teutsch,* 505–6).

51. And the first thing Baldanders has to say for himself, even as he names himself is "Leave me in peace. I am Baldanders" (Grimmelshausen, *Der Abentheurliche Simplicissimus Teutsch,* 506), an expression of a will to be precisely what he never is: still.

52. Dann verwandelt sich Baldanders vor den Augen des Simplicius der Reihe nach in einen Schreiber, der folgende Zeilen schreibt

Ich bin der Anfang und das End
und gelte
an allen Orthen
. . . .
Und dann

in einen großen Eichenbaum, in eine Sau, in eine Bratwurst, in einen Bauerndreck, in einen Kleewasen, in eine weiße Blume, in einen Maulbeerbaum und einen seidenen Teppich. Ähnlich wie in diesem fortwährenden Prozeß des Fressens und des Gefressenwerdens hat auch für Thomas Browne nichts Bestand.

(*DIE RINGE DES SATURN* 34–35G)

53. Das wunderbarste Stück aber . . . ist ein vollkommen unversehrtes Trinkglas, so hell, als habe man es soeben geblasen. Dergleichen von der Strömung der Zeit verschonte Dinge werden in der Anschauung Brownes zu Sinnbildern der in der Schrift verheißenen Unzerstörbarkeit der menschlichen Seele. . . . Browne [sucht] unter dem, was der Vernichtung entging, nach den Spuren der geheimnisvollen Fähigkeit zur Transmigration, die er an den Raupen und Faltern so oft studiert hat. Das purpurfarbene Fetzchen Seide aus der Urne des Patroklus, von dem er berichtet, was also bedeutet es wohl?

(*DIE RINGE DES SATURN* 38–39G)

54. For an answer to this question that is both intelligent and convincing see the section entitled "Seide" in Hutchinson's *W. G. Sebald – Die dialektische Imagination*, 133–35.

55. Mark McCulloh, in *Understanding W. G. Sebald,* like so many other readers of Sebald, has taken up this theme: he rightly emphasizes that not only in the theme of silk but also throughout Sebald's work one is lured into thinking one can trace the connections that run through his texts. Thus he speaks of "thematic threads [that] are taken up again and again" (74), of a "kaleidoscopic continuum of associations" (82), of "everything [fitting] into a continuum" (149), of "all things [seeming] to be interconnected" (150). See also pp. 3–4. The seeming continuities, however (this is what silk teaches us), are disturbingly disruptive. See Long on "the dense web of motivic repetitions" in *Vertigo* (Long, *W. G. Sebald,* 105–7).

56. The herring nets in chapter 3 are made of black silk (*Rings of Saturn* 56E, 73G). In part 5, when Joseph Conrad's father burns his manuscripts, a flake of ash goes up in the air like a "scrap of black silk" (*Rings of Saturn* 108E, 131G). In part 6 the Dowager Empress offers a sacrifice of silk to the gods, not to mention chapter 10, which is largely devoted to the subject. Anja Lemke gives us an excellent run-through of many of these instances of silk. (Lemke, "Figurationen der Melancholie," 264).

57. Und Thomas Browne, der als Sohn eines Seidenhändlers dafür ein Auge
gehabt haben mochte, vermerkt an irgendeiner, von mir nicht mehr auf-
findbaren Stelle seiner Schrift *Pseudodoxia Epidemica*, in Holland sei es
zu seiner Zeit Sitte gewesen, im Hause eines Verstorbenen alle Spiegel
und alle Bilder, auf denen Landschaften, Menschen oder die Früchte der
Felder zu sehen waren, mit seidenem Trauerflor zu verhängen, damit
nicht die den Körper verlassende Seele auf ihrer letzten Reise abgelenkt
würde, sei es durch ihren eigenen Anblick, sei es durch den ihrer bald
auf immer verlorenen Heimat.

     (*DIE RINGE DES SATURN* 350G)

58. Fifteen pages earlier the narrator describes the "pattern catalogues" of the
silk manufacturers, filled with pieces of woven material, somewhere between scrap and whole cloth. A two-page image is devoted to this space
where silk and writing converge (*Rings of Saturn* 284–285E, 336–337G). This,
he goes on to say, is the single true book. "That, at any rate, is what I think
when I look at the marvelous strips of colour in the pattern books, the
edges and gaps filled with mysterious figures and symbols. . . . Until the
decline of the Norwich manufactories towards the end of the eighteenth
century, these catalogues of samples, the pages of which seem to me to
be leaves from the only true book which none of our textual and pictorial
works can even begin to rival, were to be found in the offices of importers"
(*Rings of Saturn* 283–86E, 335–38G).

59. The first photo already, for example, shows this, an image of the hospital window . . . "strangely [hung] with a black net" which also could be viewed as a
sideways lightly distorted, squared writing surface, bearing a cloud pattern
but otherwise empty, on whose edge a pencil seems to lie. The photo whose
signifieds, cut-out piece of sky/writing surface, substitute for one another become a picture puzzle in the style of Magritte. For just as in the work of this
painter represented image surfaces and represented exterior world, signifier
and signified, are often indistinguishable so in the photo presented by Sebald
the cut out piece of sky can be regarded as a writing surface and also the reverse. This ambiguity of the image can in turn also be read as an allegory of
Sebald's text which as it gives an account of the journey cannot get around also
speaking of the process of its writing.

     (ALBES, "DIE ERKUNDUNG DER LEERE," 297)

60. As Mark Anderson has so suggestively noted, Sebald uses Celan's last address, "6, avenue Émile-Zola," as Austerlitz's. Anderson, "The Edge of Darkness," 107. Moreover, Sebald mentions Celan in two interviews of 2001 (Sebald, "Auf ungeheuer dünnem Eis," 201 and 256).

61. In *The Rings of Saturn* the view out the window is a test of whether the narrator's past experience, the subject matter of what he has yet to write down, is still to be found.

62. Celan, "Conversation in the Mountains" and "Gespräch im Gebirg." "Still wars also, still dort oben im Gebirg. Nicht lang wars still, denn wenn der Jud daherkommt und begegnet einem zweiten, dann ists bald vorbei mit dem Schweigen, auch im Gebirg. Denn der Jud und die Natur, das ist zweierlei, immer noch, auch heute, auch hier" (Celan,"Gespräch im Gebirg" 169–70).

63. The English translation has been radically altered here and there.

> Da stehn sie also, die Geschwisterkinder, links blüht der Türkenbund, blüht wild, blüht wie nirgends, und rechts, da steht die Rapunzel, und Dianthus superbus, die Prachtnelke, steht nicht weit davon. Aber sie, die Geschwisterkinder, sie haben, Gott sei's geklagt, keine Augen. Genauer: sie haben, auch sie, Augen, aber da hängt ein Schleier davor, nicht davor, nein, dahinter, ein beweglicher Schleier; kaum tritt ein Bild ein, so bleibts hängen im Geweb, und schon ist ein Faden zur Stelle, der sich da spinnt, sich herumspinnt ums Bild, ein Schleierfaden; spinnt sich ums Bild herum und zeugt ein Kind mit ihm, halb Bild und halb Schleier.
>
> Armer Türkenbund, arme Rapunzel! . . . Zunge sind sie und Mund, diese beiden, wie zuvor, und in den Augen hängt ihnen der Schleier, und ihr, ihr armen, ihr steht nicht und blüht nicht, ihr seid nicht vorhanden.
>
> (CELAN,"GESPRÄCH IM GEBIRG" 170)

64. We might well think Celan's "Gespräch im Gebirg" in relation to the question of hatching/*Schraffur* and the eyes of the narrator as described in *Austerlitz*.

65. It says something as well about the way Sebald's text moves in and out of unsettlingly disparate "subject matter"—bringing together historically, geographically, and conceptually unrelated texts, memories, images. What *Austerlitz* has to say about time and space has much to do with this (*Austerlitz* 98–102E, 144–48G).

4. TOWARD AN EPISTEMOLOGY OF CITATION

1. Julia Hell understands the problem well. "What is Sebald's oeuvre all about," she writes, "if not the refusal of realism?" (Hell, "Eyes Wide Shut," 28), in which she expands in the pages that immediately follow with intelligence and insight.

2. James Wood, "An Interview with W. G. Sebald," *Brick: A Literary Journal* 58 (Winter 1998): 26 (cited in Presner, "'What a Synoptic and Artificial View Reveals,'" 350).

3. Silverblatt, "A Poem of an Invisible Subject (Interview)," 80.
4. Even later, as historians documented what happened: "the images of this horrifying chapter of our history have never really crossed the threshold of the national consciousness" ("Air War" 11E, 19G]).
5. A phrase and title that Sebald took from Solly Zuckerman, the title of a book Zuckerman wanted to write but never did.
6. The eagle's-eye perspective closes *After Nature*, has its place in *The Emigrants,* and is also there at a number of critical points in *Rings of Saturn*, as we will go on to note.
7. Sebald, *The Emigrants* and *Die Ausgewanderten.*

> Voller Verwunderung schaute ich . . . hinunter auf das . . . sich erstreckende Lichternetz, dessen orangefarbener Sodiumglanz mir ein erstes Anzeichen dafür war, daß ich von nun an in einer anderen Welt leben würde. . . . In einer letzten Schleife und unter immer stärker werdendem Brausen der Motoren ging es über das offene Land hinaus. . . . Spätestens jetzt hätte man Manchester in seiner ganzen Ausdehnung erkennen müssen. Es war aber nichts zu sehen als ein schwaches, *wie von Asche nahezu schon ersticktes Glosen.* Eine Nebeldecke . . . hatte sich ausgebreitet über die . . . von Millionen von toten und lebendigen Seelen bewohnte Stadt.
>
> (*DIE AUSGEWANDERTEN* 220–21G, EMPHASIS MINE)

8. "Nossack feels that the strategy of the Allied air forces was the work of divine justice. Nor is this process of revenge solely a matter of retribution visited on the nation responsible for the Fascist regime; it is also concerned with the need for atonement felt by the individual, in this case the author, who has long yearned to see the city destroyed" (*Campo Santo* 74E, 78G).

9. The revulsion at this new life, at the "horror teeming under the stone of culture" to which Nossack gives expression in one of the most terrible passages of this text, is a pendant to the fear that the inorganic destruction of life by the firestorm, which (according to Walter Benjamin's distinction between bloody and nonbloody violence) might yet be reconcilable with the idea of divine justice, will be followed by organic decomposition caused by flies and rats.

> (*CAMPO SANTO* 81E, 85G)

> Kluge's literary record of the air raid on Halberstadt is also a model of its kind from another objective viewpoint, where it studies the question of the "meaning" behind the methodical destruction of whole cities, which authors like Kasack and Nossack omit for lack of information, and also out of a sense of personal guilt, or becomes mystified as divine justice and long overdue punishment.
>
> (*CAMPO SANTO* 86E, 90–91G)

10. Die neutralste Form der Mythologie in diesem Zusammenhang wäre wahrscheinlich die Vorstellung, dass es sich um einen Akt göttlicher Intervention handelt, wofür ja Feuer und Wasser immer die zentralen Instrumente waren. Also blutlose Gewalt von oben im biblischen Sinne. Aber selbst das, glaube ich, ist in diesem Zusammenhang und aus dieser Erfahrungsgeschichte heraus in keiner Weise aufrechtzuerhalten. Der Erzähler in meinen Texten entschlägt sich aber jeder Deutung. Er macht sich die Möglichkeiten der Erklärung der Katastrophe nicht zu nutze, er verweist darauf, dass die Leute früher in dieser oder jener Weise darüber nachgedacht haben. Was ihn selber betrifft, glaube ich sagen zu können, dass er keine Antwort auf diese Form der radikalen Kontingenz hat. Er steht dem ratlos gegenüber, kann nur beschreiben, wie es aussah, wie es dazu kam.
     (KÖHLER, "KATASTROPHE MIT ZUSCHAUER")

11. "It was the quasi-natural reflex, determined by feelings of shame and defiance against the victors to keep silent and turn away" ("Air War" 30E, 37G)

12. Thus Julia Hell has written, "W. G. Sebald thought of his 1997 lectures 'Air War and Literature' as his essay on poetics" (Hell, "The Angel's Enigmatic Eyes," 361). Hell's essay is a magisterial piece of criticism and scholarship whose concerns intersect with those of this chapter in more places than I pinpoint here. It concentrates on Sebald's description of the destruction of the 1943 Hamburg air raids and also reads with meticulous care the closing passage in which Sebald turns to Walter Benjamin's angel of history. Along the way, with a remarkably convincing overview, Hell is able to read and account for a broad spectrum of Sebald criticism and to cast all that she does into the even larger and more complex framework of postwar literature and its reception. She fully understands that we encounter here "the central concerns and constitutive conflicts of Sebald's postwar authorship" (ibid., 361).

13. See the superb essay by Presner, "'What a Synoptic and Artificial View Reveals,'" in this regard.

14. Hell wishes to separate these two exigencies in Sebald, the concrete and the documentary, which makes for an interesting reading, but is perhaps not always the case in Sebald's text (Hell, "The Angel's Enigmatic Eyes" 367).

15. "Das Ideal des Wahren, das in seiner, über weite Strecken zumindest, gänzlich unprätentiösen Sachlichkeit beschlossen ist, erweist sich angesichts der totalen Zerstörung als der einzige legitime Grund für die Fortsetzung der literarischen Arbeit. Umgekehrt ist die Herstellung von ästhetischen oder pseudoästhetischen Effekten aus den Trümmern einer vernichteten Welt ein Verfahren, mit dem die Literatur sich ihrer Berechtigung entzieht" ("Luftkrieg" 59G)

16. Barthes, *Mythologies,* 145–46.

17. "Die Bevölkerung (hätte), bei offensichtlich eingeborener Erzählkunst, die psychische Kraft, sich zu erinnern, genau in den Umrissen der zerstörten Flächen der Stadt verloren." Selbst wenn es sich bei dieser einer angeblich realen Person zugeschriebenen Vermutung um einen von Kluges berühmten pseudodokumentarischen Kunstgriffen handeln sollte, hat es sicher seine Richtigkeit mit dem solchermaßen identifizierten Syndrom, haftet doch den Berichten derer, die mit dem blanken Leben davongekommen sind, in aller Regel etwas Diskontinuierliches an, eine eigenartig erratische Qualität, die so unvereinbar ist mit einer normalen Erinnerungsinstanz, daß sie leicht den Anschein von Erfindung und Kolportage erweckt.

("LUFTKRIEG" 31–32G)

18. "It seems improbable [to us] that anyone . . . who saw the panorama of the burning city with sparks flying around them would have come away with an undisturbed mind" ("Air War" 25E, 32G).

19. In his 1997 interview with Andrea Köhler (Köhler, "Katastrophe mit Zuschauer"), we find this exchange:

AK: Ultimately that would mean that only someone who wasn't there is capable of narrating the horrific.

WGS: More or less, yes. Those who have been saved cannot narrate it. Those who have survived have the least clear picture of how it was.

20. Perhaps we should take the term concrete in its etymological senses of various elements grown together in contradistinction to the quality as mentally abstracted or withdrawn from substance.

21. Presner, "'What a Synoptic and Artificial View Reveals.'"

But I suggest that in his "synoptic and artificial view" of the firebombing of Hamburg, Sebald creates a modernist form of realism that has the effect of being "concrete" and "documentary" while radically opening up the domain of the real and the historical by way of the imaginary and the fictional. The modernism of Sebald's account does not derive from any sort of "linguistic radicalism" but rather from the multiplicity of contingent and simultaneous perspectives and the formal, literary aspects of emplotting the modernist event.

(IBID., 352–53)

What is remarkable about Sebald's description of the firebombing of Hamburg is the fact that no eyewitness could have possibly seen or experienced it in this way. In a single "synoptic" view, Sebald has spliced together information and experiences culled from a multiplicity of perspectives. . . . His description oscillates between global and local views, perspectives from above and below, points of view within and external

to the bombing, and, finally knowledge gained, before, during, and after the catastrophe. No one who was there could have seen what he describes, and yet—or for exactly this reason—it is strikingly real.

(IBID., 354)

Even while it is ultimately incomplete, it offers a "synoptic view" (and
there may be many synoptic views) of the totality of the destruction
through the multiplicity and simultaneity of its many contingent perspectives. . . . This view is utterly "artificial," because no eyewitness could
have possibly seen it as it is described. It is an imaginary, artificially constructed view of a real historical event.

(IBID., 356–57)

22. Ibid., 356.
23. Also in *Campo Santo* we read: "In such conditions writing becomes an imperative that dispenses with artifice in the interests of truth, and turns to
a 'dispassionate kind of speech' reporting impersonally as if describing 'a
terrible event from prehistoric time'" (81–82E, 86G).
24. Part of what Sebald/Nossack have in mind here is the return of the population to a prehistorical stage of human civilization, reduced as it is from a
highly developed industrial state to hunters and gatherers ("Air War" 36–
37E, 43–44G).
25. Julia Hell connects this phrasing (and similar phrasing also appears elsewhere in the essay) with Leopold von Ranke's "So had it been" ("Air War"
52E, 58G; Hell, "The Angel's Enigmatic Eyes," 367; also Presner, "'What a
Synoptic and Artificial View Reveals,'" 343), in which case Sebald would
seem to be ironizing himself by becoming the most naive of historians, at
least according to Benjamin's "On the Concept of History." Sebald turns to
Benjamin's theses (which also cite Ranke) at the close of the lectures.
26. "Der Ton, in dem hier berichtet wird, ist der des Boten in der Tragödie.
Nossack weiß, daß man solche Boten oft hängt. Eingebaut in sein Memorandum zum Untergang Hamburgs ist die Parabel von einem Menschen,
der behauptet, erzählen zu müssen, *wie es war*, und der von seinen Zuhö-
rern erschlagen wird, weil er eine tödliche Kälte verbreitet" ("Luftkrieg"
58G, emphasis mine).
27. It was Sebald , of course, who wrote "So ist es gewesen." ("Luftkrieg" 58G)
and who thereby (along with Nossack) claims that he is telling it as it was.
28. *Wir befinden uns* in der Nekropole eines fremden, unbegreiflichen Volks,
herausgerissen aus seiner zivilen Existenz und Geschichte, zurückge-
worfen auf die Entwicklungsstufe unbehauster Sammler. *Stellen wir uns
also vor* "fern, hinter den Schrebergärten, über den Bahndamm hin-
ausragend . . . die verkohlten Ruinen der Stadt, eine zerrissene finstere
Silhouette" [a footnote tells us this is a citation from Böll], davor eine

Landschaft aus niederen, zementfarbenen Schuttbergen . . . einen ein-
zelnen Menschen, der im Geröll herumstochert, [another note tells us
this is from Nossack], die Haltestelle einer Bahn, mitten im Nirgendwo,
Leute, die sich dort einfinden und von denen man, wie Böll schreibt,
nicht wußte, woher sie auf einmal kamen, die aus den Hügeln gewach-
sen schienen, "unsichtbar, unhörbar . . . aus dieser Ebene des Nichts . . .
Gespenster, deren Weg und Ziel nicht zu erkennen war. . . ." [Yet another note refers us to Böll]. *Fahren wir mit ihnen zurück* in die Stadt, in
der sie leben, durch Straßenzüge, in denen die Schutthalden bis zum
ersten Stockwerk der leergebrannten Fassaden sich türmen. *Wir sehen
Menschen*, die sich im Freien kleine Feuerstellen gebaut haben (als seien
sie im Urwald, schreibt Nossack). . . . So ungefähr muß es ausgesehen
haben, *das Vaterland*, im Jahr 1945.

("LUFTKRIEG" 43–44G, EMPHASIS MINE)

29. The multiplicity of narrative modes should be thought in relation to the
fluctuations of critical perspective discussed in chapter 7.

30. Is this gesture, like many in the essay, a plea to leave behind the economy of retribution (*Vergeltung*) so bound up with theologizing in speaking
of war?

31. "[They] are merely the setting for the superordinate plan, which is to myth-
ify a reality that in its raw form defies description" ("Air War" 48E, 54–55G).

The thesis frequently held by the "internal emigrants" that genuine literature had employed a secret language under the totalitarian regime is
thus proved true, in this as in other cases, only insofar as its own code ac-
cidentally happened to coincide with Fascist diction. The vision of a new
educational field proposed by Kasack, as it also was by Hermann Hesse
and Ernst Jünger, makes little difference to the fact, for it too is only a
distortion of the bourgeois ideal of an association of the elect operating
outside and above the state, an ideal which found its ultimate corruption
and perfection in the ordained Fascist elites.

(*CAMPO SANTO* 71E, 75–76G)

32. Presner, "Synoptic and Artificial View" 353.

33. This section was written after having given the lectures in Zurich and partly
to report on and meditate the response to those initial lectures.

34. In the opening lines of the first lecture Sebald writes: "Born in a village
in the Allgäu Alps in May 1944, I am one of those who remained almost
untouched by the catastrophe then unfolding in the German Reich. . . . I
tried to show . . . that this catastrophe had nonetheless left its mark on my
mind" ("Air War" vii–viiiE, 5G). In contrast to this, the destruction "seems
to have left scarcely a trace of pain behind in the collective consciousness"
("Air War" 4E, 12G).

35. Was den Luftangriff auf Sonthofen betrifft, so entsinne ich mich, im Alter von vierzehn oder fünfzehn Jahren den Benefiziaten, der auf dem Oberstdorfer Gymnasium Religionsunterricht erteilte, gefragt zu haben, wie es sich mit unseren Vorstellungen von der göttlichen Vorsehung vereinbaren lasse, daß bei diesem Angriff weder die Kasernen noch die Hitler-Burg, sondern, sozusagen an ihrer statt, die Pfarrkirche und die Spitalskirche zerstört worden sind, kann mich jedoch nicht mehr an die Antwort erinnern, die ich damals erhielt.

("LUFTKRIEG" 80G)

36. One of the most subtle takes on "Air War and Literature" is to be found in the several pages devoted to it by Rebecca Walkowitz (Walkowitz, *Cosmopolitan Style*, 155ff.). She places much of Sebald's work under the star of "vertigo," which will also be one of the overt gestures of Sebald's lectures ("Air War" 74E, 79–80G). Thus she understands that "Sebald's combination of panoramic and microscopic views produces a relentless vertigo" (ibid., 155). A careful commentator on Sebald's very precise use of language (see also her insights on Sebald's "unassimilation" of proper nouns [ibid., 160–61]), as well as on the role of the reader in his works, she continues later in the text with the following remarkable comment:

> Preferring a more transient vision, Sebald suggests that aerial and documentary views need to be supplemented by speculative descriptions. Writing of the firebombing of Dresden, Sebald values subjunctive observation: what someone might have seen if someone could have seen it. He will imagine the destruction not only of buildings, trees, and inhabitants, but also of "domestic pets" and "fixtures and fittings of every kind." . . . By including these objects in his narrative, Sebald hopes to rectify that paralysis (by asking readers to think and feel about loss, including the loss of rationality) and also to imitate it (by asking readers to learn about details whose significance cannot be rationalized).

(IBID., 157)

37. The structure of the lectures themselves, Sebald claims, came together as something of a jumble. At least he calls them "an unfinished gathering of diverse observations, materials and theses" ("Air War" 69E, 75G). It is perhaps not irrelevant that throughout Sebald's work, and there are several instances of it in the air war lectures, he is intrigued by and plays with coincidences of dates and names, especially those that echo his own birthday and name (ibid., 78E, 84G). Andrea Köhler speaks in 2003 of "how often Sebald gave the date of his birth to his figures as the date of their death" (Köhler, "Die Welt im Auge des Kranichs").

38. "Über den zugeschütteten Grundstücken und den durch die Trümmerwelt verwischten Straßenzügen ziehen sich nach einigen Tagen *Trampelpfade,*

die auf legere Weise an frühere *Wegverbindungen anknüpfen*" ("Luftkrieg" 73G, emphasis mine).

39. Narrative distance is also at stake in the passage that follows from *Campo Santo.* (It refers to Nossack's *Bericht eines fremden Wesens über die Menschen.*) "The wide distance between the subject and object of the narrative process implies something like the perspective of natural history, in which destruction and the tentative forms of new life that it generates act like biological experiments in which the species is concerned with 'breaking its mold and abjuring the name of man'" (*Campo Santo* 77E, 81–82G).

40. Die ironische Verwunderung, mit der er die Tatsachen registriert, erlaubt ihm die Einhaltung der für jede Erkenntnis unabdingbaren Distanz. Und doch rührt sich sogar in ihm, diesem aufgeklärtesten aller Schriftsteller, der Verdacht, daß wir aus dem von uns angerichteten Unglück nichts zu lernen vermögen, sondern, unbelehrbar, immer nur fortmachen *auf Trampelpfaden, die auf legere Weise an die alten Wegverbindungen anknüpfen.* Kluges Blick auf seine zerstörte Heimatstadt ist darum, aller intellektuellen Unentwegtheit zum Trotz, auch der entsetzensstarre des Engels der Geschichte, von dem Walter Benjamin gesagt hat. . . .

(\"LUFTKRIEG" 73G, EMPHASIS MINE)

41. Benjamin, *Gesammelte Schriften* 1.3.1232.

42. Benjamin, "On the Concept of History" 392E, "Über den Begriff der Geschichte" 697G. The connection between fascism and progress appears several times in "On the Concept of History." See , for example, also: "This vulgar-Marxist conception of the nature of labor scarcely considers the question of how its products could ever benefit the workers when they are beyond the means of those workers. It recognizes only the progress in mastering nature, not the retrogression of society; it already displays the technocratic features that later emerge in fascism" (ibid., 393E, 699G).

43. "Between History and Natural History"/"Zwischen Geschichte und Naturgeschichte" was written in 1982. Andreas Huyssen, in an intriguing and thought-provoking essay, "On Rewritings and New Beginnings: W. G. Sebald and the Literature about the *Luftkrieg*," reads this earlier piece in contrast to "Air War and Literature," viewing it as still holding out the possibility of a learning process that the later Zurich lectures, he tells us, have given up (ibid., 88–89). Other passages in the early text, however (cited shortly in this chapter), also seem skeptical about this (*Campo Santo* 80–81E and 89–90E, 84–85G and 94G). And there are passages in "Air War and Literature" that might suggest we are still between history and natural history.

44. Die Perspektive, die sich hier für einen unter Umständen möglichen, anderen Ablauf der Geschichte auftut, versteht sich, ihrer ironischen Einfärbung zum Trotz, als ernstgemeinter Appell für eine, gegen alle

Wahrscheinlichkeitsrechnung, zu erarbeitende Zukunft. Gerade Kluges detaillierte Beschreibung der gesellschaftlichen Organisation des Unglücks, die programmiert wird von den beständig mitgeschleppten und beständig sich potenzierenden Fehlleistungen der Geschichte, beinhaltet die Konjektur, daß ein richtiges Verständnis der von uns in einem fort inszenierten Katastrophen die erste Voraussetzung darstellt für die gesellschaftliche Organisation des Glücks.

("LUFTKRIEG" 70G; SEE ALSO THE SLIGHTLY VARIANT
CAMPO SANTO 95G)

45. "An dieser Divergenz, die freilich dann auch von den 'Gehirnen von morgen' nie ausgeglichen wird, bewahrheitet sich das Diktum Brechts, daß der Mensch durch Katastrophen soviel lerne wie das Versuchskaninchen über Biologie, woraus sich wiederum ergibt, daß der Grad der *Autonomie* des Menschen vor der von ihm bewerkstelligten tatsächlichen oder potentiellen Zerstörung artgeschichtlich nicht größer ist als der des Nagetiers im Käfig des Experimentators" (*Campo Santo* 94G, emphasis mine).

46. This chapter follows the concept of "natural history" as Sebald presents it in the *Campo Santo* essay "Between History and Natural History." Eric Santer, in his book *On Creaturely Life,* has this to say of "natural history: "The theme of the ending of time *within time,* a constant of the apocalyptic imagination, clearly haunts Sebald's writing and the figures that populate his work." And he goes on to add: "But there is a more specific sense of natural history at work in Sebald's vision of the nexus of the natural and the human, one that Walter Benjamin developed over the course of his career. . . . Sebald's writing is deeply indebted to the Benjaminian view that at some level we truly encounter the radical otherness of the "natural" world only where it appears in the guise of historical remnant" (ibid., xv). "In Benjamin's parlance," Santner continues later, "*Naturgeschichte* has to do with . . . the breakdown and reification of the normative structures of human life and mindedness. It refers, that is, not to the fact that nature also has a history but to the fact that the artifacts of human history tend to acquire an aspect of mute, natural being at the point where they begin to lose their place in a viable form of life" (ibid., 16). This certainly is what is at issue in the passage from "Air War and Literature," although the issue of epistemology will enlarge the stakes beyond that of artifacts to what Santner may have in mind when he writes of "human . . . mindedness." Santner's theoretical erudition takes us in other directions as well, not only to Benjamin, but also to Freud, Schmitt, Lacan, Rilke, Heidegger, Agamben, Foucault, and others, to place Sebald's *natural history* and also his understanding of *creaturely life* in a context that deeply enriches his writings and forces us to read them anew.

47. There is a footnote to Kluge here, but it refers only to the citation. It is Sebald who has introduced the phrases on the dominant species.

Die Primitivisierung des menschlichen Lebens, die damit beginnt, daß, wie Böll später erinnert, "am Anfang dieses Staates ein im Abfall wühlendes Volk stand", ist ein Anzeichen dafür, daß die kollektive Katastrophe den Punkt markiert, auf dem Geschichte in Naturgeschichte zurückzufallen droht. . . . Die Tatsache, daß es sich in der in eine Steinwüste verwandelten Stadt bald schon wieder zu rühren beginnt, daß sich Trampelpfade übers Geröll abzuzeichnen beginnen, die – wie Kluge dann vermerkt– "auf legere Weise an frühere Wegverbindungen anknüpfen", hat in dem Nossack'schen Bericht allerdings wenig Tröstliches, ist es doch zu diesem Zeitpunkt noch nicht ausgemacht, ob die überlebenden Reste der Bevölkerung oder die die Stadt beherrschenden Ratten und Fliegen aus dieser regressiven Phase der Evolution als die dominierende Gattung hervorgehen werden.

(*CAMPO SANTO* 84–85G)

48. Die Geschichte der Industrie als das offene Buch des menschlichen Denkens und Fühlens—läßt die materialistische Erkenntnistheorie oder irgendeine Erkenntnistheorie überhaupt sich aufrechterhalten angesichts solcher Zerstörung, oder ist nicht diese vielmehr das unwiderlegbare Exempel dafür, daß die gewissermaßen unter unserer Hand sich entwickelnden und dann anscheinend unvermittelt ausbrechenden Katastrophen in einer Art Experiment den Punkt vorwegnehmen, an dem wir aus unserer, wie wir so lange meinten, *autonomen* Geschichte zurücksinken in die Geschichte der Natur?

("LUFTKRIEG" 72G, EMPHASIS MINE)

49. See Hell, "The Angel's Enigmatic Eyes" on this issue.
50. The precise title of the essay is "Zwischen Geschichte und Naturgeschichte," followed by the subtitle, in smaller print, "Über die literarische Beschreibung totaler Zerstörung" (*Campo Santo* 69G). "Between History and Natural History" followed by "On the Literary Description of Total Destruction" (*Campo Santo* 65E, 69G).

51. Kluges Blick auf seine zerstörte Heimatstadt ist darum, aller intellektuellen Unentwegtheit zum Trotz, auch der entsetzensstarre des Engels der Geschichte, von dem Walter Benjamin gesagt hat, daß er mit seinen aufgerissenen Augen "eine einzige Katastrophe [sieht], die unablässig Trümmer auf Trümmer häuft und sie ihm vor die Füße schleudert. Er möchte wohl verweilen, die Toten wecken und das Zerschlagene zusammenfügen. Aber ein Sturm weht vom Paradiese her, der sich in seinen Flügeln verfangen hat und so stark ist, daß der Engel sie nicht mehr schließen kann. Dieser Sturm treibt ihn unaufhaltsam in die Zukunft, der er den Rücken kehrt, während der Trümmerhaufen vor ihm zum Himmel wächst. Das, was wir den Fortschritt nennen, ist dieser Sturm."

("LUFTKRIEG" 73–74G)

52. The temporality of the dialectic image is that of the instant. The temporality of the angel of history is that of longing to return to the past. See Hell, "The Angel's Enigmatic Eyes."

53. Benjamin, *The Arcades Project* 473E, *Das Passagen-Werk* 591–92G.

54. In a 1992 interview Sebald speaks of the many citations that found their way into *Vertigo*: "The text is one great homage to Kafka, an author whom I always, and ever again read. But in the novel in fact many smaller homages to other authors are hidden. These are testimonies of respect in the form of citation that have simply slipped themselves into the text" ("Auf ungeheuer dünnem Eis" 77). The citations here seem to slip themselves into the text as though they had a will independent of the writer. One might compare this to the way in which the pictures of the Halberstadt photographer make their way into Kluge's text.

55. The English translation fails to register either of these phrases, "into memory" and "into experience."

56. Huyssen quite astutely notes that, "unmistakably, Sebald's essay is not just an analysis of those earlier writers' work, but a hidden rewriting of both Nossack and Kluge's texts themselves" (Huyssen, "On Rewritings and New Beginnings," 83). He goes on to speak of this in terms of "Sebald's treatment of memory and his incorporation of photographs into all of his texts [as] clearly reminiscent of Kluge's text/image strategies in *Neue Geschichten*" (ibid., 83). Huyssen attributes this to the fact that Sebald, born in 1944, unlike Kluge, born in 1932, had no early childhood memories of the Third Reich, "no access to the experience or memory of the air war except through these earlier texts which he is compelled to rewrite" (ibid., 84). Perhaps one might add to this that Sebald meditates on the fact that no generation had access to experience in any simple, linguistically expressible way, not even that first generation of observers. The epistemological problems of that quandary, along with the impossibility of learning either from one's own experience or from the experience of others, are acted out in Sebald's use of citation, as Huyssen himself notes.

57. Sebald's *After Nature* does end from a crane's point of view: "with a crane's eye/one surveys his far-flung realm" (*After Nature* 115E, 98G), a superordinate position Sebald seems to abandon as a closing moment of his texts.

5. A IS FOR AUSTERLITZ

1. Antwerp is the city in which the narrator first meets the man for whom his text is named. *A* is for Andromeda Lodge, the home of Austerlitz's good friend Gerald Fitzpatrick whose father is Aldous, uncle Alphonso, and mother Adela (all four of whom share the letters *A* and *L*). *A* is also for Alderney Street where Austerlitz resides in London. Ashman is the owner

of Iver Grove, visited by Austerlitz and his teacher, André Hilary, who had given him "a triple starred *A*" (*Austerlitz*, 73E, 111G) on an essay. Two of the four characters in *Die Ausgewanderten* also point to Sebald's propensity toward the first letter of the alphabet: Ambros Adelwarth and Max Aurach. Agáta Austerlizová, with its five *A*s, lies just at the middle of the book (Sebald, *Austerlitz*, 146E, 210G).

2. The consequences of the encounter with Tereza will ultimately lead Austerlitz to Terezín.

3. As Austerlitz, having found his past, retraces the train ride of the *Kindertransport* that first brought him to England, Sebald plays on this possibility: "Zwischen Würzburg und Frankfurt . . . ging die Strecke durch eine baumreiche Gegend, kahle Eichen- und Buchenstände" (*Austerlitz* 324G). The play of words (*A*ychen-, *E*ichen-, *B*uchen-) does not carry over into the English translation: "it was between Würzberg and Frankfurt that the line ran through a densely forested region with leafless stands of oak [*Eichen-*] and beech [*Buchen*] trees" (*Austerlitz* 224E). And lest one have missed the dark suggestion, a few lines later, Sebald intersperses the syllable *Wald:* he speaks of the "gänzlich von finsteren Waldungen überwachsenen Land" that "war das Original der so viele Jahre hindurch mich heimsuchenden Bilder" ("land . . . entirely overgrown by dark forests which . . . was the original of the images that had haunted me for so many years"; *Austerlitz* 224E, 324G). Earlier the ABCs of trees is also at play when Austerlitz describes the excursions he made with Hilary: "nach langem Herumwandern in einem mit jungem *A*horn- und *B*irkengehölz dicht zugewachsenen Park" ("after walking for a long time in a park densely overgrown with young sycamore and birch trees"; *Austerlitz* 154G, 103E, emphasis mine).

4. Thus the title of a 2001 essay/interview in the *Guardian* is "Recovered Memories."

5. The Austrian writer Jean Améry left his homeland behind, but not the bitterness of his memories. Sebald's narrator leaves this story untold, but it adds yet another name beginning with *A* to those that are already explicitly at play throughout the book. After the war he rearranged the letters of his name from the stereotypical Austrian *Mayer* to its logogriph *Améry* where all the bitterness of his ressentiment might crystallize. The name is an obvious play on the French for bitter, *amer*, and bitterness, *amertume*. Sebald had written about Améry's bitter resentment elsewhere (Sebald, "Verlorenes Land," 142).

6. [Er] stellte, so gut es ging, ein Lexikon ihrer fast nur aus Vokalen und vor allem aus dem in unendlichen Variationen betonten und akzentuierten Laut A bestehenden Sprache zusammen. . . . Später, in sein Heimatland zurückgekehrt, begann Novelli mit dem Malen von Bildern. Das Hauptmotiv, dessen er sich dabei in immer neuen Ausprägungen und

Zusammensetzungen bediente . . . war das des Buchstabens A, den er . . .
hineinkratzte . . . in eng in- und übereinander gedrängten Reihen, im-
mer gleich und doch sich nie wiederholend, aufsteigend und abfallend
in Wellen wie ein lang anhaltender Schrei.
AAAAAAAAAAAAAAAAAAAAAAAAAAAAAAAAA
AAAAAAAAAAAAAAAAAAAAAAAAAAAAAAAAA
AAAAAAAAAAAAAAAAAAAAAAAAAAAAAAAA
(*AUSTERLITZ*, 43–44G)

7.   I can see that my name alone, and the fact that it was kept from me until my fifteenth year, ought to have put me on the track of my origins,
but it has also become clear to me of late why an agency greater than or
superior to my own capacity for thought, which circumspectly directs
operations somewhere in my brain, has always preserved me from my
own secret, systematically preventing me from drawing the obvious conclusions and embarking on the inquiries these conclusions would have
suggested to me.

(*AUSTERLITZ* 44E)

[Ich sehe,] daß allein mein Name und die Tatsache, daß mir dieser Name
bis in mein fünfzehntes Jahr vorenthalten geblieben war, mich auf die
Spur meiner Herkunft hätten bringen müssen, doch ist mir in der letzt-
vergangenen Zeit auch klargeworden, weshalb ein meiner Denkfähigkeit
vor- oder übergeordnete und offenbar irgendwo in meinem Gehirn mit
der größten Umsicht waltende Instanz mich immer vor meinem eigenen Geheimnis bewahrt und systematisch davon abgehalten hat, die
naheliegendsten Schlüsse zu ziehen und die diesen Schlüssen entsprechenden Nachforschungen anzustellen.

(*AUSTERLITZ* 68–69G).

8.   Amir Eshel, in a stunning and carefully reflective essay makes the connection between Austerlitz and Ulysses, though on another basis than that I
am suggesting here. Eshel speaks of "Austerlitz's Ulyssian journey back to
his past," "to Prague, where, much like Ulysses, he encounters his childhood in the figure of his nursemaid" (Eshel, "Against the Power of Time,"
78). The irony in this particular passage, which marks the moment when
Austerlitz first consciously hears of the Kindertransport, is that Austerlitz
is already with his Penelope, Penelope Peacefull, and he makes his trip to
Prague by leaving her and leaving behind what little peace he has. For the
trip "home" to Prague, which follows upon the summer of 1992 breakdown,
will precipitate an even greater breakdown. The return home to Prague has
all the ambiguity of Odysseus's embrace of Telemachus, accompanied as
it is by their shrill cries which are compared in book 16 (216–19) of Homer's
text to that of birds whose children had been stolen away.

9. "Im Alter von viereinhalb Jahren, in den Monaten unmittelbar vor dem Ausbruch des Krieges, die Stadt Prag verlassen zu haben mit einem der damals von hier abgehenden, sogenannten Kindertransporte und deshalb in das Archiv gekommen sei in der Hoffnung, die in der Zeit zwischen 1934 und 1939 in Prag wohnhaften Personen meines Namens, bei denen es gewiß nicht um allzu viele sich handle, mit ihren Anschriften aus den Registern heraussuchen zu können" (*Austerlitz* 216G).

10. "Daß die Einwohnerregister aus der fraglichen Zeit vollständig erhalten seien, daß der Name Austerlitz in der Tat zu den ungewöhnlicheren gehöre und es darum keine besonderen Schwierigkeiten bereiten dürfte, die entsprechenden Auszüge für mich bis morgen nachmittag anzufertigen" (*Austerlitz* 217G).

11. Alongside broader reflections on the concept of the archive in Sebald, J. J. Long gives us a highly intelligent meditation on the archive in *Austerlitz* in particular. See for example the section entitled "The Archive as Substitute Memory" in chapter 8. Long (*W. G. Sebald,* 152ff). What Long so cannily shows is that Austerlitz's sense of the archive has nothing of the apparent simplicity of his archival success in Prague. Rather, Long writes: "Austerlitz's substitution of scholarship for memory forms part of his wider efforts to resist the power of linear time by stressing the radically relative nature of temporality" (ibid., 154).

12. If at first the writing of the name proved something of a stumbling block to the fifteen year old, it is the spelling of the name alone which initiates the restoration of his past. With no missteps along the way, Austerlitz finds his childhood apartment by searching for his name in the state archive. "And so . . . , no sooner had I arrived in Prague than I found myself back in the place of my early childhood, every trace of which had been expunged from my memory" (*Austerlitz* 150E, 216G). A little later he calls all the details of the Sporkova 12 "pure letters and signs from the type case of forgotten things" ("lauter Buchstaben und Zeichen aus dem Setzkasten der vergessenen Dinge"; *Austerlitz* 151E, 222G).

13. Austerlitz is sixty-two at the end of Sebald's volume.

14. In his KCRW interview Sebald underscores the necessity of narrating indirectly and confirms his stylistic debt to Thomas Bernhard. Silverblatt, "A Poem of an Invisible Subject (Interview)," 80 and 82.

15. "Věra [war] selber, unwillkürlich, wie ich annehme, sagte Austerlitz, aus der einen Sprache in die andere übergewechselt, und ich, der ich . . . nicht . . . auch im entferntesten nur auf den Gedanken gekommen war, vom Tschechischen je berührt worden zu sein, verstand nun wie ein Tauber, dem durch ein Wunder das Gehör wiederaufging, so gut wie alles, was Věra sagte" (*Austerlitz* 227G).

16. See Presner's excellent reading of this passage in *Mobile Modernity,* 273–75.

17.   Erst unlängst habe ich, an der Schwelle des Erwachens, in das Innere
      eines solchen Terezíner Kasernenbaus hineingesehen. Er war von den
      Netzen dieser kunstreichen Tiere Schicht um Schicht ausgefüllt, von
      den Fußböden bis hinauf an die Decken. Ich weiß noch, wie ich im
      Halbschlaf versuchte, das . . . *erschauernde Traumbild* festzuhalten und
      zu erkennen, was in ihm verborgen war, aber es löste sich immer mehr
      auf und wurde überlagert von der zugleich in meinem Bewußtsein
      aufgehenden Erinnerung an die blinkenden Schaufenster*scheiben* des
      ANTIKOS BAZAR.

      (*AUSTERLITZ* 280–81G, EMPHASIS MINE)

18. Thus the narrator tells of Austerlitz's fascination with network as possible
     system: "But then again, it was also true that he was still obeying an im-
     pulse which he himself, to this day, did not really understand, but which
     was somehow linked to an early fascination that made itself apparent with
     the idea of a network such as that of the entire railway system" (*Austerlitz*
     33E, 52–53G).

19. "Sehen konnte ich freilich nur, was in den Auslagen zur Schau gestellt
     war. . . . Aber selbst diese vier, offenbar vollkommen willkürlich zusam-
     mengesetzten Stilleben, die auf eine, wie es den Anschein hatte, naturhafte
     Weise, hineingewachsen waren in das schwarze, in den Scheiben sich spie-
     gelnde Astwerk der rings um den Stadtplatz stehenden Linden, hatten für
     mich eine derartige Anziehungskraft, daß ich mich von ihnen lange nicht
     losreißen konnte und, die Stirne gegen die kalte Scheibe gepreßt . . ." (*Aus-
     terlitz* 282–83G).

20. The phrase suggesting relationships that cannot be explored is omitted
     in the English translation. The textual entryway to the Antikos Bazar and
     its unfathomable interrelations is a surreptitious, slightly aberrant visual
     experiment, unlike anything else we encounter in the volume. Rather than
     image as illustration, the implicit, if often failed concept throughout Se-
     bald's works, the photos here take on a life of their own.

     Elsewhere and a few pages earlier they seem to suggest a straight and
     inevitable narrative line in contrast to the involutions in the display win-
     dows to come. In a series of five photographs, as nowhere else in the vol-
     ume, the images follow one another (*Austerlitz* 190–93E, 276–79G). Under
     a double window in a decaying building we see a long row of numbered
     garbage pails stretching from one edge of the photo to the other. This is
     followed by four images that seem to morph from one to the next as the
     conceptualization of the window is slowly transformed.

     A door with a window on either side: a door with a single window above
     it; the sunlit doorways of the last two shots replaced now by a darkened
     doorway with a narrow, black, rectangular windowlike form above it that
     has lost all sense of translucence; and, finally, a door of sorts, barricaded

shut with black metal strips. The window form that in the earlier pictures was above or to the side of the doorway is now a small square at the top of the door itself: it gives off a brightness suggestive not of daylight but of flames within. The path of Terezín, we might be led to conclude, leads inexorably to the gas chambers and the incinerators.

21. "[Die] elfenbeinfarbene Porzellankomposition, die einen reitenden Helden darstellte, der sich auf seinem soeben auf der Hinterhand sich erhebenden Roß nach rückwärts wendet, um mit dem linken Arm ein unschuldiges, von der letzten Hoffnung verlassenes weibliches Wesen zu sich emporzu-ziehen und aus einem dem Beschauer nicht offenbarten, aber ohne Zweifel grauenvollen Unglück zu retten" (*Austerlitz* 284–85G).

22. "[Ich studierte] die hundert verschiedenen Dinge . . . als müßte aus irgend-einem von ihnen, oder aus ihrem Bezug zueinander, eine eindeutige Ant-wort sich ableiten lassen auf die vielen, nicht auszudenkenden Fragen, die mich bewegten" (*Austerlitz* 282–83G, emphasis mine).

23. "Auf einem Aststummel hockend [war] dieses ausgestopfte, stellenweise schon vom Mottenfraß verunstaltete Eichhörnchen, das sein gläsernes Knopfauge unerbittlich auf mich gerichtet hielt und dessen tschechischen Namens – veverka – ich nun von weit her wieder erinnerte wie den eines vor langer Zeit in Vergessenheit geratenen Freunds" (*Austerlitz* 284G).

24. "Wenn wir zu der Seite kamen, sagte Věra, sagte Austerlitz, auf der davon die Rede war, daß der Schnee durch das Gezweig der Bäume herabrieselt und bald den ganzen Waldboden bedeckt, hätte ich zu ihr aufgeblickt und gefragt: Aber wenn alles weiß sein wird, wie wissen dann die Eichhörn-chen, wo sie ihren Vorrat verborgen haben?. . . . Ja, wie wissen die Eich-hörnchen das, und was wissen wir überhaupt, und wie erinnern wir uns, und was entdecken wir nicht am Ende?" (*Austerlitz* 295G).

25. "It was six years after our farewell outside the gates of the Trade Fair in Holešovice, so Vera continued, that I learned how Agáta was sent east in September 1944." ("Es war sechs Jahre nach unserem Abschied vor dem Tor des Messegeländes in Holešovice, so berichtete Věra weiter, daß ich erfuhr, daß Agáta im September 1944. . . . nach Osten geschickt worden war"; *Austerlitz* 204E, 295G).

26. Still, when Austerlitz thinks back on Terezín, what comes to mind is a somewhat gentler version: "the framed ground plan . . . in soft tones of gray-brown" figuring "the model of a world made by reason and regulated in all conceivable respects" (*Austerlitz* 199E, 288G).

27. No reader of Sebald can fail to recognize the critical importance of this figure of interconnection throughout his work. Anne Fuchs, in *Die Schmer-zensspuren der Geschichte*, is particularly astute in this regard. She notes that structure in the Quincunx of Browne (ibid., 101), in anatomical struc-tures such as blood vessels (102) in the image of train tracks compared to strands of muscles and nerves in *Austerlitz* (48). But she understands that

the net in Sebald's writings is not simply the naming of a physical structure but also a textual practice, what she calls a network aesthetic (74), that
might bring together literature and natural history, and biography, for example (77). She develops her sense of the net as a mode of thinking and
writing in Sebald in a section entitled "Topographical Networks in *Austerlitz*" (47–54).

28. The play here, once again, is on *Buchenwald* and *Eichenwald*, with its echo
of *Aychenwald*, the family name of Austerlitz's father.

29. Nowhere is this more obvious than at the Greenwich Royal Observatory.

30. "Auch wenn ich heute an meine Rheinreisen denke, von denen die zweite
kaum weniger schrecklich als die erste gewesen ist, dann geht mir alles in
meinem Kopf durcheinander, das, was ich erlebt und das, was ich gelesen
habe, die Erinnerungen, die auftauchen und wieder versinken, die fortlau-
fenden Bilder und die schmerzhaften blinden Stellen, an denen gar nichts
mehr ist" (*Austerlitz* 327G).

31. W. G. Sebald, "Kafka Goes to the Movies," in *Campo Santo* 156E, 198G.

32. The Ghetto Museum is only one of such destinations: there are, also, the
Greenwich Royal Observatory, the veterinary museum at Maisons-Alfort,
and Breendonk.

33. Like many others, Eshel documents the parallels between Sebald and the
narrator figures in his work.

34. Tripp hat mir damals einen von ihm gefertigten Stich als Geschenk mit-
gegeben, und auf diesen Stich, auf dem der kopfkranke Senatspräsident
Daniel Paul Schreber zu sehen ist mit einer Spinne in seinem Schädel—
was gibt es Furchtbareres als die in uns immerfort wuselnden Gedanken?—auf diesen Stich geht vieles von dem, was ich später geschrie-
ben habe, zurück, auch in der Art des Verfahrens, im Einhalten einer
genauen historischen Perspektive, im geduldigen Gravieren und in der
Vernetzung, in der Manier der *nature morte*, anscheinend weit auseinander liegender Dinge.

("EIN VERSUCH DER RESTITUTION," *CAMPO SANTO* 243–44)

35. See Klaus Jeziorkowski's wonderfully intelligent commentary on the concept of web in *Austerlitz* ("'Peripherie als Mitte'"), although, to be sure, the
tone and gesture of the essay are in many senses a counterpoint to rather
than a confirmation of what is written here. Thus he speaks of a *Lesbarma-
chen* (a making readable), or of the idea of a network that is to be thought of
as all encompassing, or, in the title as in the closing line, of the periphery
as middle, which seems to solidify the concept of periphery in a manner
Sebald astutely avoids.

36. "Es nutzte mir offenbar wenig, daß ich die Quellen meiner Verstörung ent-
deckt hatte, mich selber, über all die vergangenen Jahre hinweg, mit größ-

ter Deutlichkeit sehen konnte als das von seinem vertrauten Leben von einem Tag auf den anderen abgesonderte Kind; die Vernunft kam nicht an gegen das seit jeher . . . und jetzt gewaltsam aus mir hervorbrechende Gefühl des Verstoßen- und Ausgelöschtseins" (*Austerlitz* 330G).

37. His earlier, initial, breakdown finds its retelling only towards the end of the text, given the endless involutions of narration, and disruptions of linear time.

38. It also recalls the far more benign version of such displays at Gerald's home (*Austerlitz* 82E, 125–26G). It is in this collection that Austerlitz's namesake, Jaco, has his place, though in a cardboard box rather than in glass.

39. Weitaus am entsetzlichsten jedoch, so sagte Austerlitz, ist die in einer Vitrine rückwärts in dem letzten Kabinett des Museums zu sehende lebensgroße Figur eines Reiters, dem der . . . Anatom und Präparator Honoré Fragonard auf das kunstvollste die Haut abgezogen hat, so daß, in den Farben gestockten Blutes, *jeder einzelne Strang der gespannten Muskeln* des Kavaliers sowohl als des mit panischem Blick vorwärts stürmenden Pferdes vollkommen deutlich zutage tritt mitsamt dem blauen Geäder und den ockergelben *Sehnen und Bändern.*
   (*AUSTERLITZ* 378–80G, EMPHASIS MINE)

40. "Vor Beginn der Bauarbeiten an den beiden nordöstlichen Bahnhöfen, wurden diese Elendsquartiere gewaltsam geräumt und ungeheure Erdmassen, mitsamt den in ihnen Begrabenen, aufgewühlt und verschoben, damit die Eisenbahnstrassen, die auf den von den Ingenieuren angefertigten Plänen sich ausnahmen wie Muskel- und Nervenstränge in einem anatomischen Atlas, herangeführt werden konnten bis an den Rand der City" (*Austerlitz* 194G).

41. "Fragonard . . . muß . . . Tag und Nacht über den Tod gebeugt gewesen sein, umfangen von dem süßen Geruch der Verwesung und bewegt offenbar von dem Wunsch, dem hinfälligen Leib durch ein Verfahren der *Vitrifikation* und somit durch die Umwandlung seiner in kürzester Frist korrumpierbaren Substanz in ein *gläsernes Wunder* wenigstens einen Anteil am ewigen Leben zu sichern" (*Austerlitz* 380G, emphasis mine).

42. W. G. Sebald, "The Mystery of the Red-Brown Skin," in *Campo Santo* 177E, 219G.

43. "Dem hinfälligen Leib durch ein Verfahren der Vitrifikation und somit durch die Umwandlung seiner in kürzester Frist korrumpierbaren Substanz in ein gläsernes Wunder wenigstens einen Anteil am ewigen Leben zu sichern. In den Wochen, die auf meinen Besuch in dem Veterinärwissenschaftlichen Museum folgten, [so setzte Austerlitz, {den Blick nach draußen auf den Boulevard gerichtet,} seine Geschichte fort,] war es mir unmöglich, mich an irgend etwas von dem, was ich soeben erzählt habe, zu erinnern" (Austerlitz 380–81G, emphasis, parentheses, and brackets mine).

44. This is the inverse of the Jan Peter Tripp image of a man behind a cracked glass: the crack in the glass, and it alone, reminds us that what we see is not a photograph ("As Day and Night, Chalk and Cheese" and "Wie Tag und Nacht," 82E, 176G).

45. This becomes all the more clear in a later passage that speaks this time of remarkable, perfect recall and remembers to name both the boulevard and the window through which Austerlitz gazes: "Austerlitz quoted from memory, as he looked out of the brasserie window at the Boulevard Auguste Blanqui" (*Austerlitz* 283E, 400G).

46. In den Wochen, die auf meinen Besuch in dem Veterinärwissenschaftlichen Museum folgten, [so setzte Austerlitz, {den Blick nach draußen auf den Boulevard gerichtet,} seine Geschichte fort,] war es mir unmöglich, mich an irgend etwas von dem, was ich soeben erzählt habe, zu erinnern, denn es war auf dem Rückweg von Maisons-Alfort, daß ich in der Métro den ersten der später mehrfach sich wiederholenden, mit einer zeitweiligen Auslöschung sämtlicher Gedächtnisspuren verbundenen Ohnmachtsanfälle erlitt.

    (*AUSTERLITZ* 380–81G, PARENTHESES AND BRACKETS MINE)

47. "Wieder zu mir gekommen bin ich erst in der Salpêtrière, in die man mich eingeliefert hatte und wo ich nun, irgendwo in dem riesigen, über die Jahrhunderte sozusagen aus sich selber herausgewachsenen und zwischen dem Jardin des Plantes und der Gare d'Austerlitz ein eigenes Universum bildenden Gebäudekomplex, in welchem die Grenzen zwischen Heil- und Strafanstalt von jeher unsicher gewesen sind, . . . lag" (*Austerlitz* 382G).

48. These linguistic propensities are already there in Austerlitz's first description of such excursions: a reverse alphabetical list of five metro stations is followed by the stammers of St . . . St . . . St . . . "When she was not in Paris, which always cast me into an anxious mood, I regularly set off to explore the outlying districts of the city, taking the Métro out to Montreuil, Malakoff, Charenton, Bobigny, Bagnolet, Le Pré St. Germain, St. Denis, St. Mandé, or elsewhere" (*Austerlitz* 264E, 376G). This makes the precision of stuttering and alphabetization all the more manifest in the later passage.

49. Iéna, Solferino, Stalingrad are the names of battles (with the Gare d'Austerlitz significantly omitted, named after, of course, the Battle of Austerlitz); Campo Formio is the place of the treaty of Campo Formio, Crimée is named after the Crimean War; the Musée de l'Armée at Invalides is touted as having the most important military collection anywhere in the world. Oberkampf has the German word for battle in it. And Elysées of course is the place in Greek mythology where heroes go after death—which is more or less the subject matter of the lines that follow. Simplon, although the connection is far more tenuous, is the pass in Switzerland in an area that

has one of the world's longest railroad tunnels—a link, then, to the train in *Austerlitz*, rather than the military. In a 2000 interview with Volker Hage, Sebald speaks of the Paris metro as the locus of "a French history of glory [*Ruhmesgeschichte*]" ("Auf ungeheuer dünnem Eis" 188).

50. Austerlitz's counterpart is a roofer who has felt the moment when the roof of his mind, so to speak, was suddenly torn: a critical, recurring point of Austerlitz and the narrator's experience. "Occasionally I talked to one or the other of the hospital patients, a roofer, for instance, who claimed he could recollect with perfect clarity the moment when, in the middle of his work, something that had been stretched too taut inside him snapped at a particular spot behind his forehead, and for the first time he heard, coming over the crackling transistor wedged into the batten in front of him, the voices of those bearers of bad tidings" (*Austerlitz* 230–31E, 333G).

51.   Genau kann niemand erklären, was in uns geschieht, wenn die Türe aufgerissen wird, hinter der die Schrecken der Kindheit verborgen sind. Aber ich weiß noch, daß mir damals in der Kasematte von Breendonk ein ekelhafter Schmierseifengeruch in die Nase stieg, daß dieser Geruch sich, an einer irren Stelle in meinem Kopf, mit dem mir immer zuwider gewesenen und vom Vater mit Vorliebe gebrauchten Wort "Wurzelbürste" verband, daß ein *schwarzes Gestrichel* mir vor den Augen zu zittern begann und ich gezwungen war, mit der Stirn mich anzulehnen an die von *bläulichen Flecken* unterlaufene, griesige und, wie mir vorkam, von kalten Schweißperlen überzogene Wand.
      (*AUSTERLITZ* 41G, EMPHASIS MINE)

52. And then, again, the narrator places his forehead against the iron band of the medical equipment (*Austerlitz* 38E, 60G) at the ophthalmologist's and also leans his head against the wall at the Great Eastern Hotel (*Austerlitz* 39E, 61G) where, soon thereafter, he meets Austerlitz again after twenty years.

53. As they do both on the ferry they share back to England and in scene of Van Valckenborch's painting of ice-skating on the Schelde, as Austerlitz describes it to the narrator.

54. The reader doesn't know this yet. Austerlitz describes his crisis only later in the book, although it took place several years before this encounter.

55.   Ich befand mich damals gerade in einiger Unruhe, weil ich beim Heraussuchen einer Anschrift aus dem Telephonbuch bemerkt hatte, daß, sozusagen über Nacht, die Sehkraft meines rechten Auges fast gänzlich geschwunden war. Auch wenn ich den Blick von der vor mir aufgeschlagenen Seite abhob und auf die gerahmten Photographien an der Wand richtete, sah ich mit dem rechten Auge nur eine Reihe dunkler, nach

oben und unten seltsam verzerrter Formen—die mir bis ins einzelne vertrauten Figuren und Landschaften hatten sich aufgelöst, unterschieds-
los, in eine bedrohliche schwarze Schraffur.

(*AUSTERLITZ* 54–55G)

56. We have seen this theme at work in Sebald's writings since the opening
chapter, "Like the Snow on the Alps." In a 1992 interview Sebald spoke of
his own fears, of "this feeling of being blinded [*Blendung*], the fear of no
longer being able to see" ("Auf ungeheuer dünnem Eis" 74).

57. As laden as the name *Gregor* seems with unlikely Kafkan overtones, Zdeněk
Gregor maintained, at the time of this writing, a place in what we call reality—or at least a virtual place on the Web. After all, what difference would
there be in Sebald? (The entry was subsequently modified, for who can
trust to the stability of the Net?)

Zdenek J Gregor. Area(s) of specialism/subspecialism: Vitreoretinal Surgery and Medical Retina. (diabetic retinopathy, macular surgery, retinal
detachment . . .)

58. Retina: from the Latin RETE = net.

59. "[Es] herrsche weitgehend Unklarheit, sagte Zdenek Gregor. Man wisse ei-
gentlich nur, daß sie fast ausschließlich auftrete bei Männern mittleren
Alters, die zuviel mit Schreiben und Lesen beschäftigt seien. Im Anschluß
an diese Konsultation mußte zur genaueren Bestimmung der schadhaften
Stelle in der Retina noch . . . eine Reihe photographischer Aufnahmen meiner Augen oder vielmehr . . . des Augenhintergrunds durch die Iris, die Pu-
pille und den Glaskörper hindurch [gemacht werden]" (*Austerlitz* 59–60G).

60. The technical assistant assigned to this task, an exceptionally noble man
who wore a white turban (*Austerlitz* 38E, 60G), has an uncanny resemblance
to the gatekeeper of Austerlitz's past, the porter at the Liverpool Street Station who also wore a snow white turban (*Austerlitz* 132E, 196G) and who
opens to view for Austerlitz the scene of his first arrival from Prague on the
Kindertransport.

61. Ich bildete mir ein, ich sähe dort draußen in der zunehmenden Dunkelheit die von ungezählten Straßen und Bahnwegen durchfurchten Areale
der Stadt, wie sie sich ostwärts und nordwärts übereinanderschoben, ein
Häuserriff über das nächste und übernächste und so fort . . . und daß nun
auf diesen riesigen steinernen Auswuchs der Schnee fallen würde . . . bis
alles begraben und zugedeckt wäre . . . London a lichen mapped on mild
clays and its rough circle without purpose . . . Einen ebensolchen, an seinem Rand ins Ungefähre übergehenden Kreis zeichnete Zdenek Gregor
auf ein Blatt Papier, als er mir . . . die Ausdehnung der grauen Zone in
meinem rechten Auge zu veranschaulichen suchte.

(*AUSTERLITZ* 58–59G)

62. Watts, "Fragment."

63. This is, perhaps, a visual metaphor for Sebald's insistence that all must be narrated indirectly.

64. There is, for example, no correct correspondence between the number of windows the childhood house in Wales appears to have from the outside and how many actually allow access to the view of an outside from within.

65. The praise of Marcel Proust's *À la recherche du temps perdu* is suggested, perhaps, by the last lines of the book that inscribe the name of Lob, Marcel de St. Nazaire (*Austerlitz* 298E, 421G).

66.   Weiter in der Geschichte Moses, sagte Austerlitz, hat besonders der Abschnitt mich angezogen, in dem berichtet wird, wie die Kinder Israel eine furchtbare Einöde durchqueren. . . . Ich . . . versenkte mich, alles um mich her vergessend, in eine ganzseitige Illustration, in der die Wüste Sinai mit ihren kahlen, ineinander verschobenen Bergrücken und dem grau gestrichelten Hintergrund, den ich manchmal für das Meer und manchmal für den Luftraum gehalten habe, ganz der Gegend glich in der ich aufgewachsen bin. Tatsächlich, sagte Austerlitz bei einer späteren Gelegenheit, als er die walisische Kinderbibel vor mir aufschlug, wußte ich mich unter den winzigen Figuren, die das Lager bevölkern, an meinem richtigen Ort. Jeden Quadratzoll der mir gerade in ihrer Vertrautheit unheimlich erscheinenden Abbildung habe ich durchforscht. In einer etwas helleren Fläche an der steil abstürzenden Bergseite zur Rechten glaubte ich, einen Steinbruch zu erkennen und in den gleichmäßig geschwungenen Linien darunter die Geleise einer Bahn. Am meisten aber gab mir der umzäunte Platz in der Mitte zu denken und der zeltartige Bau am hinteren Ende, über dem sich eine weiße Rauchwolke erhebt. Was damals auch in mir vorgegangen sein mag, das Lager der Hebräer in dem Wüstengebirge war mir näher als das mir mit jedem Tag unbegreiflicher werdende Leben in Bala, so wenigstens, sagte Austerlitz, dünkt es mir heute.

   (*AUSTERLITZ* 85–88G)

67. *Forschung* (research) has a strange resonance throughout the work as a failed attempt at restitution and connection—and not only in relation to Austerlitz's writings on the history of architecture: as when Austerlitz speaks of his failure to research his past—"that I had blocked off the investigation [*Erforschung*] of my most distant past for so many years, not on principle, to be sure, but still of my own accord" (*Austerlitz* 339G), or when Vera's *Nachforschung* to trace the family didn't work, or when Austerlitz speaks of the unfathomable connections (*unerforschliche Zusammenhänge*, a phrase omitted in the English translation) of objects in the Antikos Bazar window (*Austerlitz* 285G).

68. "Jedenfalls war eines Tages dann unter der Post diese Ansichtskarte aus den zwanziger oder dreißiger Jahren, die eine weiße Zeltkolonie zeigte in der ägyptischen Wüste, ein Bild aus einer von niemandem mehr erinnerten Kampagne, auf dessen Rückseite nichts stand als *Saturday 19 March, Alderney Street*, ein Fragezeichen und ein großes *A* für Austerlitz" (*Austerlitz* 173–74G).

69. "Nein, man sah auch, so sagte Věra, berichtete Maximilian, aus der Vogelschau eine im Morgengrauen bis gegen den Horizont reichende Stadt von weißen Zelten, aus denen, sowie es ein wenig licht wurde, einzeln, paarweise und in kleinen Gruppen die Deutschen hervorkamen und sich in einem schweigsamen, immer enger sich schließenden Zug alle in dieselbe Richtung bewegten, als folgten sie einem höheren Ruf und seien, nach langen Jahren in der Wüste, nun endlich auf dem Weg ins Gelobte Land" (*Austerlitz* 247–48G).

70. J. J. Long notes the return of the figure of the tent in *Austerlitz* (Long, *W. G. Sebald,* 164).

71. They are like the Nazi followers in the earlier passage who go singly, in couples, and in groups.

72. Nowhere is the capacity for the shift of the network from plan to confusion clearer than in Austerlitz's description of a scholar's work in the Paris Bibliothèque Nationale:

> I went daily to the Bibliothèque Nationale . . . and usually remained in my place there until evening . . . losing myself in the small print of the footnotes to the works I was reading, in the books I found mentioned in those notes, then in the footnotes to those books in their own turn, and so escaping from factual, scholarly description of reality to the strangest of details, in a kind of continual regression expressed in the form of my own marginal remarks and glosses, which increasingly diverged into the most varied and impenetrable of ramifications.
>
> (*AUSTERLITZ* 260E, 370–71G)

73. Presner shows this both by way of extended theoretical reflections on the nature of memory and narrative in Sebald and also by way of specific readings in *Austerlitz*. His commentary on Austerlitz at Breendonk as he speaks of the experience of Jean Améry is a particularly beautiful example: Presner, *Mobile Modernity,* 266–68.

74. This language of the river and its flow that is about to become so central to Austerlitz's critique of linear time continues into the next lines: "Then we walked the rest of the way in silence, going on downstream from Wapping and Shadwell to the quiet basins which reflect the towering office blocks of the Docklands area, and so to the Foot Tunnel running under the bend in the river" (*Austerlitz* 98E, 147–48G).

75. Wenn Newton gemeint hat, sagte Austerlitz und deutete durch das Fenster hinab auf den im letzten Widerschein des Tages gleißenden Wasserbogen, . . . wenn Newton wirklich gemeint hat, die Zeit sei ein Strom wie die Themse, wo ist dann der Ursprung der Zeit und in welches Meer mündet sie endlich ein? Jeder Strom ist, wie wir wissen, notwendig zu beiden Seiten begrenzt. Was aber wären, so gesehen, die Ufer der Zeit? Wie wären ihre spezifischen Eigenschaften, die etwa denen des Wassers entsprächen, das flüssig ist, ziemlich schwer und durchscheinend? In welcher Weise unterscheiden sich Dinge, die in die Zeit eingetaucht sind, von solchen, die nie berührt wurden von ihr? Was heißt es, daß die Stunden des Lichts und der Dunkelheit im gleichen Kreis angezeigt werden? Warum steht die Zeit an einem Ort ewig still und verrauscht und überstürzt sich an einem andern? Könnte man nicht sagen, sagte Austerlitz, daß die Zeit durch die Jahrhunderte und Jahrtausende selber ungleichzeitig gewesen ist?

    (*AUSTERLITZ* 150–151G)

76. Und unter all diesen Symbolbildern, sagte Austerlitz, stehe an höchster Stelle die durch Zeiger und Zifferblatt vertretene Zeit. An die zwanzig Meter oberhalb der . . . Treppe . . . befinde sich genau dort, wo im Pantheon in direkter Verlängerung des Portals das Bildnis des Kaisers zu sehen war, die Uhr; als Statthalterin der neuen Omnipotenz rangiere sie noch über dem Wappen des Königs und dem Wahlspruch *Eendracht maakt macht*. Von dem Zentralpunkt, den das Uhrwerk im Antwerpener Bahnhof einnehme, ließen sich die Bewegungen sämtlicher Reisender überwachen, und umgekehrt müßten die Reisenden alle zu der Uhr aufblicken und seien gezwungen, ihre Handlungsweise auszurichten nach ihr.

    (*AUSTERLITZ* 21–22G)

Earlier, in the Antwerp station, Austerlitz declares the buffet attendant the goddess of past time. Behind her a clock, decoratively one with the insignias of power, performs repeated executions.

And on the wall behind her, under the lion crest of the kingdom of Belgium, there was indeed a mighty clock, the dominating feature of the buffet, with a hand measuring some six feet traveling round a dial which had once been gilded. . . . During the pauses in our conversation we both noticed what an endless length of time went by before another minute had passed, and how alarming seemed the movement of that hand, which resembled a sword of justice, even though we were expecting it every time it jerked forward, slicing off the next one-sixtieth of an hour from the future and coming to a halt with such a menacing after-quiver that one's heart almost stopped.

(*AUSTERLITZ* 8–9E, 16–17G)

77. "Es war für mich von Anfang an erstaunlich, wie Austerlitz seine Gedanken beim Reden verfertigte, wie er sozusagen aus der Zerstreutheit heraus die ausgewogensten Sätze entwickeln konnte, und wie für ihn die erzähleri-sche Vermittlung seiner Sachkenntnisse die schrittweise Annäherung an eine Art Metaphysik der Geschichte gewesen ist, in der das Erinnerte noch einmal lebendig wurde" (*Austerlitz* 22–23G).

78. "Er deutete auf das breite, in der Morgensonne blinkende Wasser hinaus und sprach davon, daß auf einem gegen Ende des 16. Jahrhunderts . . . ge-malten Bild die zugefrorene Schelde vom jenseitigen Ufer aus zu sehen sei. . . . und dort draußen auf dem Strom, auf den wir jetzt vierhundert Jahre später hinausblicken, sagte Austerlitz, vergnügen sich die Antwerpe-ner auf dem Eis" (*Austerlitz* 23–24G).

79. Im Vordergrund, gegen den rechten Bildrand zu, ist eine Dame zu Fall gekommen. Sie trägt ein kanariengelbes Kleid. . . . Wenn ich nun dort hi-nausschaue und an dieses Gemälde und seine winzigen Figuren denke, dann kommt es mir vor, als sei der von Lucas van Valckenborch darge-stellte Augenblick niemals vergangen, als sei die kanariengelbe Dame gerade jetzt erst gestürzt oder in Ohnmacht gesunken . . . als geschähe das kleine, von den meisten Betrachtern gewiß übersehene Unglück im-mer wieder von neuem, als höre es nie mehr auf und als sei es durch nichts und von niemandem mehr gutzumachen.

    (*AUSTERLITZ* 24G)

80. Alle Momente unseres Lebens scheinen mir dann in einem einzigen Raum beisammen, ganz als existierten die zukünftigen Ereignisse be-reits und harrten nur darauf, daß wir uns endlich in ihnen einfinden, so wie wir uns, einer einmal angenommenen Einladung folgend zu einer bestimmten Stunde einfinden in einem bestimmten Haus. Und wäre es nicht denkbar, fuhr Austerlitz fort, daß wir auch in der Vergangenheit, in dem, was schon gewesen und größtenteils ausgelöscht ist, Verabredun-gen haben und dort Orte und Personen aufsuchen müssen, die, quasi jenseits der Zeit, in einem Zusammenhang stehen mit uns?

    (*AUSTERLITZ* 367G)

    In another passage time also gives way to space and the promise of the interpenetration of the present and the past. "It does not seem to me, said Austerlitz, that we understand the laws governing the return of the past, but I feel more and more as if time did not exist at all, only various spaces interlocking according to the rules of a higher form of stereometry, be-tween which the living and the dead can move back and forth as they like" (*Austerlitz* 185E, 269G).

81. See Presner's beautiful reading of three photographs in relation to this sense of layering: Presner, *Mobile Modernity*, 279–82.

82. Manchmal, sagte Lemoine, sagte Austerlitz, sei es ihm als spüre er he-
roben die Strömung der Zeit um seine Schläfen und seine Stirn, doch
wahrscheinlich, setzte er hinzu, ist das nur ein Reflex des Bewußtseins,
das sich im Laufe der Jahre in meinem Kopf ausgebildet hat von den verschiedenen Schichten, die dort drunten auf dem Grund der Stadt überei-
nandergewachsen sind. Auf dem Ödland zwischen dem Rangiergelände
der Gare d'Austerlitz und dem Pont Tolbiac, auf dem heute diese Biblio-
thek sich erhebt, war beispielsweise bis zum Kriegsende ein großes Lager, in dem die Deutschen das gesamte von ihnen aus den Wohnungen
der Pariser Juden geholte Beutegut zusammenbrachten.

(AUSTERLITZ 406-10G)

83. Throughout *Austerlitz* the repeated stratification of time arouses a sense of
"disjunction and of having no ground beneath [one's] feet" (*Austerlitz* 109E,
161G).

84. This is the title of the 1956 movie by Alain Resnais about the Bibliothèque Nationale: *The Complete Memory of the World;* see *Austerlitz*
286E, 404G.

85. Es war gegen halb vier Uhr nachmittags und die Dämmerung senkte sich
herab, als ich die Sternwarte mit Austerlitz verließ. Eine gewisse Zeitlang
standen wir noch auf dem ummauerten Vorplatz. Man hörte in der Ferne
das dumpfe Mahlen der Stadt und in der Höhe das Dröhnen der großen
Maschinen, die in Abständen von kaum mehr als einer Minute sehr nied-
rig und unglaublich langsam, wie es mir erschien, aus dem Nordosten
über Greenwich hereinschwebten und westwärts nach Heathrow hinaus
wieder verschwanden.

(AUSTERLITZ 152G)

86. Und als man diese Paravents . . . im Herbst 1951 oder 1952 entfernte und
er zum erstenmal seit zehn Jahren das Kinderzimmer wieder betrat, da,
sagte Ashman, hätte nicht viel gefehlt, und er wäre um seinen Verstand
gekommen. Beim bloßen Anblick des Eisenbahnzugs mit den Wag-
gons der Great Western Railway und der Arche, aus der paarweise die
braven, aus der Flut geretteten Tiere herausschauten, sei es ihm gewesen, als öffne sich vor ihm der Abgrund der Zeit . . . und ehe er auch
nur wußte, was er tat, habe er draußen auf dem hinteren Hof gestanden und mehrmals mit seiner Flinte auf das Uhrtürmchen der Remise
geschossen.

(AUSTERLITZ 160-61G)

87. Es war, als sei hier die Zeit, die sonst doch unwiderruflich verrinnt, ste-
hengeblieben, als lägen die Jahre, die wir hinter uns gebracht haben,
noch in der Zukunft, und ich entsinne mich, sagte Austerlitz, daß Hi-

lary, als wir mit Ashman in dem Billardzimmer von Iver Grove gestanden sind, eine Bemerkung machte über die sonderbare Verwirrung der
Gefühle, die selbst einen Historiker überkämen in einem solchen, vom
Fluß der Stunden und Tage und vom Wechsel der Generationen so lange
abgeschlossen gewesenen Raum.

(AUSTERLITZ 160G).

88. Jacobson, *Heshel's Kingdom.*

89. Die gesamte von Heschel auf den Enkel gekommene Hinterlassenschaft
besteht aus einem Taschenkalender, einem russischen Ausweispaper, einem abgewetzten Brillenfutteral, in welchem nebst den Brillengläsern,
ein verblaßtes, halb schon zerfallenes Fetzchen Seide liegt, und aus einer
Studiophotographie, die Heschel zeigt. . . . Sein eines Auge, so wenigstens scheint es auf dem Einband des Buchs, ist verschattet; im anderen
kann man, als ein weißes Fleckchen, das Lebenslicht noch erkennen, das
erlosch, als Heschel . . . an einem Herzschlag verstarb.

(AUSTERLITZ 419G)

90. They appear both in *Austerlitz* and elsewhere in Sebald's writings. See chapters 6 and 7 where one of the eyes of a painted dog lies in shadow.

91. "Yes, there . . . are an incredible number of hidden, obliterated citations,"
Sebald says to his interlocutor Walther Krause ("Auf ungeheuer dünnem
Eis" 152), referring to a line borrowed from Büchner's *Woyzeck*. And it is
here he makes clear the attention he pays to the smallest nuances of linguistic shadings, emphasizing as he does the power of the grammatical error in Büchner's sentence: "Ja, wenn einer gelehnt steht an den Strom der
Zeit." We already touched upon the role of citation while reading "Air War
and Literature" as we thought through the role of the Halberstadt photographer and Sebald's gesture of closing his texts with a citation.

92. 1941 kamen [die Forts] in deutsche Hand, auch das berüchtigte Fort IX,
in dem zeitweise Kommandostellen der Wehrmacht sich einrichteten
und wo in den folgenden drei Jahren mehr als dreißigtausend Menschen
ums Leben gebracht wurden. . . . Bis in den Mai 1944 hinein, als der Krieg
längst verloren war, kamen Transporte aus dem Westen nach Kaunas.
Die letzten Nachrichten der in die Verliese der Festung Gesperrten be-
zeugen es. Nous sommes neuf cents Français schreibt Jacobson, habe
einer von ihnen in die kalte Kalkwand des Bunkers geritzt. Andere hinterließen uns bloß ein Datum und eine Ortsangabe mit ihren Namen;
Lob, Marcel, de St. Nazaire; Wechsler, Abram, de Limoges; Max Stern,
Paris, 18.5.44.

(AUSTERLITZ 421G)

93. See Andrea Köhler, among others: Köhler, "Penetrating the Dark," 99–100. As we have seen elsewhere, Sebald plays with the coincidence of dates quite often. One of the richest examples is the passage about the narrator's visit to Michael Hamburger in *The Rings of Saturn.*

94. Jacobson, *Heshel's Kingdom,* 161.

95. As any reader of Sebald knows, the eighteenth of May appears elsewhere in his works—In *After Nature* see, for example section VII of "Like the snow on the Alps."

96. It is presumably a question of Adler's *Theresienstadt.*

97. Sebald often seems to pigeonhole evil as the highly rational and organized. Here is the longer version of the passage cited earlier: "I saw balance sheets, registers of the dead, lists of every imaginable kind, and endless rows of numbers and figures, which must have served to reassure the administrators that nothing ever escaped their notice. And whenever I think of the museum in Terezín now, said Austerlitz, I see the framed ground plan of the star-shaped fortifications . . . the model of a world developed by reason and regulated in all conceivable respects" (*Austerlitz* 199, 287–88G).

98. This is so despite the temptation to contrast, for example, the rigidly organized file room at Theresienstadt (*Austerlitz* 284–85E, 402–3G) and Austerlitz's office with its endearing professorial helter-skelter (*Austerlitz* 32E, 51G).

99. "I remember to this day how easily I could grasp what he called his tentative ideas when he talked about the architectural style of the capitalist era, a subject which he said had fascinated him since his own student days, speaking in particular of the compulsive sense of order and the tendency towards monumentalism evident in law courts and penal institutions, railway stations and stock exchanges, opera houses and lunatic asylums, and the dwellings built to rectangular grid patterns for the labor force" (*Austerlitz* 33E, 52G). Still, the description of the Palace of Justice in Brussels, an architectural monstrosity in the style of the capitalist era, also, it seems, suffers from a compulsive sense of disorder (*Austerlitz* 29–30E, 46–47G).

100. It would be easy enough to try to organize not only text but also images from Austerlitz according to such an order: the different architectural plans, for example, of fortresses—Breendonk (*Austerlitz* 21E and 24E, 3G and 40G), Saarlouis (*Austerlitz* 15E, 26G), Theresienstadt (*Austerlitz* 234–35E, 336–37G)—in contrast to the pixelated images from the slowed-down version of the Theresienstadt film (*Austerlitz* 248–49E, 354–55G; 251E, 358G). This could be extended in comparisons of such doubles as the blanket of snow-white anemone blooms in Prague to the disturbing image of intertwined roots that precedes it (*Austerlitz* 163E, 238–39G).

6. DÉJÀ VU OR . . .

1. "In order to call on [death] the painter had to pass over the border. On the way to the other side. . . ." ("As Day and Night" 86E, 180G).
2. The accident that took Sebald's life left behind, actually, not one but two shorter projects published in close proximity to the final major work. In their questioning of the relation between the text and what one observes, they are remarkably similar both to *Austerlitz* and also to one another, yet also at odds with one another. *Unerzählt* appeared in 2003. Reminiscent of the first images in *Austerlitz*, thirty-three pairs of eyes by Jan Peter Tripp, who also determined the order of the pages (Köhler, "Penetrating the Dark," 97), stare out, accompanied by thirty-three brief poems by Sebald, written between 1999 and 2001. An English edition (Sebald and Tripp, *Unrecounted*) with translations by Michael Hamburger, came out soon thereafter (2004). Shortly before his death in 2001, his collaborative work with Tess Jaray, *For Years Now*, had been published: *Poems by W. G. Sebald, Images by Tess Jaray.*

Most of the poems appeared in both volumes. No doubt, they raise once again Sebald's question—What's the point of literature?—and raise it more profoundly if we juxtapose the two volumes. The abstract artwork of Jaray might consist of rows of repeated dots or of small marks suggesting woven material or, say, evenly bespeckled rectangles repeated within a larger enclosure. No act of imagination can with any certitude take these out of an abstract field into a scene of representation. We cannot help but link these figures with the flecks and hatch marks of Austerlitz's world and with the quadrilateral of Browne's quincunx and the figure of woven cloth in *Rings of Saturn*. The Tripp volume, however, seems at least to land us squarely in clear-sighted, realistic reproduction, bordering, as Tripp's work so often does, on the illusion of photographic fidelity. That it is the organ of sight that is figured here has an inescapable irony. One tends to place Tripp's images on the side of clarity, order, representation in its most seductive form. Sebald's essay "Like Day and Night" is about this if nothing else. Still, on the cover of *Unrecounted* the image of Sebald gives us the whole show and unsettles that proclivity: not just his eyes but a full sense of the man, it reveals, as Tripp's work more rarely does, the strokes and marks of the artist's hand, perhaps a hatchwork after all.

The two books have this in common: each poem of Sebald alternates with an image produced by the artist. In *Unrecounted* text and image lie on facing pages, as though to solicit the obvious response. *For Years Now* presents a more complex pattern: blank page, poem, double-paged image—alternating with a poem facing a single-page image. This purposeful choice of repeated form, first confronting text with an emptiness and then with a visual figure, reminds us there is no steadfast, implicit claim of juxtaposing text with its apparent illustration or image with its apparent textual description. It suggests that the written word may or may not have a counterpart in a more tangible world—and, even when it does, that relation is at best a mystery. A glance at the abstract art in *For Years Now* could have told us so, though its wit now and again teases with a suggested correlation to the text ("my grandfather's coffin," for example, juxtaposed with a light brown shape suggestive of that form). In *Unrecounted* this is made all the more complex: we strain toward the possibility of linking image and text, a possibility made infinitely richer by the accompanying list: the names of the writers, artists, scraps of pilfered artworks, and even that of Maurice (Moritz), that most loyal of pet dogs, to whom the eyes presumably belong. They are displayed in the table of contents, an excuse to believe text and image purposeful. Still, Andrea Köhler, in the beautiful essay entitled "Penetrating the Dark" ("Die Durchdringung des Dunkels") that closes the volume, reminds us of Tripp's and Sebald's intentions: "their declared aim was that text and image should not explain, let alone illustrate, each other but enter into a dialogue that would leave each his own space for reverberations" (Köhler, "Penetrating the Dark," 97).

Perhaps the most instructive meditation on those spaces for reverberation is to be found in the translator's note of Michael Hamburger: it prefaces the English edition of *Unrecounted*. He casts a veil of uncertainty over the whole project, even as he introduces it, and one feels his sense of shock. A number of the texts in *Unrecounted*, he warns us from the outset, overlap with those in *For Years Now*. Moreover, it was Tripp who asked Hamburger to translate (not Sebald). Hamburger speaks guardedly of "enigmas, conflicts and contradictions" (Hamburger, "Translator's Note," 1) in the last years of Sebald's life that might explain the duplicity of the project. That Hamburger suggests a moral lapse is perhaps understandable, particularly from his own personal point of view. "[Sebald] never so much as mentioned the writing of these miniatures to me and gave me no copy of *For Years Now* (ibid., 2), he goes on to write. His "total reticence about these texts" (ibid.), "his collaboration with two very different artists," begins to bespeak a betrayal. "The mere duplication of some of these texts for the two projects is out of character in the Max I knew, scrupulous as he was in all his dealings and so meticulous over the editing of his writings that he spent hundreds of hours on the checking of their English versions" (ibid., 1). That betrayal extends, then, to the question of translation and to its theory as fidelity to an original. "Again, I had to establish for myself that the English versions in *For Years Now* were done by Sebald himself, with a freedom or latitude I could not allow myself as translator of the German texts. No translator's name appears" (ibid., 2). Sebald's translations of his own German originals show a deviation that Hamburger could never have permitted himself. Thus, whereas earlier translation projects always required the careful oversight and approval of the author, now different translated versions of the same German poem are striking in their dissimilarity. The trajectory of the lament goes from (in)fidelity to a friend, to lack of fidelity in translation, and now, in this rather brilliant reflection on to the relation of literature and life, a question of the responsibility of the literary work to its source of inspiration.

What "distinguished Sebald the imaginative writer from Sebald the scholar" was a "freedom from literalness" (ibid., 3). Hamburger himself had noted that in the imprecise account of their meeting described in *Rings of Saturn* where factual accuracy bows to the demand of "such departures from the source material," for this is "the very nature of all Sebald's [imaginative] writings" (ibid., 3). Thus Hamburger claims himself happy "to be a character in [Sebald's] work of fiction" (ibid., 4). One senses less joy or at least greater puzzlement in the contradictory sense of the seemingly same piece in the two volumes of poetry. In the Tess Jaray volume, "stars . . . guide us / only under / a dark sky" (*For Years Now* 48), whereas, true to the German text, Hamburger is forced to write "only / in brightest daylight" (ibid., 3). Michael Bates ("Unerzählt") notes other wild deviations between the volumes. Can night and day be interchangeable?

We expect too much, or is it too little, of a literary text—when we imagine that it might reliably record and explain the world (visualized or lived) or, at the very least, as a translation, echo its textual source. This has much to do with the works that came before and is surely the complex lesson of reading Sebald's last two volumes side by side. They seem to reprise the clarity of sight in contrast to the flecks and hatch marks that in *Austerlitz* challenge the narrator's vision and challenge the sanity of his character. The volumes themselves are no standard-bearers of either view. They come as something of an epitaph or, if not that, they come as what Sebald, writing of Tripp, spoke of as a *Hinterlassenschaft*, an estate ("As Day and Night" 80E, 174G). He left them behind, though for which inheritors it is difficult to say. Perhaps we have to relinquish, as Sebald goes on to suggest, perhaps we must give up not our will to know but what Sebald spoke of as our *all too facile* will to know.

3. *Logis in einem Landhaus* first appeared in 1998 but "Wie Tag und Nacht" was first published in 1993 in Tripp, *Die Aufzählung der Schwierigkeiten.*

4. Und vorab als Leser entrichte ich darum im Folgenden meinen Tribut an die vorangegangenen Kollegen in Form einiger ausgedehnter und sonst keinen besonderen Anspruch erhebenden Marginalien. Daß am Ende ein Aufsatz steht über einen Maler, das hat auch seine Ordnung, nicht nur weil Jan Peter Tripp und ich eine ziemliche Zeitlang in Oberstdorf in dieselbe Schule gegangen sind und weil Keller und Walser uns beiden gleichviel bedeuten, sondern auch weil ich an seinen Bildern gelernt

habe, daß man weit in die Tiefe hineinschauen muß, daß die Kunst ohne
das Handwerk nicht auskommt und daß man mit vielen Schwierigkeiten
zu rechnen hat beim Aufzählen der Dinge.
(*LOGIS IN EINEM LANDHAUS* 7G)

5. It was Thomas Fries, who, in a superb paper given in Zurich in spring of
   2008, made me aware of the strangeness of this phrase, the modesty of
   Sebald speaking of his own commentary as "marginalia" combined with
   claiming himself the colleague of such pivotal figures in world literature.
6. Michael Hamburger translates Sebald's title as "As Day and Night, Chalk
   and Cheese: On the Pictures of Jan Peter Tripp" because, as he explains in
   his translator's note, as chalk and cheese is the British idiom that would
   best render the German "wie Tag und Nacht." The American usage "as different as night and day" is much closer to the German (Hamburger, "Translator's Note," 6–7).
7. Sebald, "As Day and Night" and "Wie Tag und Nacht."
8. "Und das in einen Text (oder in ein Bild) einmontierte Zitat zwingt uns . . .
   zur Durchsicht unserer Kenntnisse anderer Texte und Bilder und unserer
   Kenntnisse der Welt. Das wiederum erfordert Zeit. Indem wir sie aufwen-
   den, treten wir ein in die erzählte Zeit und in die Zeit der Kultur" ("Wie Tag
   und Nacht" 184G).
9. A counterpart in this, no doubt, to Van Gogh's *Peasant Shoes.*
10. Throughout the essay Sebald plays on *Erklären* and *Erklärung* (explain and
    explanation or declaration). The most obvious instance is the German of
    Déclaration de guerre, Kriegserklärung (186G). We see elsewhere the weight
    Sebald places on *Erklärung.* See chapter 7.

11.   Versuchen wir das zuletzt zu zeigen an dem 370 x 220 cm messenden Bild
       'La déclaration de guerre', auf welchem ein feines Paar Damenschuhe zu
       sehen ist, das auf einem gekachelten Fußboden steht. Das blaßblau-na-
       turweiße Ornament der Kacheln, die grauen Linien der Verfugung, das
       Rautennetz der Bleiverglasung eines Fensters, das vom Sonnenlicht über
       den mittleren Teil des Bildes gebreitet wird, in welchem die schwarzen
       Schuhe zwischen zwei Schattenbereichen stehen, all das ergibt zusam-
       men ein geometrisches Muster von einer mit Worten nicht zu beschrei-
       benden Komplexität.
       ("WIE TAG UND NACHT" 184–85G)

12. We might think of this as well as the struggle between a positive presence
    of an object (the tile, the shoes) and the absence of an object (the window
    frames). Those frames leave their mark as shadow, the light they refuse to
    let pass.
13. "Aus diesem, den Schwierigkeitsgrad der verschiedenen Verhältnisse, Ver-
    bindungen und Verstrickungen illustrierenden Muster und dem mysteriö-

sen Paar schwarzer Schuhe entsteht eine Art *Bilderrätsel*, das der *Betrachter*, der die *Vorgeschichte* nicht kennt, kaum wird auflösen können. Welcher Frau haben die Schuhe gehört? Wohin ist sie gekommen? Sind die Schuhe übergegangen in den Besitz eines anderen?" ("Wie Tag und Nacht" 185G, emphasis mine).

To be sure, there is the throwaway answer that follows: "Or, ultimately, are they nothing more than the paradigm of that fetish which the painter is forced to make out of everything he produces?" ("As Day and Night" 91E, 185G). But this formal explanation, held onto for a moment, completely disappears.

14. Zwei Jahre später allerdings rückt der Maler sein Rätselbild ein Stückchen weiter wenigstens in die Öffentlichkeit. In einem Werk von bedeutend kleinerem Format (100 x 145 cm) taucht das große Bild noch einmal auf, nicht bloß als Zitat, sondern als vermittelnder Gegenstand der Darstellung. Es hängt, die oberen zwei Drittel der Leinwand ausfüllend, offenbar jetzt an seinem Platz, und vor ihm, vor der ‚Déclaration de guerre' sitzt, vom Betrachter abgewandt, seitwärts auf einem weißgepolsterten Mahagonisessel eine flammend rothaarige Frau. Elegant ist sie gekleidet, aber doch jemand, der müd ist am Abend von des Tages Last. Sie hat einen ihrer Schuhe—und es sind dieselben, die sie betrachtet auf dem großen Bild—ausgezogen.

("WIE TAG UND NACHT" 185-86G)

15. "Das photographische Bild verwandelt die Wirklichkeit in eine Tautologie. . . . Roland Barthes sah in dem inzwischen omnipräsenten Mann mit der Kamera einen Agenten des Todes und in den Photographien so etwas wie Relikte des fortwährend absterbenden Lebens" ("Wie Tag und Nacht" 178G).

16. All this assumes, of course, that the woman's shoes were the source for Tripp's first painting, its prehistory. Ultimately, can one say that this is the case? The painting of the two shoes, after all, preexisted the painting that incorporates it. Both are paintings. Perhaps the woman is the result of the pair of shoes; that is, she is their pretext.

17. "Ursprünglich, so habe ich mir sagen lassen, hat sie diesen ausgezogenen Schuh in der linken Hand gehalten, dann war er rechts neben dem Sessel am Boden gelegen, und schließlich war er ganz verschwunden" ("Wie Tag und Nacht" 186G)

18. "Die Frau mit dem einen Schuh, mit sich und der rätselhaften Kriegserklärung allein, allein bis auf den treuen Hund an ihrer Seite, der sich freilich nicht interessiert für die gemalten Schuhe, sondern gerade herausschaut aus dem Bild und uns in die Augen . . ." ("Wie Tag und Nacht" 186G).

The dog is not true to the painted shoes—in the *Déclaration de guerre*. True to what, then? Not her. He looks at us. Nor is there any obvious sign of marriage (whose fidelity the dog might be a symbol of) as in van Eyck's painting of Arnolfini and his Giovanna Cenami.

19. *"Inzwischen* ist er *unterwegs* gewesen und hat eine Art Holzsandale herbeigebracht, aus dem 15. Jahrhundert beziehungsweise aus dem in der Londoner Nationalgalerie hängenden Hochzeitsbild, das Jan van Eyck 1434 . . . gemalt hat" ("Wie Tag und Nacht" 186–87G, emphasis mine).

20.   [Der Hund] hat eine Art Holzsandale herbeigebracht, aus dem 15. Jahrhundert beziehungsweise aus dem in der Londoner Nationalgalerie hängenden Hochzeitsbild, das Jan van Eyck 1434 für Giovanni Arnolfini und die ihm in morganatischer Ehe ,zur linken Hand' angetraute Giovanna Cenami gemalt hat zum Zeichen seiner Zeugenschaft. *Johannes de Eyck hic fuit* heißt es auf dem Rahmen des Rundspiegels, in dem die Szene auf Miniaturformat reduziert von rückwärts noch einmal zu sehen ist. Im Vordergrund, nahe dem linken unteren Bildrand, liegt die hölzerne Sandale, dieses seltsame Beweisstück, neben einem kleinen Hündchen, das in die Komposition hineingeraten ist wahrscheinlich als ein Symbol ehelicher Treue.

("WIE TAG UND NACHT" 187G)

21. Could this be a case of those divergences and differences that distinguish art from photography of which Sebald spoke earlier in the essay ("As Day and Night" 84–85E, 178–79G)?

22. In an interview of 1993, the same year that the essay on Tripp was first published, Sebald made the following remark, which suggests that the citation of van Eyck by Tripp is also metaphorical for his own work.

Moreover, in the case of painters, for example, to my mind, it is a long cultivated virtue that they refer to one another in their works, that they take over themes from a colleague in their own work as a gesture, so to speak, of reverence. And that is something that I also enjoy doing as a writer.

Außerdem ist es bei den Malern zum Beispiel eine seit langem gepflogene Tugend, meines Erachtens, daß sie sich in ihren Werken aufeinander beziehen, daß sie Motive aus dem einen Werk eines Kollegen in das eigene Werk übernehmen, sozusagen als Geste der Ehrerbietung. Und das ist etwas, was ich also auch sehr gerne mache als Schreibender.

("AUF UNGEHEUER DÜNNEM EIS" 97–98)

23. It is a double gaze of left and right eyes similar to that of the narrator in Austerlitz.

24. "Aufmerksam ist sein linkes (domestiziertes) Auge auf uns gerichtet; das rechte (wilde) hat um eine Spur weniger Licht, wirkt abseitig und fremd.

Und doch fühlen wir uns gerade von diesem überschatteten Auge durchschaut" ("Wie Tag und Nacht" 188G).
25. The English translation has the odd but interesting choice of "unrelatedly" here.
26. "Die *nature morte* ist bei Tripp . . . das Paradigma unserer Hinterlassenschaft. An ihr geht uns auf, was Maurice Merleau-Ponty . . . den 'regard préhumain' genannt hat, denn umgekehrt sind in solcher Malerei die Rollen des Betrachters und des betrachteten Gegenstands. Schauend gibt der Maler unser allzu leichtfertiges Wissen auf; unverwandt blicken die Dinge zu uns herüber. 'Action et passion si peu discernable . . . qu'on ne sait plus qui voit et qui est vu, qui peint et qui est peint'" ("Wie Tag und Nacht" 174G).
27. "Bedenkenswert daran scheint mir einzig . . . die . . . Vermutung, wonach die inhärente Qualität eines Bildes von Tripp, gerade in Anbetracht seiner, wie man meinen könnte, rein objektiven und affirmativen Beschaffenheit, sich wahrscheinlich nicht bestimmen läßt in der von allen Betrachtern unfehlbar bewunderten Identität mit der Wirklichkeit (oder ihrem photographischen Abzug), sondern in den weit weniger offensichtlichen Punkten der Abweichung und Differenz" ("Wie Tag und Nacht" 178G).

The almost identical phrase, but in the plural, "divergences and differences," appears a page later.

7. A CRITICAL EYE

1. It is Austerlitz who speaks of the possibility "that all moments of our life occupy the same space" (*Austerlitz*, 257E, 363G) or even that time does not exist at all, only various interlocking spaces (*Austerlitz* 185E, 265G). The narrator of *After Nature* tells us that figures in paintings step out of their frames to enter our world five centuries later, a jumping of centuries that the narrator of *Vertigo* also invokes. But for Sebald, whose literary activity spanned a scant decade and a half, justifications for reading his works side by side are perhaps in any case not necessary.
2. Several volumes of his interviews have been published: "Auf ungeheuer dünnem Eis" and Schwartz, *The Emergence of Memory.*
3. Talking with Andreas Isenschmid in 1990 about *Vertigo*, Sebald explains that the sections on Stendhal and Kafka were those he wrote first.

SEBALD: Ja, ja. Those were the first two, because as a writer literature was not my point of departure, rather, actually, literary criticism.
ISENSCHMID: Because you are a professor of German literature, as I might say once more.
SEBALD: And, given that, I have naturally certain reservations about setting out to fabricate, as you can probably imagine. That's a certain form of

cheating and an absolutely unscientific procedure which one shrinks away from. Thus to begin with I wrote these two first texts, Kafka and Stendhal ("Auf ungeheuer dünnem Eis" 64).

4. One need only read his scathing assessment of Kafka criticism. With a vituperative attack on the travesties of both scholarly endeavor and theory, he praises exclusively those critics who "[keep] to the facts alone and [refuse] to indulge in attempts at elucidation [*Erklärung*]" or the "fatal inclination to speculate about meaning [*Bedeutung*]" ("Kafka Goes to the Movies" 153–54E, 195–96G). What counts is "reconstructing a portrait of the author in his own time" ("Kafka Goes to the Movies" 154E, 196G). The remarkable, lengthy passage is cited below. How is it possible that the author could have written the lines that follow, around the same time as *Schwindel. Gefühle.*, a volume in which lengthy sections are devoted to both Stendhal and Kafka and in which the reading is hardly, simply, *sachlich*, realistic, matter-of-fact, objective? One might say the same for Sebald's writings on Matthaeus Grünewald in *After Nature* or Rembrandt in *Rings of Saturn*, not to mention Jan Peter Tripp, in which what we encounter is hardly criticism by way of reconstruction of a portrait of the author or painter. Still, this limited concept of the role of the critic is one that is always at play in Sebald's work.

> Unlike the general run of German critics, whose plodding studies regularly become a travesty of scholarship, and unlike the manufacturers of literary theory applying their astute minds to the difficulty of Kafka, Hanns Zischler confines himself to a restrained commentary which never tries to go beyond its particular subject. It is this restraint, keeping to the facts alone and refusing to indulge in attempts at elucidation, that we can now see, looking back, distinguishes the best of Kafka scholars. Today, if you pick up one of the many Kafka studies to have appeared since the 1950s, it is almost incredible to observe how much dust and mold have already accumulated on these secondary works, inspired as they are by the theories of existentialism, theology, psychoanalysis, structuralism, post-structuralism, reception aesthetics, or system criticism, and how unrewarding is the redundant verbiage on every page. Now and then, of course, you do find something different, for the conscientious and patient work of editors and factual commentators is in marked contrast to the chaff ground out in the mills of academia. To me at least—and I cannot claim to be entirely innocent of the fatal inclination to speculate about meanings—[those who] have concentrated mainly on reconstructing a portrait of the author in his own time, have made a greater contribution to elucidating the texts than those exegetes who dig around in them unscrupulously and often shamelessly.
>
> ("KAFKA GOES TO THE MOVIES" 153–54E, 195–96G)

One might look to a text like Judith Ryan's *The Novel After Theory* as a response to this. Ryan carefully and expressly sidesteps the notion of "mechanical translations of a theoretical model into the fictional mode" (ibid., 7) or the crass application of theory to the literary text. What she is after, rather, is to "show how novelists themselves engage with theory" (ibid., 5). She does this elegantly and convincingly as she reads Sebald's engagement with Deleuze and Guattari. The irony of Sebald's invective against theory in relation to Kafka is Ryan's revelation about Sebald's interest in those same theorists: "It is not clear to what extent Sebald knew other publications by the two theorists; the Kafka book is the only one of their works included among volumes from his private library currently housed in Marbach. He read and marked the Kafka book intensively. Careful study of his annotations reveals . . . how closely he read the book" (ibid.).

I would like to believe that the beautifully written and constructed essay by Mary Jacobus entitled "Pastoral, After History" might have escaped Sebald's cynicism about literary criticism. It is an essay that floats among Rilke, Michael Hamburger, Sebald's imaginary Michael Hamburger, Seamus Heaney's translations, Hoffmannsthal, Tacita Dean's film *Michael Hamburger,* and much else as well. She touches upon a number of Sebald's works, and one comes away feeling all the wiser (Jacobus, *Romantic Things,* 36–56).

5. See also Sebald's conversation with Joseph Cuomo in which he compares his own "form of unsystematic searching" with "the same way in which, say, a dog runs through a field" (Cuomo, "A Conversation with W. G. Sebald," 94).

6. On the relation between the photograph and verification that seems to convince people, the photo and a legitimization of the story, see Wachtel, "Ghost Hunter," 41.

7. Walkowitz, in *Cosmopolitan Style,* puts it this way: "And, second, there is the effort to generate, instead of judgment and order, an ethos of embodied uncertainty that is sometimes at odds with political action and the affects of critical theory" (169).

8. To conceive the function of photographs in Sebald simply as occupying two possible, polar positions—either as document or as falsification—is, of course, a blatant error, as this essay will go on to say. Marianne Hirsch's concept of "postmemory" (*The Generation of Postmemory*) takes us a long way in understanding the complexity of reading photographs. Her exceptional analysis of images in Sebald's *Austerlitz* in relation to Art Spiegelman's *Maus* (and these in relation to Roland Barthes) proves just how rich and problematic the uncertainty of images might be.

9. Speaking to Eleanor Wachtel of *The Emigrants,* Sebald says: "It's a form of prose fiction . . . dialogue plays hardly any part in it at all. Everything is related round various corners in a periscopic sort of way. In that sense it doesn't conform to the patterns that standard fiction has established.

There isn't an authorial narrator. And there are various limitations of this kind that seem to push the book into a special category. But what exactly to call it, I don't know" (Wachtel, "Ghost Hunter," 37). Later in the conversation Sebald calls it "a work of documentary fiction" (ibid., 39).

10. It is of course Kluge whom Sebald takes as his model for a "legitimate intellectual coming to terms with this German past." "This same getting closer to the past . . . is much clearer in the case of Alexander Kluge who has always been a model author for me, whose work about the German past I value very very highly and which in my estimation demonstrates the only line of a legitimate intellectual coming to terms with this German past" ("Auf ungeheuer dünnem Eis" 257).

11. It is worth returning to Austerlitz's account of his work in the Bibliothèque Nationale through regressive layers of footnotes: they move him from factual descriptions of reality to "the most varied and impenetrable of ramifications" (*Austerlitz* 260E).

12. We saw this in the ambiguities of works signed with different signatures; in the suggestion that Mathis Nithard and Matthaeus Grünewald might well have been one and the same; in a young Jewess who might at first have fallen in love with his "green-colored name"; and in Sebald's play with the fragments of the last name, *grün*, *Wald*, once the artist's end is in sight.

13. As they were in the diatribe against academic literary criticism in the essay "Kafka Goes to the Movies" ("Kafka im Kino").

14. For a rather remarkable and productive meditation on genre in Sebald's work, see Kilbourn, "The Question of Genre in Sebald's Prose."

15. Is it worth noting that Sebald writes the essay in 1993—just in the midst of his years of literary production? He wrote the first part of *After Nature* in 1986 and published *Austerlitz* in 2001.

16. There are elements of literary criticism in many of Sebald's works. Sebald says this himself with respect to the sections on Stendhal and Kafka in *Vertigo*. But we also find descriptions of literary and art works in *After Nature*, in *Vertigo*, in "Air War and Literature," and in *Rings of Saturn* as the narrator speaks of Rembrandt's famous painting, of Browne's *Garden of Cyrus*, and of Grimmelshausen's *Simplicissimus* and various postwar writers.

17. In *Rings of Saturn* Baldanders also offered a puzzle, the text whose solution was readable by the selection of the first and last letter of each word. The answer to the puzzle, of course, is an ironic commentary on the desire to solve the puzzle in the first place.

18. This is similar to the shift in *Austerlitz* from the As of Novelli, from the impaired vision of the narrator and the hatch marks that pervade the text, to the recovered memories of the prose fiction's unproblematic narrative in its central pages.

19. One needs to think this confrontation of Tripp's dog with the spectator in relation to the role of the photograph throughout Sebald's work. Over and

over images speak to and compel the observer. In a 1997 conversation with Christian Scholz, Sebald put it this way. "Yes, but in the dead hours of the day I have rummaged about in such a box. Doing that it has always struck me that an enormous call goes out from these pictures; a demand directed at the observer to tell or imagine to himself what one might be able to narrate taking these pictures as a point of departure" ("Auf ungeheuer dünnem Eis" 165).

It is not only that the images call on the observer to stand apart and tell of them, leaving her untouched; the images call us as well into their world. We saw this especially in *The Emigrants*. "This feeling I always have with photographs, that they exert a pull on the viewer and in this enormous way so to speak lure him out of the real world into an unreal world, that is into a world in which one doesn't exactly know how it is constituted, of which one however suspects that it exists" ("Auf ungeheuer dünnem Eis" 167).

20. This, too, of course, is something of a tale, since, in actuality, the "domesticated eye" looks askance and not directly at the spectator.

21. Like the right eye of the narrator in *Austerlitz* who is plagued with a menacing crosshatching.

22. The essay on Tripp was first published in 1993, *The Emigrants* in 1992.

23. The boundary between the observer and the object observed, which often appears as a pane of glass, but not always, is also challenged throughout Sebald's work. Sometimes that challenge comes with a sense of benign wonder, as in the opening lines of *After Nature*.

> Foremost at the picture's edge he stands
> above the world by a hand's breadth
> and is about to step over the frame's
> threshold. Georgius Miles. . . .
> (*AFTER NATURE* 5E, 7G)

Sometimes crossing that boundary is associated with an ominous threat, as in *The Emigrants* when Cosmo retells the scene from the film *Dr. Mabuse, the Gambler* in which a caravan passes from the mirage of an oasis on stage out into the audience. Sometimes it comes in a moment of surprise, as when the glass slide cracks at Henry Selwyn's slide show. This in turn echoes the "slight crack" in the image "Ein leiser Sprung" (1974), cited in the Tripp essay.

24. Cuomo, "A Conversation with W. G. Sebald," 99.

25. Breaking the frame is rather what is called for: in the opening lines of *After Nature*, in the slide show in *The Emigrants*, in the travels of Tripp's dog in *Déjà vu or the Incident*, not to mention all the variations on the frame in *Rings of Saturn*.

WORKS CITED

Albes, Claudia. "Die Erkundung der Leere. Anmerkungen zu W. G. Sebalds "eng-lischer Wallfahrt" *Die Ringe des Saturn.*" *Jahrbuch der deutschen Schillergesellschaft* 46 (Jahrgang 2002): 279–305.

Adler, H. G. *Theresienstadt. 1941–1945. Das Antlitz einer Zwangsgemeinschaft, Geschichte Soziologie Psychologie.* Tübingen: Mohr, 1955.

Anderson, Mark. "The Edge of Darkness: On W. G. Sebald." *October* 106 (2003): 102–21.

Barthes, Roland. *Mythologies.* Trans. Annette Lavers. New York: Hill and Wang, 1972.

Bates, Michael. "Unerzählt: The Unannounced Translator of Sebald's Late Poetry." http://sheffield.academia.edu/MichaelBates/Papers/582831/Unerzahlt_The_Unannounced_Translator_of_Sebalds_Late_Poetry.

Benjamin, Walter. *The Arcades Project.* Trans. Howard Eiland and Kevin McLaughlin. Cambridge: Harvard University Press, 1999.

——. *Gesammelte Schriften.* Ed. Rolf Tiedemann and Hermann Schweppenhäuser. Frankfurt: Suhrkamp, 1974.

——. "On the Concept of History." In *Selected Writings*, 4:389–400. Ed. Howard Eiland and Michael W. Jennings. Cambridge: Harvard University Press, 2003.

——. "On the Image of Proust." In *Selected Writings*, 2:237–47. Ed. Michael W. Jennings, Howard Eiland, and Gary Smith. Cambridge: Harvard University Press, 1999.

——. *Das Passagen-Werk.* Ed. Rolf Tiedemann. In *Gesammelte Schriften,* 5:1. Frankfurt: Suhrkamp, 1989.

———. "Über den Begriff der Geschichte." In *Gesammelte Schriften,* 1.2:691–704. Ed. Rolf Tiedemann and Hermann Schweppenhäuser. Frankfurt: Suhrkamp, 1974.

———. "Zum Bilde Prousts." In *Gesammelte Schriften,* 2.1:310–24. Ed. Rolf Tiedemann and Hermann Schweppenhäuser. Frankfurt: Suhrkamp, 1989.

Browne, Thomas. "THE GARDEN OF CYRUS, or, the Quincunciall, Lozenge, or Net-work Plantations of the Ancients, Artificially, Naturally, Mystically Considered. With Sundry Observations. 1658." In *Religio Medici and Other Writings,* 185–252. New York: Dutton, 1951.

———. "HYDRIOTAPHIA, Urne-Buriall, or, A Discourse of the Sepulchrall Urnes lately found in Norfolk. 1658." In *Religio Medici and Other Writings,* 131–84. New York: Dutton, 1951.

Celan, Paul. "Conversation in the Mountains." In *Selected Poems and Prose of Paul Celan,* 397–400. Trans. John Felstiner. New York: Norton, 2001.

———. "Gespräch im Gebirg." In *Gesammelte Werke in fünf Bänden,* 3:169–73. Ed. Beda Allemann and Stefan Reichert. Frankfurt: Suhrkamp, 1983.

Cuomo, Joseph. "A Conversation with W. G. Sebald." In *The Emergence of Memory,* 93–117. Ed. Lynne Sharon Schwartz. New York: Seven Stories, 2007.

Dante, Alighieri. *The Divine Comedy of Dante Alighieri, Inferno.* Trans. Allen Mandelbaum. New York: Bantam, 1981.

Dickey, Colin. "The Fate of His Bones." *Cabinet* 28 (2007/2008). http://www.cabinetmagazine.org/issues/28/dickey.php.

Eshel, Amir. "Against the Power of Time: The Poetics of Suspension in W. G. Sebald's 'Austerlitz.'" *New German Critique* 88 (2003): 71–96.

Finch, Jeremiah S. "Sir Thomas Browne and the Quincunx." *Studies in Philology* 37, no. 2. (1940): 274–82.

Franklin, Ruth. "Rings of Smoke." In *The Emergence of Memory,* 119–43. Ed. Lynne Sharon Schwartz. New York: Seven Stories, 2007.

Freud, Sigmund. *The Interpretation of Dreams.* Ed. and trans. James Strachey. New York: Basic Books, 1955.

Fuchs, Anne. *"Die Schmerzensspuren der Geschichte": Zur Poetik der Erinnerung in W. G. Sebalds Prosa,* 99–107. Cologne: Böhlau, 2004.

Gray, Richard T. "From Grids to Vanishing Points: W. G. Sebald's Critique of Visual-Representational Orders in *Die Ringe des Saturn.*" *German Studies Review* 32 (2009): 497–526.

Grimmelshausen, Hans Jakob Christoph von. *Der Abentheurliche Simplicissimus Teutsch und Continuatio des abentheurlichen Simplicissimi.* Ed. Rolf Tarot. Tübingen: Max Niemeyer, 1967.

Hamburger, Michael. "Translator's Note." In W. G. Sebald and Jan Peter Tripp, *Unrecounted,* 1–9. Trans. Michael Hamburger. London: Penguin, 2005.

Hart, Matthew and Tania Lown-Hecht. "The Extraterritorial Poetics of W. G. Sebald." *Modern Fiction Studies* 58, no. 2 (2012): 214–38.

Heckscher, William S. *Rembrandt's ANATOMY OF DR. NICOLAAS TULP, an Iconological Study.* New York: New York University Press, 1958.

Hell, Julia. "The Angel's Enigmatic Eyes; or, The Gothic Beauty of Catastrophic History in W. G. Sebald's 'Air War and Literature.'" *Criticism* 46, no. 3 (2004): 361–92.

———. "Eyes Wide Shut." *New German Critique* 88 (2003): 9–36.

Hirsch, Marianne. *The Generation of Postmemory: Writing and Visual Culture After the Holocaust.* New York: Columbia University Press, 2012.

Hoffman, Eva. "Curiosity and Catastrophe." *New York Times Book Review*, September 22, 2002.

Hutchinson, Ben. *W. G. Sebald – Die dialektische Imagination.* Berlin: Walter de Gruyter, 2009.

Huyssen, Andreas. "On Rewritings and New Beginnings: W. G. Sebald and the Literature About the *Luftkrieg*." *Zeitschrift für Literaturwissenschaft und Linguistik* 124 (2001): 72–90.

Jacobs, Carol. *In the Language of Walter Benjamin.* Baltimore: Johns Hopkins University Press, 1999.

———. *Telling Time.* Baltimore: Johns Hopkins University Press, 1993.

———. "Walter Benjamin: Image of Proust." In *In the Language of Walter Benjamin.* Baltimore: Johns Hopkins University Press, 1999.

Jacobson, Dan. *Heshel's Kingdom.* London: Hamish Hamilton, 1998.

Jacobus, Mary. *Romantic Things: A Tree, a Rock, a Cloud.* Chicago: University of Chicago Press, 2012.

Jaggi, Maya. "Recovered Memories." *Guardian Unlimited.* September 22, 2001. http://www.guardian.co.uk/saturday_review/story/0,3605,555861,00.html

Jewish Museum in Frankfurt. *"Unser einziger Weg ist Arbeit": Das Getto in Łódź 1940–1944.* Ed. Hanno Loewy and Gerhard Schoenberner. Vienna: Jüdisches Museum Frankfurt am Main and Löcker Verlag, 1990.

Jeziorkowski, Klaus. "'Peripherie als Mitte': Zur Ästhetik von Zivilität—W. G. Sebald und sein Roman *Austerlitz*." In *Verschiebebahnhöfe der Erinnerung. Zum Werk W.G. Sebalds,* 69–80. Ed. Sigurd Martin and Ingo Wintermeyer. Würzburg: Königshausen & Neumann, 2007.

Kafka, Franz. *Sämtliche Erzählungen.* Ed. Paul Raabe. Frankfurt: Fischer, 1970.

Kilbourn, Russell J. A.. "The Question of Genre in Sebald's Prose (Towards a Post-Memorial Literature of Restitution)." In *A Literature of Restitution: Critical Essays on W.G. Sebald,* 247–64. Ed. Jeanette Baxter, Valerie Henitiuk, and Ben Hutchinson. Manchester: University of Manchester Press, 2013.

Köhler, Andrea. "Katastrophe mit Zuschauer: Ein Gespräch mit dem Schriftsteller W. G. Sebald." *Neue Zürcher Zeitung,* November 22–23, 1997.

———. "Penetrating the Dark." In W. G. Sebald and Jan Peter Tripp, *Unrecounted,* 95–103. Trans. Michael Hamburger. London: Penguin, 2005.

———. "Die Welt im Auge des Kranichs. W. G. Sebalds nachgelassene Prosa und verstreute Essays." *Neue Zürcher Zeitung,* October 7, 2003.

Krauss, Nicole. "Arabesques of Journeys." *Partisan Review* 68, no. 4 (2001). http://www.bu.edu/partisanreview/archive/2001/4/krauss.html

Lemke, Anja. "Figurationen der Melancholie. Spuren Walter Benjamins in W. G. Sebalds 'Die Ringe des Saturn.'" *Zeitschrift für deutsche Philologie* 2 (2008): 239–67.

Lévi-Strauss, Claude. *Tristes Tropiques*. Paris: Plon, 1955.

——. *Tristes Tropiques*. Trans. John and Doreen Weightman. New York: Atheneum, 1974.

Long, J. J., *W. G. Sebald: Image, Archive, Modernity*. New York: Columbia University Press, 2000.

Martin, James. "*Campi deserti:* Polar Landscapes and the Limits of Knowledge in Sebald and Ransmayr." In *The Undiscover'd Country: W. G. Sebald and the Poetics of Travel*, 142–60. Ed. Markus Zisselsberger. Rochester: Camden House, 2010.

McCulloh, Mark R. *Understanding W. G. Sebald*. Columbia: University of South Carolina Press, 2003.

North, Paul. *The Problem of Distraction*. Stanford: Stanford University Press, 2012.

Öhlschläger, Claudia. "Der Saturnring oder Etwas vom Eisenbau. W. G. Sebalds poetische Zivilisationskritik." In *W. G. Sebald. Politische Archäologie und melancholische Bastelei*, 189–204. Ed. Michael Niehaus and Claudia Öhlschläger. Berlin: Erich Schmidt, 2006.

Presner, Todd Samuel. "'What a Synoptic and Artificial View Reveals': Extreme History and the Modernism of W. G. Sebald's Realism." *Criticism* 46, no. 3 (2004): 341–60.

——. *Mobile Modernity: Germans, Jews, Trains*. New York: Columbia University Press, 2007.

Ryan, Judith. *The Novel After Theory*. New York: Columbia University Press, 2011.

Santner, Eric. *On Creaturely Life: Rilke/Benjamin/Sebald*. Chicago: University of Chicago Press, 2006.

Sebald, W. G. *After Nature*. Trans. Michael Hamburger. New York: Random House, 2002.

——. "Air War and Literature." In *On the Natural History of Destruction*. Trans. Anthea Bell. New York: Random House, 2003.

——. "An Attempt at Restitution." In *Campo Santo*, 197–205. Trans. Anthea Bell. New York: Random House, 2005.

——. "As Day and Night, Chalk and Cheese: On the Pictures of Jan Peter Tripp." In W. G. Sebald and Jan Peter Tripp, *Unrecounted*, 78–94. Trans. Michael Hamburger. New York: Penguin, 2004.

——. "Auf ungeheuer dünnem Eis." In *Gespräche 1971 bis 2001*. Ed. Torsten Hoffmann. Frankfurt: Fischer Taschenbuch, 2012.

——. *Die Ausgewanderten: Vier lange Erzählungen*. Frankfurt: Fischer, 2002.

——. *Austerlitz*. Frankfurt: Fischer, 2003.

——. *Austerlitz*. Trans. Anthea Bell. New York: Random House, 2001.

——. "Between History and Natural History: On the Literary Description of Total Destruction." In *Campo Santo*, 65–96. Trans. Anthea Bell. New York: Random House, 2005.

———. *Campo Santo.* Munich: Carl Hanser, 2003.

———. *Campo Santo.* Trans. Anthea Bell. New York: Random House, 2005.

———. "Ein Versuch der Restitution." In *Campo Santo*, 240–48. Munich: Carl Hanser, 2003.

———. *The Emigrants.* Trans. Michael Hulse. New York: New Directions, 1996.

———. *For Years Now: Poems by W. G. Sebald, Images by Tess Jaray.* London: Short, 2001.

———. "Kafka Goes to the Movies." In *Campo Santo*, 151–67. Trans. Anthea Bell. New York: Random House, 2005.

———. "Kafka im Kino." In *Campo Santo*, 193–209. Munich: Carl Hanser, 2003.

———. *Logis in einem Landhaus.* Frankfurt: Fischer Taschenbuch, 2002.

———. *Luftkrieg und Literatur.* Frankfurt: Fischer Taschenbuch, 2002.

———. *Nach der Natur.* Frankfurt: Fischer Taschenbuch, 2002.

———. *Die Ringe des Saturn.* Frankfurt: Fischer Taschenbuch, 1997.

———. *The Rings of Saturn.* Trans. Michael Hulse. New York: New Directions, 1998.

———. *Schwindel. Gefühle.* Frankfurt: Fischer, 1994.

———. "Verlorenes Land – Jean Améry und Österreich." In *Unheimliche Heimat: Essays zur österreichischen Literatur*, 131–44. Frankfurt: Fischer Taschenbuch, 2003.

———. *Vertigo.* New York: New Directions, 1999.

———. "Wie Tag und Nacht—Über die Bilder Jan Peter Tripps." *Logis in einem Landhaus*, 169–88. Frankfurt: Fischer Taschenbuch, 2002.

———. "Zwischen Geschichte und Naturgeschichte – Über die literarische Beschreibung totaler Zerstörung." In *Campo Santo*, 69–100. Munich: Carl Hanser, 2003.

Sebald, W. G., and Jan Peter Tripp. *Unerzählt.* Munich: Carl Hanser, 2003.

———. *Unrecounted.* Trans. Michael Hamburger. New York: Penguin, 2004.

Schwartz, Lynne Sharon, ed. *The Emergence of Memory: Conversations with W. G. Sebald.* New York: Seven Stories, 2007.

Silverblatt, Michael. "A Poem of an Invisible Subject (Interview)." In *The Emergence of Memory*, 77–86. Ed. Lynne Sharon Schwartz. New York: Seven Stories, 2007. KCRW interview with W. G. Sebald, December 6, 2001. http://www.kcrw .com/etc/programs/bw/bw011206w_g_sebald.

Steinmann, Holger. "Zitatruinen unterm Hundsstern. W. G. Sebalds Ansichten von der Nachtseite der Philologie." In *W. G. Sebald. Politische Archäologie und melancholische Bastelei*, 145–56. Ed. Michael Niehaus and Claudia Ohlschläger. Berlin: Erich Schmidt, 2006.

Theisen, Bianca. "A Natural History of Destruction: W. G. Sebald's *The Rings of Saturn*." *MLN* 121 (2006): 563–81.

Tripp, Jan Peter, with Max Bense, Manfred Esser, Wendelin Niedlich, Peter Renz, W. G. Sebald, Kurt Weidemann, and Kurt Zein. *Die Aufzählung der Schwierigkeiten: Arbeiten von 1985–92.* Offenburg: Reiff Schwarzwaldverlag, 1993.

von Mücke, Dorothea. "History and the Work of Art in Sebald's *After Nature*." *Nonsite.org*1(2011).nonsite.org/issues/issue-1/sebalds-after-nature-authorship -at-the threshold-of-representation.

Wachtel, Eleanor. "Ghost Hunter (Interview)." In *The Emergence of Memory*, 37– 62. Ed. Lynne Sharon Schwartz. New York: Seven Stories, 2007.

Walkowitz, Rebecca L. *Cosmopolitan Style: Modernism Beyond the Nation*. New York: Columbia University Press, 2006.

Watts, Stephen. "Fragment." http://spitalfieldslife.com/2010/11/30/stephen-watts -poet/.

Wiki. "Les Invalides." http://en.wikipedia.org/wiki/Les_Invalides.

———. "Simplon Tunnel." http://en.wikipedia.org/wiki/Simplon_Tunnel.

INDEX